Research Series on the Chinese Dream and China's Development Path

Drawing on a large body of empirical studies done over the last two decades, this Series provides its readers with in-depth analyses of the past and present and forecasts for the future course of China's development. It contains the latest research results made by members of the Chinese Academy of Social Sciences. This series is an invaluable companion to every researcher who is trying to gain a deeper understanding of the development model, path and experience unique to China. Thanks to the adoption of Socialism with Chinese characteristics, and the implementation of comprehensive reform and opening-up, China has made tremendous achievements in areas such as political reform, economic development, and social construction, and is making great strides towards the realization of the Chinese dream of national rejuvenation. In addition to presenting a detailed account of many of these achievements, the authors also discuss what lessons other countries can learn from China's experience.

Yunxian Wu

A Financial History of China (1949–2019)

SSAP

Springer

Yunxian Wu
Business School
China University of Political Science and Law
Beijing, China

Translated by
Wen Tao
Beijing, China

ISSN 2363-6866 ISSN 2363-6874 (electronic)
Research Series on the Chinese Dream and China's Development Path
ISBN 978-981-99-6570-0 ISBN 978-981-99-6571-7 (eBook)
https://doi.org/10.1007/978-981-99-6571-7

Jointly published with Social Sciences Academic Press
The print edition is not for sale in China (Mainland). Customers from China (Mainland) please order the print book from: Social Sciences Academic Press.

This work was supported by B&R Book Program.

This Springer imprint is published by the registered company Springer Nature Singapore Pte Ltd.
The registered company address is: 152 Beach Road, #21-01/04 Gateway East, Singapore 189721, Singapore

Paper in this product is recyclable.

Series Preface

Since China's reform and opening began in 1978, the country has come a long way on the path of Socialism with Chinese characteristics, under the leadership of the Communist Party of China. Over 30 years of reform, efforts and sustained spectacular economic growth have turned China into the world's second-largest economy, and wrought many profound changes in the Chinese society. These historically significant developments have been garnering increasing attention from scholars, governments, and the general public alike around the world since the 1990s, when the newest wave of China studies began to gather steam. Some of the hottest topics have included the so-called "China miracle", "Chinese phenomenon", "Chinese experience", "Chinese path", and the "Chinese model". Homegrown researchers have soon followed suit. Already hugely productive, this vibrant field is putting out a large number of books each year, with Social Sciences Academic Press alone having published hundreds of titles on a wide range of subjects.

Because most of these books have been written and published in Chinese, however, readership has been limited outside China—even among many who study China—for whom English is still the lingua franca. This language barrier has been an impediment to efforts by academia, business communities, and policy-makers in other countries to form a thorough understanding of contemporary China, of what is distinct about China's past and present may mean not only for her future but also for the future of the world. The need to remove such an impediment is both real and urgent, and the *Research Series on the Chinese Dream and China's Development Path* is my answer to the call.

This series features some of the most notable achievements from the last 20 years by scholars in China in a variety of research topics related to reform and opening. They include both theoretical explorations and empirical studies, and cover economy, society, politics, law, culture, and ecology, the six areas in which reform and opening policies have had the deepest impact and farthest-reaching consequences for the country. Authors for the series have also tried to articulate their visions of the "Chinese Dream" and how the country can realize it in these fields and beyond.

All of the editors and authors for the *Research Series on the Chinese Dream and China's Development Path* are both longtime students of reform and opening and recognized authorities in their respective academic fields. Their credentials and expertise lend credibility to these books, each of which having been subject to a rigorous peer review process for inclusion in the series. As part of the Reform and Development Program under the State Administration of Press, Publication, Radio, Film, and Television of the People's Republic of China, the series is published by Springer, a Germany-based academic publisher of international repute, and distributed overseas. I am confident that it will help fill a lacuna in studies of China in the era of reform and opening.

Beijing, China Shouguang Xie

Preface

Over the 70 years since the founding of the People's Republic of China in 1949, and under the leadership of the Communist Party of China, China's financial sector has achieved remarkable accomplishments in serving the Chinese people and supporting the country's economic growth and social development.

As of the end of 2019, China's foreign exchange reserves stood at US$ 3,107.9 billion, No. 1 in the world. In the same year, China's inbound FDI was RMB 941.5 billion (US$ 138.1 billion), making China the second largest foreign capital recipient country in the world. From 2015 to 2017 alone, China's investment in "Belt and Road" countries exceeded US$ 48.6 billion, accounting for more than 10 % of China's total overseas investment over the same period.[1] In 2019, China's non-financial outbound foreign direct investment reached US$ 763 billion, making it the third largest foreign investor in the world.

Despite its late start, China's modern financial sector does have a second mover advantage and it made great strides in the past seven decades, emerging in the global financial sector as a distinctive development model with Chinese characteristics. This is a historical and practical case that cannot be fully elucidated by modern western financial theories. Due to its high theoretical value and practical significance, the evolutionary trajectory of China's financial sector is an important area of research.

The development, reform, and opening up of China's financial sector was the subject of research interest as early as the 1980s, and foreign scholars have been studying these issues from different angles. Some international organizations, think tanks, and government agencies also conducted the research into this subject area, including the International Finance Corporation of the World Bank Group, the Peterson Institute for International Economics, the RAND National Security Research Division, the Deutsche Bank, and the Foreign and Commonwealth Office of the UK.

---

[1] National Bureau of Statistics of China: Frog-leap in Foreign Trade and Comprehensively Stepping up Opening up to the Outside World-Report Series on China's Social and Economic Accomplishments in Forty Years of Reform and Opening up (Part III), http://www.gov.cn/xinwen/2018-08/30/content_5319212.html, August 30, 2018.

Although foreign scholars have published an array of valuable research findings on issues associated with the seven-decade development of China's financial sector, due to language barriers and limited acquaintance with China's history and situation, most of these studies have been limited to certain areas in the financial sector and tended to focus on major issues in a specific period, thus requiring both in depth and in breadth. To date, there has been no published treatise which is as holistic and systematic as *A Financial History of China, 1949–2019*.

Chinese scholars have been studying the financial history of the People's Republic of China for quite some time. There are two types of basic research literature in this area, including: ① Data and research reports published by the statistics authorities, trade groups, and financial institutions. ② Historical documents and laws and regulations on the development trajectory of the financial sector compiled by the People's Bank of China and China Legal Publishing House.[2] However, the bulk of research works published by the academic and theoretical circles on the theme of China's 70-year financial development history only covered short periods or special events. Likewise, intensive research and publications were often associated with the commemorative events of important years. For example, the 30th and 40th anniversaries of reform and opening up and the 60th and 70th anniversaries of the founding of the People's Republic of China came into focus of academic researches, and related research publications primarily explored the theme of financial reform in specific periods. However, there were few innovative and theoretical findings of comprehensive in-depth studies of China's financial history over a long period of time.

Through an analysis of existing research findings and the logical architecture of the financial system in the dimensions of spatial, temporal, and industrial development, this book is intended to examine and elaborate on the long-term evolutionary trajectory of China's financial sector, as well as the overall structure and gradual transitions in different research areas (e.g. financial institutions, financial markets, the central banking system, financial regulation and the opening up of the financial sector to the outside world) since the founding of the People's Republic of China in 1949. In addition, the book explores the different development stages and related issues in the trajectory of financial evolution, delves into the laws of financial industry evolution, and summarizes China's financial development experience in the past seven decades, with a view to providing a basis and reference for nudging in the future correct orientation of China's financial sector and conducting theoretical research thereinto.

In the Tang Dynasty, Chancellor Wei Zheng once remarked, using bronze as a mirror, one can primp one's attire and headwear; using history as a mirror, one can discern the rise and fall of dynasties; using people as a mirror, one can learn about

---

[2] The People's Bank of China and the CCCPC Party Literature Research Office: *Selected Literature on Financial Work (1978–2005)*, China Financial Publishing House, 2007; China Legal Publishing House: *Laws and Regulations on Finance (Including Relevant Policies)*, China Legal Publishing House, 2017.

gains and losses. As the British historian Niall Ferguson argued, money is the "root of most human progress" and behind all history there lies a financial backstory.

By reviewing and studying the evolutionary trajectory of China's financial sector, we can trace a slice of history in those days and pave the way ahead in the future, thereby providing historical experience and shedding light on how to realize the great Chinese Dream of national rejuvenation.

Beijing, China Yunxian Wu

Contents

Chapter 1
Evolutionary Trajectory of China's Financial Sector Over Seven Decades

From 1949 to 2019, China's financial sector underwent two distinct development periods, namely the first 30 years, and the latter 40 years. Specifically, it moved through six main development stages.

1.1 Institutional Reconstruction and Monolithic Financial System

From 1949 to 1978, China's financial institutional regime was being rebuilt, and a monolithic financial system was established for operation. In retrospect, these 30 years witnessed the establishment of a financial system and its operating regime compatible with the then planned economic system, albeit with twists and turns, kicking off China's financial reform and opening up.

1.1.1 Establishing the Credit Monetary System: Renminbi as Fiat Money

On December 1, 1948, the People's Bank of China (PBoC) was established in Shijiazhuang, Hebei province and thereafter the first edition of the *renminbi* was also issued. As the People's Liberation War raged on, the Communist Party of China (CPC) also launched a war without smoke in the financial sector in 1949—a struggle to unify the national financial market with the *renminbi*. Needless to say, this war was no easier than the decisive Huaihai Campaign in the Chinese Civil War.

Y. Wu, *A Financial History of China (1949–2019)*, Research Series on the Chinese Dream and China's Development Path,
https://doi.org/10.1007/978-981-99-6571-7_1

By the end of 1949, the *renminbi* had been in circulation nationwide. In 1950, it became legal tender in most regions of the country. Meanwhile, the Chinese government also withdrew or exchanged old currencies still in circulation which had been issued in the Kuomintang's reign, and a series of measures were taken to carry out the unified management of legal tender, finance and foreign currencies.

In March 1951, the Government Administration Council (today's the State Council), China's then cabinet, ordered the PBoC to withdraw all the local currency notes from circulation and exchange them for the *renminbi.* On March 1, 1955, the PBoC issued a new edition of the *renminbi.* On June 10, 1955, all the circulating old *renminbi* was superseded by the new edition of the *renminbi.* At the end of October 1959, the Chinese government withdrew Tibetan currency circulating in Xizang and replaced it with the *renminbi* as legal tender there.

By 1960, the Chinese government eventually had introduced the *renminbi*, a fiat currency across the whole country (excluding the Taiwan region). In other words, the PBoC monopolized the issue of the *renminbi* on state credit, making it hitherto legal tender (also known as fiat money) in China. It is worth mentioning that the PBoC also became the sole authority for regulating gold, silver, legal tender and foreign currencies in the country, and administering the circulation of the *renminbi* and withdrawal of the *renminbi* from circulation through two channels.

The first channel was through compiling cash disbursement and withdrawal plans under the guidance of the Finance and Economics Committee of the Government Administration Council. In 1953, the PBoC stipulated that all state-owned enterprises, supply and marketing cooperatives, and state organs and organizations must draw up their own cash disbursement and withdrawal plans, while provincial financial and economic departments were required to formulate provincial comprehensive cash disbursement and withdrawal plans, or furnish relevant materials. The PBoC's head office, provincial branches, and county and city sub-branches were respectively responsible for compiling comprehensive cash disbursement and withdrawal plans for the whole country, specific provinces (autonomous regions, and municipalities directly under the Central Government), and various counties and cities. Additionally, they were also mandated to organize the issue and circulation of the *renminbi* and withdrawal of the *renminbi* from circulation in cash as planned.

The second channel was through the imposition of administrative measures for cash transfer by banks with the help of Soviet experts. It was stipulated that banks at all levels could only transfer treasury funds issued within the issuance quotas as specified in their cash disbursement and withdrawal plans subject to the approval from the PBoC's head office. In this way, cash transfer was effectuated in accordance with the cash disbursement and withdrawal plan. Following trial implementation, the administrative measures for cash transfer were officially instituted for nationwide implementation in July 1954, imposing an important management regime for the *renminbi.*

1.1.2 A PBoC-Centered Financial System

From 1949 to 1958, the Chinese government progressively established a PBoC-centered monolithic financial institution system and an operational management regime while taking over and reforming the old financial system.

First, the Chinese government established the PBoC's vertical organizational structure. As early as December 1949, the PBoC already set up 4 regional branches in East China, Central South China, Northwest China, and Southwest China, 40 provincial and municipal branches, and over 1,200 county (city) sub-branches and business offices according to then China's regional administrative divisions. In 1951, the PBoC set up branches nationwide (excluding Taiwan and Xizang) and it thereby effectively established a four-tiered vertical organizational structure consisting of head office, regional branches in major administrative regions, branches in provinces, autonomous regions, and municipalities directly under the central government, and sub-branches at the county level.

Second, the Chinese government reorganized financial institutions and set up new ones. The Chinese government took over from the Kuomintang government and reorganized the Bank of China (BOC) and the Bank of Communications (BCM). In December 1949, the BOC's General Administrative Office was moved from Shanghai to Beijing city. Additionally, the Chinese government officially established the People's Insurance Company of China (PICC) on October 20, 1949 and subsequently set up its branches across the country. Moreover, the Agricultural Cooperative Bank of China was established with approval in August 1951, becoming China's first state-owned specialized commercial bank. Nevertheless, it had no regional branches. In addition to the PBoC, these reorganized and newly established financial institutions constituted a PBoC-centered monolithic financial institution system. Altogether, they had 1,380 branches nationwide.

Third, the central government reformed the financial institution system and relevant regulatory regime. In 1952, the BOC and the PBoC's Overseas Business Bureau worked in a united office under the administration of the PBoC. The BCM and PICC were administered by the Ministry of Finance (MoF), while the Agricultural Cooperative Bank of China was streamlined and dissolved, and the General Administrative Office for Public–Private Partnership Banks was established therefrom.

In June 1954, the PBoC dissolved its regional branches to strengthen its head office' unified leadership and centralized regulation of financial activities throughout the country, establishing a vertical regulatory regime for regulating the PBoC's internal financial institutions. After the socialist transformation of the financial sector was completed, public–private partnership banks were progressively incorporated into the PBoC's administrative system.

On February 1, 1955, the public–private partnership banks in fourteen cities across China commenced to work in a united office with local PBoC branches, shifting their role into the savings agencies of the PBoC. In July 1956, the General Administrative Office for Public–Private Partnership Banks and the PBoC's Private Business Administration Division worked in a united office.

Fourth, the Chinese government merged and dissolved financial institutions and set up new ones. In March 1955, the Agricultural Bank of China (ABC) was established with approval to primarily conduct the business of granting short-term rural loans in support of agricultural production, while all other rural financial business was still conducted by the PBoC. However, the ABC was dissolved on April 12, 1957, and its rural credit loan business was handed over to the PBoC for handling. On August 1, 1957, the PBoC set up the Rural Finance Administration Bureau to administer rural finance across the whole country. On October 1, 1954, the People's Construction Bank of China (the predecessor of today's CCB) was established with approval to manage a huge amount of funds earmarked for China's 156 key construction projects.

By 1958, a PBoC-centered "1 + N" organizational structure had been basically established in China's financial sector. In other words, the PBoC was not only national currency issuer and financial regulator, but also a core economic organization for operating in the financial business across the whole country. This highly centralized monolithic financial institution system and the operational management regime continued to be in place until 1978.

1.1.3 The Fund Management Regime of Unified Deposit and Unified Lending

"Unified deposit and unified lending", also known as "unified collection and unified allocation", was a fund management regime adopted by the Chinese government in a planned economy erato pool and allocate credit in a uniform and planned way. "Unified deposit" (unified collection) means that PBoC branches at all levels must turn over all their funds to the PBoC's head office for centralized utilization, while "unified lending" (unified allocation) means that the PBoC's head office imposed credit quotas according to the national comprehensive economic development plan and specific targets, and then allocated credit loan quotas level by level to each branch and sub-branch, with credit loans being granted in strict accordance with the quotas imposed by the PBoC's head office.

The system of "unified deposit and unified lending" originated from 1952 to 1953, and it was finally established in 1955. This system was established and applied depending on a combination of factors such as the PBoC's credit loan plan regulatory regime, funds mainly derived from government financial appropriation and bank credit loans, and highly centralized fund allocation and management requirements during the First Five-Year Plan period. Following the abolishment of commercial credits in 1955, the Chinese government stipulated that all the credit loans must be brought under the control of central bank. In this regard, the PBoC proposed the establishment of a monolithic credit loan plan regulatory regime.

Under the vertical credit fund management regime of "unified deposit and unified lending", the PBoC branches at different levels were not allowed to arrange for or grant loans at their discreet. Instead, all of planed credit loan quotas must be subject to the approval from the PBoC's head office and must be allocated in a hierarchical manner. The PBoC's branches at all levels must grant loans within the credit loan quotas as allocated.

Funds settlement was mainly conducted through central bank. For state-owned commercial enterprises, all commodity purchase and sales loans as well as fund transfers must be handled and settled through the PBoC. All the credit loans and fund settlement of the whole country was centralized granted and handled through the PBoC, thus establishing a centralized fiscal and financial development model.

1.1.4 Exploring Policy to Cope with Abnormal Times

From 1958 to 1978, China's economy entered an "abnormal" development period. During this period, major political events and upheavals such as the Great Leap Forward, the People's Commune Movement and the Cultural Revolution all militated against the development of the financial sector, resulting in uncontrolled credit lending and excessive money issuance which have disrupted the national economy. To address such a volatile situation, the Chinese government and the financial authorities commenced to explore some effective countermeasures.

First, the credit loan management regime was duly reformed. In August 1958, with a view to addressing the ongoing decentralization of enterprises and public institutions and to further optimizing the financial management and bank credit loan management regime, the Chinese government decreed that all deposits of the PBoC, other than the deposits of central revenues, national defense, central enterprises and government organs and organizations, must be allocated to the local governments for unified management, while the local governments were required to fulfill their quotas for deposit-loan gap. In April 1961, however, the PBoC decided to cease imposing the measures of "delegation of deposit and lending powers, quota allocation plan, deposit-loan gap management, and unified allocation" and "fulfilling deposit-loan gap quotas and prohibiting from exceeding loan-deposit gap quotas".

Second, "Six Banking Measures" were issued to cease delegation of powers and tighten up financial regulation. On March 10, 1962, the Central Committee of the Communist Party of China and the State Council issued the Decision on Reinforcing the Uniformity of Banking Work and Strictly Controlling the Issue of Currencies, which was known as the "Six Banking Measures". These six measures were imposed as follows: Ordering the PBoC to regain all the powers which had been delegated before, resorted to a rigorous credit loan plan and management regime for the banking industry and cease "full-amount loans"; explicitly defining the boundary between bank funds and fiscal funds, strengthening cash management and strictly operating the fund settlement system; reinforcing the banking working system at all levels; allocating and managing agricultural funds in a unified way, and strengthening the leadership in rural credit cooperatives; proactively participating in and pushing forward with the warehouse inventory verification and proper disposal work; and revising and amending the internal rules and regulations of banks.

The implementation of the "Six Banking Measures" discontinued lax financial regulation. It was only after 1962 when national financial work progressively returned to normal, and circulation of money was brought under normal control. This move has nudged national economy into correct orientation towards "reform, rectification, restructuring and revitalization".

Third, the PBoC's financial management regime were maintained and imposed. During the Cultural Revolution, the financial sector was widely and substantially impacted. In July 1969, the PBoC and the MoF worked in a united office. The bulk of the staff were sent to work in the countryside, with only 87 left to attend to financial affairs at the headquarters. As such, the financial work has almost discontinued. Meanwhile, the PBoC's local branches and functional departments and bureaus were either merged or dissolved, and only two large political work and business departments were retained, which has materially weakened the operational and centralized regulation systems of the PBoC. Thanks to the strenuous efforts of the remaining departments and staff, the PBoC managed to maintain its financial regulation regime and run it until the end of the Cultural Revolution.

Fourth, the PBoC and the MoF were officially "separated" from each other. In accordance with the relevant provisions as prescribed by the State Council on December 31, 1977, the PBoC's head office and the MoF officially worked separately from January 1, 1978 onwards. In the meantime, all PBoC branches at or below the provincial, autonomous region or municipalities directly under the central government level were required to complete the separation from the departments of the MoF at the corresponding level at the end of 1978. Following the separation, a bank-led indirect financing channel and a hierarchical financial management regime both have been progressively established in the country. Additionally, the separation this time has also enabled the PBoC to reinforce its backbone force, as well as its leadership and administration of the financial work.

1.2 The Period of Recovery and Restructuring Reforms

From 1978 to 1983, the internal structure of the financial sector was adjusted, and the financial sector, which had been hit by political movements, was restored to a normal development state. Additionally, the financial management regime and the financial institution system were restructured and reformed, while the order of the financial market was rectified.

1.2.1 Clarifying Functions and Regulatory Authority

First, the functions of the PBoC and important financial institutions were redefined. On March 13, 1979, the State Council decided to separate the BOC from the PBoC. As a specialized bank designated by the state to specialize in conducting the foreign exchange business, the BOC's former function for regulating China's foreign exchange was taken over by the State Administration of Foreign Exchange (SAFE), which was established in 1980. Both the BOC and the SAFE were directly under the leadership of the State Council but were administered by the PBoC on behalf of the State Council. Meanwhile, the China Banknote Printing and Minting Corporation was established with approval.

Second, national specialized banks were established and their regulatory authorities were designated. On April 20, 1983, China Construction Bank (CCB) and the ABC were both established with approval.[1] In January 1984, the Industrial and Commercial Bank of China (ICBC) was set up to undertake the commercial banking business which had been originally conducted by the PBoC. As a result, the BOC, CCB, ABC and ICBC have emerged as China's four large state-owned specialized banks, all of which were registered with the MoF and were also subject to the administration of the MoF.

Third, the PBoC was designated as China's central bank. On September 17, 1983, according to the Decision on the People's Bank of China Exclusively Exercising Central Bank Functions issued by the State Council, the PBoC was designated as China's central bank and it commenced to officially perform its functions as the central bank of the country. Specifically, the four large state-owned specialized banks conducted business under the leadership of the PBoC yet they were not subject to the administration of the PBoC.

Fourth, the affiliation and administrative functions of the PICC were clarified. From January 1984 onwards, all affiliates of the PICC established in 1949 were brought under the direct leadership of the PICC, and they were registered with the MoF, Additionally, they also carried out systematic management in respect of infrastructure, raw materials, labor relationship and wages, accounting, personnel and foreign-related affairs.

Among the financial institutions mentioned above, only the PICC and the China Banknote Printing and Minting Corporation were categorized as corporations, which imposed a regulatory regime for corporate entity.

[1] The CCB was under the dual leadership of the MoF and the PBoC, yet the ABC was only under the leadership of the PBoC.

1.2.2 Deposit-Loan Gap Quota Management Regime and Policy on Replacement of Appropriation by Loans

From 1979 to 1984, the government imposed a policy of shifting profits turned over to the state to taxes levied on incomes on state-owned enterprises. Against such a backdrop, the credit loan management regime has undergone reforms twice.

First, the credit loan management regime was reformed. In 1979, the PBoC adopted a deposit-loan gap quota management regime to replace the "unified deposit and unified lending" regulatory regime which had been in place since the 1950s. In 1980, the deposit-loan gap quota management regime was imposed in all provincial branches of the PBoC with two available options, namely total deposit-loan gap quota, and partial deposit-loan gap quota. The PBoC's branches were at liberty to choose either one at their discretion.

From 1981 to 1984, the deposit-loan gap quota management regime was imposed nationwide. Under this new regime, the PBoC's head office was designated to incorporate some deposit and lending projects into the national comprehensive credit loan plan, which were then allocated to specialized banks and the PBoC's branches for quota management.

Second, a "loans-in–place-of-appropriation" policy for managing financial funds was pursued. This policy shifted the government infrastructure investment model for infrastructure construction from fiscal appropriations to loans granted by the CCB. In 1979, the CCB was designated as the pilot agency for operating the scheme on replacement of appropriation by loans. In the process, it came as a proactive advocate and organizer of the reform.

By the end of 1980, the pilot reform on replacement of appropriation by loans had been carried out in 28 provinces, autonomous regions, and municipalities directly under the central government. Altogether, the CCB signed loan contracts worth RMB3.2 billion for 619 projects in ten industries, involving electric power, light textile, building materials, commerce, coal, oil, transportation, metallurgy, and chemicals. In the year of 1980, the CCB granted loans totaling RMB1.5 billion.

In 1981, the State Council stipulated that the policy on replacement of appropriation by loans shall be carried out by all the state-owned enterprises that accounted for independently and were solvent. The pilot scheme on replacement of appropriation by loans was up-scaled in 1982 and rolled out nationwide in 1985. As of the end of 1993, the **"loans-in–place-of-appropriation"** scheme operated by the CCB had an outstanding investment balance of RMB111.6 billion.

The reform on replacement of appropriation by loans marked a departure from the original investment model of the government in charge of making appropriations to state-owned enterprises. On the contrary, all the entities had to pay interest and principal to obtain bank loans, making a creative exploration into the market-oriented reform of state-owned enterprises.

1.2.3 Traditional Financial Institutions and Indirect Financing

In the early stages of reform and opening up, with a view to putting in place multiple ongoing pilot reforms (e.g. the household contract accountability system in rural areas and the expansion of autonomy for urban and township enterprises), it was imperative to pool idle funds from enterprises and urban and rural residents, and leverage them in funds-lacking industrial sectors according to national macro-regulation policies. To that end, the Chinese government proactively encouraged the establishment of traditional financial institutions and the development of an indirect financing system.

First, specialized savings institutions were established in urban and rural areas. After the country's first urban credit cooperative was established in Zhumadian, Henan province in 1979, the Chinese government subsequently set up urban and rural credit cooperative systems across China and made efforts to improve these systems. On March 10, 1979, the PBoC decided to restore the ABC, whose predecessor was the Agricultural Cooperative Bank of China established in 1951. In this way, a rural financial system has progressively taken shape.

Second, banks were encouraged to conduct the trust business. In 1980, the State Council and the PBoC both encouraged the governments at all levels, specialized banks and enterprises to conduct the trust business. In March 1981, Shanghai Investment Trust Corporation Limited (today's Shanghai International Trust Co., Ltd.) was established with approval. Subsequently, all sorts of local investment companies and international trust and investment companies were successively set up in different provinces and cities, and all leading specialized banks also proactively commenced to conduct the trust and investment business as well. By the end of 1982, the commercial banking system alone had contributed to almost 90% of all trust and investment companies in the country.

Third, domestic insurance business was resumed. In April 1979, the PBoC made a decision to allow the establishment of insurance institutions, kicking off the resumption and development of insurance business in the country. As of October 1981, there were 477 specialized insurance institutions, 803 banking agencies and more than 5,700 insurance practitioners in 28 provinces, autonomous regions, and municipalities directly under the central government (excluding Xizang) and a few counties in the country. Meanwhile, insurance business such as enterprise property insurance, family property insurance, and automobile insurance were also resumed for handling, providing RMB200 billion worth of property coverage for nearly 100,000 enterprises, more than 900,000 households and 130,000 vehicles. Among them, the property insurance for state-owned enterprises amounted to RMB193.5 billion, accounting for 23% of their fixed assets and working capital.[2]

In 1982, insurance business operations were actively carried out throughout the country and China's economic compensation system was progressively established.

[2] Wu Xiaoling (ed): *A Chronicle of Major Events in China's Financial Reform and Opening up*, China Financial Publishing House, 2008, p. 55.

This system could not only safeguard the normal production and operation of enterprises, secure the people's livelihood and reduce the loss of social wealth, but also open up an important indirect financing channel for pooling construction funds.

1.2.4 Regulating the Market and Overhauling the Trust Industry

In the early 1980s, unswerving government policy support stimulated the rapid development of the financial sector. However, disorderly development occasionally surfaced in the financial market mainly as a result of a backward management regime. Therefore, it was urgent to strengthen market management and overhaul some fairly chaotic industrial sectors.

With a view to safeguarding a unified *renminbi* market in the foreign-related economy sector, the State Council and the PBoC rolled out a policy to prohibit the denomination and circulation of all foreign currencies in the domestic market on January 5, 1980. Additionally, they also ordered the BOC to issue foreign exchange certificates, and prohibit enterprises and individuals from directly receiving foreign currencies. From 1983 to 1985, the government issued several relevant laws and regulations to progressively bring in and regulate foreign financial institutions according to the law.

Rather than acting as financial institutions for "managing wealth for customers" as planned, trust and investment companies that emerged in the early 1980s as a result of policy incentives have developed into banks that made deposits and granted loans in disguise, going beyond their business scope of trusts contrary to expectations. In this way, they have exacerbated the overload operations by using short-term funds to grant long-term loans, thereby resulting in a spiral of fixed asset investment. Additionally, there were too many trust and invest companies established in different regions, and they operated in a chaotic state. In reality, these financial institutions have disrupted the normal financial market order by competing with banks for funds and artificially aggravating fund shortage.

On April 10, 1982, the PBoC made its first attempt to overhaul the trust industry, with a focus on overhauling trust and investment companies set up by non-financial institutions and reversing the situation of too many trust financial institutions and too chaotic operation of trust financial institutions. For the overhauling campaign, the following provisions were laid down: Except for those trust and investment companies approved by the State Council or its authorized departments, the local governments and different government departments were not allowed to conduct the trust investment business. Those that have already conducted the trust and investment business must be overhauled by the people's governments at the levels of provinces, autonomous regions, and municipalities directly under the central government within the prescribed time limit; all the trust and investment business must be conducted by the PBoC or specialized banks designated by the PBoC; all the fund-related activities associated with approved trust investment business must be incorporated into the national comprehensive credit loan plan and the fixed assets investment plan for overall balancing. Following the overhauling campaign, the trust market was in much better order.

With the affirmation and support of the PBoC, the trust industry saw a new round of development from 1983 to 1984. Although banking financial institutions at all levels operated in their trust business, such business was no more than bank deposit and lending under a banking-dominated mixed operation model, which failed to reflect the essential characteristics and specialty of trust. Most funds were channeled to the fixed asset sector, causing credit loans and currency issuance to run out of control, thus intensifying an already "overheated" economy and fueling the ballooning of fixed assets.

In December 1985, the PBoC initiated its comprehensive overhauling of the trust industry for the second time, with a focus on overhauling the irregular business operations of trust companies, and concurrently requiring banks to cease conducting the trust loan and investment business. However, the overhauling campaign was of little avail. In 1986, while the overhauling campaign was still on, the trust industry re-emerged again. Nevertheless, the main business in the trust industry was still concentrated on securities investment by banks in the name of trust, thus deviating from the real trust business. As such, a lack of separation of "banks from securities business" has affected the imposition effectiveness of China's then national macro-regulation policies.

In 1986, the third overhauling campaign of the trust industry was put on the agenda. The PBoC stepped up its overhauling efforts to separate banks from securities business by rigorously regulating the business operations of trust companies, dissolving or merging some trust financial institutions, and imposing policies to contain their survival. However, this overhauling campaign has failed to curb the rapid development momentum of trust and investment companies. By the end of 1988, there had been 1,000 trust and investment companies in China altogether, 745 of which were independent legal entities approved by the PBoC. Actually, trust and investment companies served as the main channel for specialized banks to transfer funds, which resulted in fixed asset investment running out of control again.

As national economic overhaul campaign was launched in 1988, the overhauling of trust and investment companies continued until 1990. As such, the number of trust and investment institutions in the country fell to 339 in 1990 from more than 1,000 in 1988, basically achieving the target of "separating banks from securities business".

1.3 Incremental Changes and Market-Oriented Reform

From 1984 to 1991, with the continuous thrust of China's economic system reform, the financial sector entered a period of incremental changes, edge innovation, and the reform of the red-ocean market.

1.3.1 Establishing Different Types of Financial Markets

In 1981, the commercial bill acceptance and discount business was conducted in Shanghai for the first time. In 1985, interbank lending intermediaries were successively set up in Guangzhou city, Wuhan city, Shanghai, and other medium-sized and large cities, progressively forming a cross-regional and cross-system interbank lending market mainly in central cities or economically developed cities. In 1986, the PBoC officially gave its official sanction for specialized banks to operate in the commercial bill acceptance and discount business. Thereafter, the business was widespread conducted in most regions of the country, especially in some economically developed coastal provinces and cities, becoming the primary settlement and financing model for enterprises.

In 1981, the Chinese government resumed the issuance of treasury bonds, while an annual treasury bond issuance system was introduced. From 1985 onwards, state key construction bonds, fiscal bonds, special bonds, and inflation-indexed bonds were successively issued. In 1993, a secondary market system for treasury bonds basically took shape. Meanwhile, enterprise bonds were approved for issuance. On January 20, 1987, Shanghai Jinshan Petrochemical Plant won approval to issue RMB138 million worth of long-term enterprise bonds for its 300,000 t/a ethylene project, setting a precedent for self-financing through bond issuance for key projects. At the end of 1986, enterprise bonds worth approximate RMB10 billion were issued in the country.[3]

In 1984, Beijing Tianqiao Department Store Co., Ltd. and Shanghai Feile Acoustics Co., Ltd. both issued irredeemable shares to the public, heralding a new era for the stock market in China. In the 1990s, the government commenced to develop the stock market on a pilot basis. In 1990 and 1991, Shanghai and Shenzhen Stock Exchanges were respectively inaugurated with approval. As of the end of 1991, there were a total of sixty-nine joint-stock enterprises that had issued shares to the public in the two pilot cities of Shanghai and Shenzhen. Specifically speaking, the initial shares traded on the Shanghai and Shenzhen exchanges totaled RMB8,405 million, and the shares traded had a total market capitalization of approximately RMB65 billion.

From 1990 to 1992, Zhengzhou Commodity Futures Exchange, Shenzhen Non-Ferrous Metals Exchange and Shanghai Metals Exchange were successively established with approval. With the establishment of these exchanges, China's futures market has progressively took shape. From 1992 onwards, the stock and futures markets kept the irreversible momentum going in China, emerging from scratch and progressively carrying out regulated operations in business. However, the government took a positive yet prudent attitude towards fundraising through issuing stocks.

[3] *A Chronicle of Major Events in China's Financial Reform and Opening up*, China Financial Publishing House, 2008, p. 131.

1.3.2 Setting Up More Banking and Non-banking Financial Institutions

In addition to existing state-owned specialized banks, all kinds of banking and non-banking financial institutions were also established with approval in the 1980s. Specifically, banking financial institutions included national joint-stock commercial banks like the BCM (1986), China Merchants Bank (1987) and CITIC Industrial Bank (1987); regional joint-stock commercial banks established by local governments such as Yantai Housing Savings Bank (1987), Shenzhen Development Bank (1987), Fujian Industrial Bank (1988), and China Guangfa Bank (1988); and joint venture banks such as Xiamen International Bank (1985).

Non-banking financial institutions included securities companies, trust and investment companies, financial companies affiliated to enterprise group, insurance companies, and financial leasing companies. Examples of such institutions included Shenzhen Special Economic Zone Securities Company (1985), Shanghai AJ Financial Trust Co., Ltd. (1986), Dongfeng Motor Finance Co., Ltd. (1987), Ping An Insurance Company of China Ltd. (1988), China Orient Leasing Company (1981), China Development Bank Financial Leasing Co., Ltd. (1984), China Electronics Leasing Co., Ltd. (1986), and South China International Leasing Co., Ltd. (1989).

In addition, a good number of urban and rural credit cooperatives were also established with approval. As of the end of April 1987, there were 59,000 independently accounted rural credit cooperatives and 334,000 dependently accounted credit cooperative outlets across China,[4] which mainly engaged in the deposit, lending, settlement and personal savings business in rural areas. At the end of 1989, there were 3,330 urban credit cooperatives altogether, with a total asset value of RMB28.4 billion.

1.3.3 Enterprise-Oriented Reform of State-Owned Specialized Banks

In 1984, four large state-owned specialized banks in China, namely the ICBC, BOC, ABC and CCB, which concurrently conducted the policy-based and commercial business and performed administrative functions, embarked on enterprise-oriented reforms under the leadership of the State Commission for Economic Restructuring and the PBoC.

On May 7, 1984, the pilot reform of the business model of state-owned specialized banks was approved for initial implementation in the Shenzhen Special Economic Zone. Through the pilot reform scheme, state-owned specialized banks have accumulated practical experiences such as special handling procedures for special matters,

[4] Wu Xiaoling (ed): *A Chronicle of Major Events in China's Financial Reform and Opening up*, China Financial Publishing House, 2008, p. 137.

flexible operation mechanism, and market-oriented operation. The government employed the tactics of initiating the reform in a few pilot cities, then progressively up-scaling it to more pilot cities, and eventually rolling out it to the whole country.

In January 1986, the first batch of five pilot cities such as Guangzhou, Chongqing, Wuhan, Shenyang and Changzhou was selected to initiate the reform, with a focus on reforming the credit fund management regime. While the necessity to coalesce planning with market-orientation in the allocation of financial resources was highlighted, an incentive mechanism was introduced as a complement to deposit and lending plans.

In August 1986, eight cities such as Dalian, Nanjing, Dandong, Suzhou, Wuxi, Ningbo, Wenzhou and Baoji were selected as the second batch of pilot reform cities, increasing the number of pilot cities in the country to thirteen from five.

In December 1986, fourteen cities including Shanghai, Beijing and Tianjin were selected to undertake pilot reform for the third time, raising the total number of pilot cities to twenty-seven. In the meantime, Guangdong province was designated as a pilot province for financial system reform.

In practice, the enterprise-oriented reform of state-owned specialized banks was instituted to mainly define their operational autonomy. The autonomy in operations involved: Progressive operation of the bank governor and manager accountability system; the power to allocate credit funds or to set forth insurance provisions; the power to float the interest rate and insurance premium rate in a range of 20% either based on the existing interest rate or insurance premium rate; the power to appoint and remove middle-ranking managerial personnel from office, recruit workers, provide rewards and mete out punishments, and the power to set up internal departments; the power to internally allocate retained profits, remuneration, rewards and welfare funds, and the power to internally impose various forms of economic accountability systems and quota management regime.

From 1988 to 1989, the State Commission for Economic Restructuring called for accelerating the reform of state-owned specialized banks, requiring all of state-owned specialized banks and other financial institutions to progressively carry out enterprise-oriented operations in business, and ameliorate the situation of "paying fixed wage regardless of work done" internally and monopolizing externally.[5] The ABC continued to optimize its quota management regime, while specialized banks were required to establish and improve their management accountability systems and effectively carry out all kinds of fundamental enterprise-oriented operations in business.

In the first half of 1988, the pace of state-owned specialized banks' enterprise-oriented reform was temporarily slowed down due to spiraling inflation, financial market instability and a complex political situation at the time. It was not until 1992 that a substantive reform proceeded.

---

[5] The People's Bank of China and the CCCPC Party Literature Research Office (eds): *Selected Literature on Financial Work (1978–2005)*, (Overall Plan of the State Commission for Economic Restructuring on Deepening the Reform of the Economic System in 1988), China Financial Publishing House, 2007, p. 72.

1.3.4 The Credit Fund Borrowing and Lending Management Regime

In 1985, the PBoC decided to impose a credit fund borrowing and lending management regime to replace the original deposit-loan gap management regime which had been in place since 1979. The newly imposed regime involved unified planning, allocation of funds, borrowing and lending, and mutual financing.

"Unified planning" requires the incorporation of all the RMB credit funds of specialized banks into the national comprehensive credit loan plan, with the PBoC's head office comprehensively balancing credit quotas and approving the credit loan plans of specialized banks and their plans of borrowing from the PBoC. "Allocation of funds" means that specialized banks operated and accounted for their proprietary funds and credit funds independently as their working capital of the banks, subject to the approval from the PBoC's head office. "Borrowing and lending" refers to the PBoC's shifting its management model from allocating planed credit loan quotas level by level to granting loans by the PBoC to specialized banks provided that specialized banks were required to open deposit and loan accounts with the PBoC, borrow money from the PBoC, and deposit the lent money with the PBoC prior to use. "Mutual financing" was effectuated to allow the inter-bank transfer of funds to effectively leverage surplus funds, and enable regional capital financing to mainly rely on inter-bank borrowing in a region. With a view to espousing the above philosophies of credit fund management, specialized banks needed to establish an inter-bank system.

The borrowing and lending credit loan management regime has shifted the fund management mode of allocating planed credit loan quotas to borrowing and lending credit funds, thus directly expediting the process of exercising the central bank's indirect regulation of finance. In this way, the PBoC has shifted the macro-regulation model from direct regulation to indirect regulation. Nevertheless, it is impossible to establish a market-oriented macro-regulation mechanism overnight and there is still a long way to go ahead.

1.3.5 Clearing Triangular Debt among Enterprises

From the later 1980s to the early 1990s, high inflation, disorder in the financial market and rampant "triangular debt" among enterprises became prominent problems in China's financial sector.

High inflation cropped up due to an extensive operation as well as a rampant growth of the financial sector. Additionally, another contributor to high inflation was the government's encouragement of all sorts of financing for tackling the shortage of funds and the imbalance between supply and demand in the early 1980s, which led to irregularities in private financing and investment fund activity. In the first half of 1988, raging inflation placed an onerous burden on the Chinese government. In the second half of 1988, strategic moves such as controlling money supply and credit loans and overhauling the financial sector were put on top agenda by the government, with a view to stabilizing the economic order and deepening reform.[6]

At the Third Plenary Session of the Thirteenth CPC Central Committee held in September 1988, the Chinese government made a decision on shifting the focus to economic environment improvement and financial market order rectification in the reform and construction work in 1989 and 1990. Additionally, it also set out the guidelines of "controlling credit loan quotas and adjusting the underlying structure" to guide the financial work in those days. Starting from 1989, an objective of basically completing the overhauling tasks in the economic and financial sector in the coming three years or more was specified at the Fifth Plenary Session of the Thirteenth CPC Central Committee held in November 1989.

At the request of the government, the PBoC prioritized the overhauling of urban credit cooperatives in the first half of 1989. A call was made for all local governments to control the number of newly established urban credit cooperatives, and disband or merge poorly operated urban credit cooperatives. From 1990 to 1991, 75 out of the 253 newly established financial institutions were dissolved. As of the end of 1991, there were over 3,500 urban credit cooperatives altogether in the country, which had assets totaling RMB49.7 billion and employed a staff of more than 77,000. These figures showed that the overhauling campaign had basically attained its objective.

In the mid-1980s, the issue of "triangular debt" among enterprises was exacerbated. According to incomplete statistics, "triangular debt" in China totaled RMB300 billion altogether at the end of June 1991, which has seriously affected the normal operation of national economy and undermined the stability of financial market order. To address such an issue, the government decided to launch a campaign of clearing "triangular debt" across the country and put it high on the agenda for the overall financial work in a bid to control, overhaul and stabilize finance.

In a narrow sense, "triangular debt" usually refers to an economic phenomenon that state-owned enterprises defaulted on each other and fell into huge arrears from the 1980s to the early 1990s, which has seriously affected the normal production and operation of enterprises and militated against the development of China's national economy.

The reasons for the "triangular debt" are manifold. Among them, the underlying ones lay in the problems and loopholes in the investment, finance, raw materials, finance and circulation management systems and the enterprise operation and management system, which were not compatible with a planned commodity economy.

With a view to clearing the "triangular debt" of enterprises, the State Council deliberately set up a leading group in charge of this work, striving to resolve the issue at source. Specifically, priority was given to overhauling the defaults on fixed

[6] The State Council Approved and Forwarded the People's Bank of China's Report on Some Measures to Control Currency and Stabilize Finance, August 11, 1988. The People's Bank of China and the CCCPC Party Literature Research Office (eds): *Selected Literature on Financial Work (1978–2005)*, China Financial Publishing House, 2007; pp. 77–78.

asset investment projects, and key debt clearing work such as substantially production curtailment, warehouse inventory reduction, sales promotion, product structure adjustment, reversal of losses, and increase in profits were also put on top agenda.

In the second half of 1991, nationwide efforts to clear "triangular debt" achieved the desired effect. By December 1992, all the "triangular debt" owed prior to the end of 1991 had been basically cleared. During two years of the clearing work, the Chinese government earmarked a total of RMB55.5 billion funds for clearing debts (including RMB52 billion of bank loans) nationwide, covering 14,121 defaulted projects in arrears (including 5,420 infrastructure projects), and recovering RMB183.8 billion in triangular debt. Additionally, the asset investment and working capital arrears totaling RMB219 billion have been recovered, achieving a debt clearing ratio of 1:4.[7]

In 1993, the "chain debt" problems were basically resolved, ushering in a period of a high growth for the China's economy.

1.4 Expansion and Commercialization Reform

From 1992 to 2001, China's financial sector shifted its original long-standing inhibited development period to a rapid development period characterized by an expansion and commercialization reform.

1.4.1 Expansion of Financial Markets and Institutional System

In the spring of 1992, Xiaoping Deng made an important speech during his tour of South China. In the meantime, a reform objective of establishing a socialist market economic system was set forth at the Fourteenth National Congress of the CPC Central Committee held in October 1992. These two moves provided policy dividends for the financial sector and spurred on a rapid development.

First, the securities market was booming as a result of hot-selling stocks. In 1992, a "stock fever" rapidly spread across China, especially in coastal cities opened up to the outside world. With short supply of stocks being a contributing factor, a more important reason for the "stock fever" was the restraints imposed on pilot joint-stock enterprises. In old days, only three types of enterprises were allowed to pilot a joint-stock system reform. Specifically, the first type enterprises were confined to joint-stock enterprises in Shanghai and Shenzhen which were allowed to issue shares

[7] The Master Plan of the State Commission for Economic Restructuring for Deeping the Economic System Reform in 1988, the People's Bank of China and the CCCPC Party Literature Research Office (eds): *Selected Literature on Financial Work (1978–2005)*, China Financial Publishing House, 2007; p. 154.

to the public and whose shares were also traded in the stock market; the second type enterprises were restricted to pilot enterprises in Guangdong province, Fujian province and Hainan province which were allowed to issue shares to the public but whose shares were non-tradable in the market; and the third type enterprises primarily refer to joint-stock enterprises in other regions with the shareholdings held by legal person or employees.

In early 1992, there were 3,220 joint-stock enterprises of all types (excluding joint-stock companies, Sino-foreign joint ventures, and domestic joint ventures which were categorized as township enterprises), of which more than 95% were piloting enterprises with the shareholding held by legal person or their employees.[8] At the end of 1992, there were a total of 247 enterprises which illegally issued RMB5.6 billion worth of shares without the approval from the central government in 33 provinces and cities other than Shanghai and Shenzhen. Among them, 38 enterprises issued shares worth RMB 1,217 million publicly, while 209 enterprises issued shares internally, with a total market capitalization of RMB 4,385 million.[9]

Due to the shortage of new shares, the Shanghai government had to issue share warrants in 1992, and only those who bought share warrants were eligible to draw lots to buy new shares. This led to a frenzy of stock trading and a restless speculative mood in the market, with many people rushing blindly into the securities market. As the local governments across the country scrambled to issue shares, the "stock fever" was intensified, causing market disruption and unregulated and illegal trading activities. In 1993, the government commenced to curb the unregulated and irregular fund-raising activities associated with employee shareholdings and tighten the regulation of share issue.

In 1992, special RMB shares (B shares) totaling $200 million were issued in Shanghai and Shenzhen in a bid to open up new channels for leveraging foreign capital. By the end of June 1992, thirteen enterprises had issued RMB950 million worth of B shares, with seven of these B shares being traded in the market. In January 1997, thirty-three enterprises were on the pre-selected B-share shortlist, covering eleven industries such as power and energy development, transportation, electronics, and communication.

As the "stock fever" was raging on, national foreign exchange trading centers, bond trading markets and interbank lending market all entered into online transactions.

Second, different kinds of joint-stock commercial banks were established with approval. The joint-stock commercial banks included China Everbright Bank, Shanghai Pudong Development Bank and Huaxia Bank established in 1992, as well as Hainan Development Bank (1995) and China Minsheng Banking Corp. Ltd. (1996). In addition, local joint-stock commercial banks such as Beijing City Cooperative

[8] Wu Xiaoling (ed): *A Chronicle of Major Events in China's Financial Reform and Opening up*, China Financial Publishing House, 2008, p. 235.

[9] The Master Plan of the State Commission for Economic Restructuring for Deeping the Economic System Reform in 1988, the People's Bank of China and CCCPC Party Literature Research Office (eds): *Selected Literature on Financial Work (1978–2005)*, China Financial Publishing House, 2007; p. 128.

Bank (1996) were also established with approval. By 1999, urban cooperative banks had been approved for establishment in nineteen cities such as Xi'an, Chengdu, Guiyang, Changchun, and Dalian.

From 1996 to 2001, Sino-foreign joint venture commercial banks were successively established, including Sino-Korean joint venture Qingdao International Bank (1996), First Sino Bank (established in 1996 and renamed Fubon Bank (China) Co., Ltd. in 2014) jointly set up by banks and industrial enterprises across the Taiwan Strait, and HANA Bank China (2000).

Third, many securities and insurance companies were established with approval. These kinds of securities and insurance companies included Huaxia Bond Corporation Limited, Guotai Securities Company and China Southern Securities Co. Ltd. established in September 1992, and China Chengxin Securities Rating Co., Ltd. established in October 1992; AIA Shanghai Branch (1992), the first foreign-funded insurance company in China; and the People's Insurance (Group) Company of China Limited, Huatai Property Insurance Co., Ltd., Dazhong Insurance Company Ltd., Taikang Life Insurance Co., Ltd., Yong An Insurance Co., Ltd., Yong An Property Insurance Co., Ltd., Manulife-Sinochen Life Insurance Co., Ltd. and others established in succession from 1996 to 2001.

Fourth, futures markets and futures exchanges were established. These futures exchanges included Dalian Commodity Exchange (today's second largest soybean futures market in the world) established in 1993, and Beijing Commodity Exchange, Shanghai Metals Exchange, Shanghai Grain and Oil Commodity Exchange, Shenyang Commodity Exchange, Dalian Commodity Exchange, Suzhou Commodity Exchange, Zhengzhou Commodity Exchange, Guangdong Unite Futures Exchange, Shenzhen Non-Ferrous Metal Futures Unite Exchange, Hainan Zhongshang Futures Exchange and Chongqing Commodity Exchange established on October 20, 1994.

On May 4, 1999, Shanghai Futures Exchange was opened for trial operation and it is the third futures exchange still in operation in China today, with 233 members and 341 trading seats.

Over a short spell of just a decade, the Chinese financial sector has kept on the momentum going, progressively building up financial markets and organizational systems in line with the actual situation in China.

1.4.2 Redefining Financial System Orientation and Bank Roles

According to the Decision on Financial Institutional Reform issued by the State Council on December 25, 1993, the government decided to press ahead with the reform on the existing financial sector, while effecting incremental changes. This mainly involved defining the roles and orientations of three types of national banks.

First, the PBoC was designated as China's central bank. As the central bank of China, the PBoC was mandated to perform the following functions: Leading and attending to the national financial affairs, scientifically formulating and implementing monetary policy and maintaining monetary stability; tightening up the regulation of financial institutions to ensure the security and effective operation of the financial system; independently pursuing monetary policy under the leadership of the State Council, and ceasing to directly grant policy loans or perform other fiscal financing functions; making up the shortfall between the central government's revenue and expenditure by issuing treasury bonds rather than bank overdrafts; and establishing a macro-regulation regime for central bank independently pursuing monetary policies under the leadership of the State Council.

Second, policy financial institutions were established and different roles of policy and commercial financial institutions were defined. This mainly involved separating the policy financial business previously undertaken by the PBoC and state-owned specialized banks, and handing over such business to deliberately established policy financial institutions for transacting. In 1994, three policy banks were successively established with approval, including China Development Bank (CDB) established on April 14, 1994, the Export-Import Bank of China (China Ex-Import Bank) established on July 1, 1994, and the Agricultural Development Bank of China (ADBC) established on November 18, 1994. With the establishment of these policy-oriented financial institutions, policy finance and commercial finance have been essentially separated.

Third, state-owned specialized banks were reorganized into wholly state-owned commercial banks. The separation of policy operations has severed the direct link between the central bank's base money supply and policy lending. Specifically, the four state-owned specialized banks of the ICBC, the ABC, the BOC and the CCB were reorganized into wholly state-owned commercial banks and their orientations were legally laid down in the Law of the People's Republic of China on Commercial Banks promulgated in May 1995. The government called on them to carry out reform in line with the operational mechanisms of modern commercial banks, so as to reorganize themselves into true state-owned commercial banks which would operate independently, bear their own risks, self-finance and exercise self-regulation.

1.4.3 Commercialized Restructuring of State-Owned Commercial Banks

The commercialized restructuring and reorganization of state-owned commercial banks was inextricably bound up with the reform of medium-sized and large state-owned enterprises, aiming to address the prominent problems of insufficient proprietary funds and high non-performing loan ratio. As of the end of June 1996, the four large state-owned commercial banks had a balance of outstanding loans of RMB3.4 trillion, with an outstanding balance of RMB840 billion in non-performing loans, accounting for 24.75% of the total outstanding loan balance. Actually, some banks were insolvent at that time.

With a view to carrying out reorganization smoothly, the government decided to take measures to sink capital into wholly state-owned commercial banks. In March 1998, the Standing Committee of the National People's Congress deliberated and adopted the plan proposed by the State Council to inject RMB270 billion of capital into state-owned commercial banks by issuing special treasury bonds. In other words, the deposit reserve requirement ratio of commercial banks was reduced from 13 to 8%, whereby commercial banks used the curtailed funds to purchase special treasury bonds issued by the MoF, while the MoF used the funds raised to sink capital into four state-owned commercial banks.

At the end of 1998, the capital adequacy ratios of four large state-owned commercial banks were still below 8% and their non-performing loan ratio exceeded 20%, which severely affected their business performance. What is more, the non-performing loan ratio tended to spiral upwards while the capital adequacy ratio was tapering off. And how could this thorny problem be solved when the central government had no capacity to inject large amounts of money every year?

There were two possible options. One was to establish a shareholding system to raise funds beyond central budgeting, which needed to lift the ownership restrictions on wholly state-owned enterprises; the other was to issue long-term bonds as supplementary capital, but there were also certain restrictions on bond issuance.

In 1999, the Chinese government worked out a viable solution for solving this thorny issue by stripping off the non-performing loans from the four large state-owned commercial banks, and selling them to newly established specialized asset management companies according to the overall timetable. Subsequently, those specialized asset management companies raised funds to purchase these non-performing loans by issuing bonds guaranteed by the MoF or financial bonds, or applying for loans from central bank, and then disposed of these non-performing loans through debt collection, debt-to-equity swap, securitization, auction, debt swap and debt restructuring.

In April 1999, China Cinda Asset Management Co., Ltd. (Cinda) was approved for establishment with a mission of acquiring and operating in the CCB's non-performing assets business. On July 21, 1999, China Huarong Asset Management Co., Ltd., China Great Wall Asset Management Co., Ltd. and China Orient Asset Management Co., Ltd.[10] were successively established to acquire, manage and dispose of the non-performing assets stripped off from the ICBC, ABC and BOC. Their main business aimed to maximize asset preservation and minimize losses.

In the second half of 1999, four financial asset management companies, namely China Huarong Asset Management Company Limited, China Great Wall Asset Management Company Limited, China Oriental Asset Management Company Limited and China Cinda Asset Management Company Limited, acquired a total

---

[10] These financial asset management companies are respectively abbreviated as Huarong, GreatWall and Orient.

of RMB1,393.9 billion of non-performing loans stripped off from the four state-owned commercial banks and the CDB, with RMB100 billion being stripped off from the CDB. The acquisition of non-performing loans by the asset management companies was partially financed by RMB 573.9 billion worth of loans granted by the PBoC to the commercial banks concerned, which were then transferred to the asset management companies, and RMB 820 billion worth of bonds issued by the asset management companies to the corresponding commercial banks.

With a view to implementing the policy of reorganization and commercialized restructuring, the four large wholly state-owned commercial banks also commenced to downsize their staff. By the end of 2000, the ICBC, ABC, BOC and CCB all had basically completed the mergers or dissolutions of their branches, with 1,586 county sub-branches being disbanded. Through the streamlining and merging of inefficient and overlapping business outlets, the number of their business outlets was reduced by 34,000 at the end of 1997, and there were 1,878,000 on-the-job employees, down by 127,000 from the end of 1997.[11]

By 2001, the non-performing loan ratios of the four large wholly state-owned commercial banks had fallen to 25.4%. In 2002, the banking regulatory authorities released the data on non-performing loans of banks in Class-V loans category. Meanwhile, commercial banks also carried out assets–liability ratio management, and progressively established self-regulation and risk liability mechanisms. With a view to supporting the joint-stock system reform and IPO of wholly state-owned commercial banks, the government subsequently stripped off large amounts of non-performing loans from them through various means. By strengthening internal management and external supervision, the asset quality of the wholly state-owned commercial banks has reached a certain level and their commercial restructuring has achieved the desired results.

Although the above-mentioned measures were imposed to temporarily solve the problems of capital inadequacy and non-performing loans of commercial banks, there were still other underlying issues to be grappled with, such as "How can specialized asset management companies recover these non-performing loans? How to define the obligations, functions and powers of central bank, commercial banks and asset management companies?". All these issues need to be explored to find a solution through carrying out reforms and optimizing relevant operation and management systems.

[11] Wu Xiaoling (ed): *A Chronicle of Major Events in China's Financial Reform and Opening up*, China Financial Publishing House, 2008, p. 565.

1.4.4 Inflation Control and Soft Landing Through Macro-regulation

Following Xiaoping Deng's speech during his South China tour, the Chinese economy experienced a new round of "overheating", which led to a spiral in direct financing and inflation.

In 1992, domestic cash injection jumped to RMB120 billion from RMB53 billion a year earlier. In 1993, the amount of currencies issued reached RMB115.8 billion, and bank loans amounted to RMB354.7 billion, up 36% and 19.7% from the previous year respectively. Meanwhile, negative interest rates on savings deposit occurred in the capital market. Nevertheless, some enterprises still substantially increased their interest rates to raise more funds from bond issuance. In the end, annual interest rates were abnormally as high as 15%, 20% or even 25% in the market. Even more, some banks also got involved in direct investment. For state-owned commercial banks with a proprietary capital ratio of less than 6%, the risks were too high to bear, causing a surge in cash injection, fund supply shortage, and a spike in price.

According to the data from the National Bureau of Statistics for the year 1994, the consumer price rose by 24.1% that year in China, with a price spike of 25% in cities. In thirty-five medium-sized and large cities, consumer price climbed by 24.8%; commodity retail price rose by 21.7%; and national agricultural and sideline products saw price rise across the country, an increase of 31.8%, 50.7%, 41.6% and 64.1% in food, grain, poultry and its products, and edible vegetable oil respectively, and 10% higher than that in 1993.

It was not until 1996 that this round of inflation trend was halted. Even more, "IOUs" were sometimes issued to farmers in many regions when state food administrations purchased grain, or supply and marketing cooperatives procured cotton and wool. This has incurred serious economic losses on the farmers and triggered a series of crimes.

On June 24, 1993, the CPC Central Committee and the State Council issued the Opinions on Rectifying the Current Economic Situation and Tightening up Macro-Regulation, which was widely known as "Central Government Document No.6". In this document, sixteen measures were proposed to curb inflation, the first nine of which were intended to exercise macro-regulation and rectify the financial market order.[12]

While implementing the sixteen measures, the government reformed the credit fund management regime as follows: ① Restoring the PBoC to the powers to adjust and control credit loan quotas which had been delegated to its provincial branches before, and centralized the powers to allocate credit loan quotas, grant loans to commercial banks, determine and adjust benchmark interest rates, and issue currencies in the hands of its head office; ② Establishing the targets of monetary policy as maintaining monetary stability and promoting economic growth; and ③ Tightening the control over credit loans by rigorously imposing the credit loan quotas on

[12] The People's Bank of China and CCCPC Party Literature Research Office (eds): *Selected Literature on Financial Work (1978–2005)*, China Financial Publishing House, 2007, pp. 170–178.

commercial banks while effecting their asset-liability restructuring to meet the asset-liability ratio requirements. From the third quarter of 1993 onwards, the government published the data regarding hierarchical money supply monitoring targets on a quarterly basis, and shifted the previous model of macro-regulation based on credit loan quota plan control.

Meanwhile, the government employed multiple measures to control inflation, including the operation of moderately tight monetary and fiscal policies, deepening the reform of economic and financial systems, and establishing a PBoC-led macro-regulation regime through using such policy instruments as the deposit reserve requirement ratio system, the central bank lending system and the foreign currencies and foreign debt management regime.

By 1996, the policy package pursued by the government to curb inflation had accomplished remarkable achievements, and price rises had continued to suffer a pullback. In 1996, commodity retail price and consumer price rose by 6.1% and 8.3% respectively from the previous year. The objectives for price control were basically fulfilled, and "soft landing" was achieved through macro-regulation, without provoking massive economic upheavals.

1.4.5 Clamping Down on Three Financial Irregularities and Stabilizing Financial Market Order

In 1993, "irregular borrowing", "irregular fundraising" and "irregular approval for establishing financial institutions", which were also known as "Three Irregularities", surfaced in the financial sector. From 1993 to 2000, these irregularities permeated everywhere and disrupted the financial market order for eight years, not far from a financial crisis in China.[13]

"Three Irregularities" have been bubbling away for a long time, mainly reflected in the following five aspects.

First, many financial institutions and practitioners engaged in falsification, illegal operations, off-balance-sheet operations and illegal borrowing. From 1992 to 1993 alone, illegal borrowing in the interbank lending market topped RMB100 billion. With a view to evading financial regulation and credit loan quota control, some financial institutions accounted for cash and loan out of balance sheet. By the end of 1995, a total of more than RMB 100 billion of off-balance-sheet funds illegally operated by state-owned commercial banks had been investigated and handled nationwide.

Second, crimes such as illegal and irregular fundraising, offering high interest rates to attract deposits and financial fraud were on the upswing, and there were a spiral trend of serious and major cases. For instance, funds in excess of RMB1.2 billion and RMB3.2 billion were illegally raised in the Shen Taifu case in Beijing

[13] Dai Xianlong, *A Personal Recollection of Eight Years of Overhauling Financial Market Order*, *China Finance*, Issue 7, 2018.

city in 1993 and the Deng Bin case in Wuxi city in 1994 respectively, causing huge losses to the public and enterprises. Thereafter, both Shen Taifu and Deng Bin were sentenced to death. Meanwhile, there were also widespread irregularities that had surfaced in the stock, trust and futures markets, and vicious cases were spiking at that time.

Third, irregular operations sparked off the payment crises and shutdowns of financial institutions. For example, Enping City Rural Credit Cooperative in Guangdong province had a deposit balance of RMB 6.63 billion in August 1996, of which deposits with extortionate interest rates and deposits with interest rates paid on the deposit date amounted to RMB5.58 billion in total and such deposits were charged an average interest rate as high as 20–25%. The local municipal government ordered to have these funds earmarked for the construction of small cement plants in different townships and villages. As the central government tightened the control on infrastructures construction scale, the small cement plants built in the city were successively closed down, which has eventually provoked two payment crises to the relevant banks and rural credit cooperatives. In the end, local financial institutions have suffered approximately RMB10 billion in losses. To address such a grave situation, state-owned commercial banks had to temporarily suspend business operations at their Enping branches, and all local rural credit cooperatives have been shut down as a result.

Fourth, illegal approvals for establishing financial institutions and irregular operation in financial business bubbled away in China. For instance, rural cooperative funds at different levels were set up to manage the rural collective economy, and render mutual fund assistance to farmers. Therefore, they were not categorized as a financial institution. However, with the intervention of local governments, rural cooperative funds at different levels attracted and grew deposits from the public by hiking interest rates, which were earmarked for local construction, or even were misappropriated by township governments to build office buildings and public roads. In the end, the bulk of rural cooperative funds at different levels were unable to return principal of their deposits to depositors as well as pay interest rates as they fell due, triggering demonstrations by depositors, vandalism against township governments and bank runs involving hundreds of people in a number of cities.

Fifth, financial institutions faced a risk of too high non-performing asset ratio. In particular, wholly state-owned commercial banks held a disproportionately high percentage of non-performing assets, with a spike in outstanding interest receivables and growing operational difficulties. Even more, non-banking financial institutions like trust and investment companies and urban credit cooperatives were plagued by more serious knotty problems of non-performing loans.

The various forms of "Three Irregularities" mentioned above have put unrelenting pressure on China's economic and financial development. To cope with the stressful situation, the Chinese government decided to concentrate on overhauling these irregularities and establishing an orderly financial market.

The first stage (1993–1996) of clamping down on "Three Irregularities" and overhauling financial market order commenced in June 1993 to make a breakthrough in overhauling the money lending business.

On the one hand, one-off overhaul was unleashed on those investment funds and trust beneficiary bonds that were not approved for issue, as well as investment fund management companies that were not approval for establishment prior to April 1993. On the other hand, the PBoC ordered all its provincial branches to cease approving the establishment of new urban credit cooperatives, effective July 1, 1993, and suspend the use of quotas that had been allocated yet not used up. Meanwhile, the PBoC grappled with the issue of overstepping authority to approve the establishment of urban credit cooperatives.

In his speech at the National Conference on Financial Work held on July 5, 1993, Rongji Zhu, then Vice Premier of the State Council and concurrently Governor of the PBoC, called on leaders in banking establishments to strictly implement the sixteen measures proposed in "Central Document No.6" in a bid to tighten financial regulation, and rectify financial market order. Meanwhile, Zhu also imposed a three-point rule: First, prohibiting and overhauling all illegal lending activities; second, prohibiting financial institutions from waging the "deposit-grabbing wars" by hiking deposit and loan interest rates without authorization or in disguise; and third, forbidding the injection of funds into economic entities set up by banks, which must completely decouple from their affiliated economic entities.

In the second half of 1993, efforts to clamp down on "Three Irregularities" and rectify financial market order accomplished an achievement.

First, irregular inter-bank lending was clamped down on. From July 20 to August 15, 1993, more than 400 loans irregularly granted were recovered from the non-banking system alone. In the national banking system, RMB72.7 billion worth of borrowed inter-bank funds were recovered. The objective of "Four Cessations" were basically achieved, i.e. cessation of newly irregular borrowing, cessation of borrowing from non-financial institutions and non-banking financial institutions, cessation of borrowing in interbank lending markets below the provincial level, and cessation of injection of new funds into the affiliated economic entities of banks.

While clamping down on irregularities, the Chinese government also imposed effective measures to solve the problem of working capital shortages facing banks and enterprises. From August to November 1993, Rongji Zhu successively presided over eight financing meetings. From August 21 to October 15, 1993, the PBoC arranged for lending RMB97 billion worth of credit funds to wholly state-owned commercial banks, while treasury and local bonds totaling RMB21.2 billion were swapped for bank loans.

Second, irregularly established financial institutions were cracked down on. Under relevant policy provisions, the Chinese government ordered the PBoC to decouple itself from all types of its affiliated economic entities in terms of their affiliation and accounting relationships in July 1993. Additionally, the PBoC's officials were not allowed to hold a concurrent position in affiliated economic entities, nor were they allowed to lend credit funds to affiliated economic entities or render special financial policy support to them. Nevertheless, some qualified securities institutions in the financial system were allowed to be retained. All securities business offices set up by commercial banks, urban cooperative banks, urban cooperatives, insurance companies, financial companies affiliated to enterprise group, financial leasing companies, pawnshops and other financial institutions and financing hubs (financial markets) must be either dissolved or transferred prior to December 31, 1996.

Third, irregular fundraising activities were clamped down on. The State Council called for clamping down on paid fundraising activities, effective on September 3, 1993. Specifically, it resolutely imposed a ban on irregular fundraising and a moratorium on all paid fund-raising activities organized by all local governments, government departments and social organizations that undertook to return principal and pay interest rates or pay dividends and bonuses to contributors.

Fourth, market manipulations were clamped down on. In 1995, the government launched a major overhaul campaign in the futures industry, and severely cracked down on market manipulations; meted out penalties to crimes that had disrupted the financial market order such as currency forgery, financial instrument fraud, fraud associated with letters of credit, and illegal fundraising scam; strictly pursued moderately tight fiscal and monetary policies, controlled money supply, and guarded against risks arising in economic operations.

After three years of strenuous efforts, the first stage of the campaign of clamping down on "Three Irregularities" came to a standstill in 1996. In the end, violations newly committed have been effectively contained, all major violators have been duly punished, and the financial market order has been rectified. However, financial risks arose from grave violations of discipline and law, and there were still many financial enterprises that were seriously insolvent and unable to repay their debts as they fell due. Therefore, the task of financial overhaul has not yet fully fulfilled.

The campaign for clamping down on "Three Irregularities" and rectifying the financial market order entered the second stage (1997–2000). Building on the work outcomes of the first stage, the second stage focused on addressing the issue of "irregular establishment of financial institutions" and overhauling the financial market market.

In January 1997, the four large wholly-owned commercial banks basically completed the decoupling from their trust and investment companies. Altogether, 148 out of their 186 trust and investment companies were disbanded. Meanwhile, the PBoC ordered the four large wholly state-owned commercial banks and the BCM to decouple from their affiliated economic entities prior to the end of June 1997.

Following the Asian financial crisis in July 1997, the Chinese government viewed 1997 as "the Year of Rectifying the Financial Market Order and Preventing Financial Risks". Efforts were intensified to solve the problems of the operation management regime and breach of discipline and regulations in the financial sector.

With a view to thoroughly carrying out the tasks of clamping down on "Three Irregularities" and rectifying the financial market order, the following five requirements were set forth at the National Conference on Financial Work held in November 1997: ① Banking, trust, securities and insurance industries shall follow the business philosophy of separate operation and management, and banks were no longer allowed to invest in non-banking financial institutions and non-financial enterprises, or directly conduct the trust, securities and insurance business; ② The PBoC and all commercial banks must completely decouple from their affiliated trust, securities and insurance companies and other economic entities in 1998; ③ Trust and investment companies were not allowed to conduct the deposit and lending business other than those entrusted by legal entities; ④ Financial companies affiliated to enterprise groups were not allowed to make personal deposits or make short-term deposits for enterprises; and ⑤ Urban and rural credit cooperatives are financial cooperatives that provide traditional banking services to their members and follow a basic business model that members pool their money—technically, they are buying shares in the cooperative—in order to be able to provide loans, demand deposit accounts, and other financial products and services to each other. Any income generated is used to fund projects and services that will benefit the community and the interests of its members. Additionally, they shall carry out management in a democratic manner.

On December 6, 1997, the CPC Central Committee and the State Council jointly put forward fifteen measures to deepen reform, rectify financial market order and prevent financial risks. On December 8, 1997, the State Council decided to set up twelve special groups for deepening financial reform and rectifying financial market order nationwide, with a mission of studying and drawing up specific schemes for solving financial problems.

Through in-depth survey and full consultation with relevant departments, the twelve special working groups formulated nineteen overhauling schemes, including the implementing scheme for reforming the PBoC's provincial branches, the reform scheme for branches of wholly state-owned commercial banks, the implementing scheme for cracking down on irregular fund-raising, illegal approval for the establishment of financial institutions and irregular financial business operations, the implementing scheme for clamping down on the off-balance-sheet accounts and the irregular operations in business of banks, the scheme for overhauling illegal over-the-counter stock trading and securities trading centers, the scheme for overhauling securities companies and futures markets, the scheme for overhauling urban credit cooperatives, and the scheme for overhauling rural cooperative funds at different levels.

Meanwhile, the PBoC also rolled out supporting solutions. On December 20, 1997, the PBoC issued relevant policies, requiring banks to verify and identify the outstanding balances of irregularly borrowed funds that they had not been recovered by the end of 1993, and resolutely remedy irregular borrowing contracts. On May 22, 1998, the PBoC held a national teleconference to arrange for the work for overhauling the financial market order.

In July and August 1998, the State Council issued the Measures for Banning Illegal Financial Institutions and Financial Business Activities, which set forth specific provisions on illegal financial institutions and illegal financial business established and conducted without the approval of the PBoC. Additionally, it also approved and forwarded the Implementing Plan for Cracking down on Irregular Fundraising, Irregular Approval for the Establishment of Financial Institutions and Irregular Operation of Financial Business promulgated by the PBoC.

From the second half of 1998 onwards, work to clamp down on "Three Irregularities" was carried out in three stages: self-examination and self-remedy, debt repayment, as well as experience summarization and acceptance inspection. All the overhauling work was scheduled for completion as of the end of 2000.

On September 30, 1998, the campaign for overhauling the securities market was launched. A centralized overhaul was carried out on all securities trading centers and their affiliated securities registration companies which were established without the approval of the PBoC or the China Securities Regulatory Commission (CSRC) yet still engaged in online trading on the Shanghai or Shenzhen Stock Exchanges via the Internet, as well as dealt in non-listed companies' stocks, stock certificates and funds.

In October 1998, the overhauling of urban and rural credit cooperatives was commenced. At the request of the State Council and the PBoC, 2,893 urban credit cooperatives were overhauled, with more than 1,700 being either dissolved or merged. In the meantime, over 28,000 rural cooperative funds at different levels were overhauled, with 7,469 being disbanded, and 4,891 being merged into rural credit cooperatives.

In 1999, work was done to overhaul financial institutions that needed to decouple from state authorities and separate government functions from enterprise management. According to the relevant statistics, there were a total of 27 central Party and government organs and relevant organizations which needed to decouple from their 36 affiliated financial enterprises by way of transfer, reorganization, dissolution, close-down, or otherwise. Additionally, there were 80 government departments which needed to decouple from their non-financial enterprises, of which 52 government departments reported 530 directly affiliated enterprises and enterprise groups for the decoupling scheme, involving 3,151 directly affiliated subsidiaries with a total net profit of RMB10.52 billion as well as 2.85 million in-service employees and 1.06 million retired employees. These affiliated enterprises were decoupled through reorganization, transfer, overhauling or shutdown for overhaul, dissolution, merger and acquisition or declaration of bankruptcy.[14]

In 1999, the insurance industry was overhauled. On July 2, 1999, the State Council called for severely investigating and punishing insurance companies for unfair competition practices, involving charging high commissions, granting high rebates, and lowering premium rates. Additionally, a call was also made to crack down on underground insurance intermediary activities.

Meanwhile, the government took decisive measures to merge or close down financial enterprises that were insolvent and incapable of repaying due debts for a long period as well as difficult to be bailed out. For instance, Hainan Development Bank, Guangdong Trust and Investment Company, the Agricultural Trust Bank of China and China Innovative Technology Venture Capital Investment Company were all shut

---

[14] Wu Xiaoling (ed): *A Chronicle of Major Events in China's Financial Reform and Opening up*, China Financial Publishing House, 2008, pp. 483–484.

down. Meanwhile, effective countermeasures such as debt-to-equity swap, reorganization or local financial aids were employed to overhaul some financial institutions with poor financial performance, involving China Everbright Bank International Trust and Investment Corporation, Fujian International Trust and Investment Corporation, and Hubei International Trust and Investment Corporation, etc.

While cracking down on illegal and irregular financial institutions and disposing of their debts, the Chinese government adhered to the principles that "whoever takes charge must undertake the overhauling work; whoever grants approval must take responsibility; whoever uses money must clear debts incurred therefrom, and whoever provides a guarantee must bear corresponding liability". Provided that overhauling costs were rationalized and the legitimate rights and interests of citizens were safeguarded, natural person's legitimate debts have been tackled and social stability has been preserved through loans from commercial banks, the PBoC's loans to commercial banks, deductions from central fiscal rebates offered to provincial governments, or otherwise. As of the end of 2000, the actual loans granted by the PBoC amounted to RMB150 billion, of which 95% were eventually recovered.

The second stage of the work has pulled off great feats. According to incomplete statistics, more than 5,200 persons in charge were dealt with nationwide during the overhaul of off-balance-sheet accounts; more than 4,000 cases of illegal fund-raising topping RMB50 billion were investigated and handled; 797 illegally established financial institutions were banned or disbanded; 7,966 cases of violating law and discipline were opened a file and handled by the disciplinary inspection and supervision departments at all levels in the financial sector, with penalties imposed on 17,484 violators; all 41 illegitimate stock exchanges in the country were closed down nationwide, and the number of futures exchanges was reduced from 14 to 3 through dissolutions or mergers; and insurance companies were investigated and handled for all kinds of unfair competition and underground intermediary activities. From 1998 to 2001, Chinese enterprises raised a total of RMB503 billion from domestic and overseas securities markets, and national premium income increased to RMB210.9 billion in 2001 from RMB124.7 billion in 1998.[15]

By 2001, the Chinese government had basically succeeded in fulfilling the tasks of clamping down on "Three Irregularities" and overhauling the financial market order. Specifically speaking, China had successfully withstood the impact of the 1997 Asian financial crisis, guarded against systemic financial risks, and safeguarded national financial security and stability. Meanwhile, all the efforts had also provided strong support for the country to stimulate domestic demand, implement the Western Development Strategy and help state-owned enterprises to put into practice the reform on getting out of difficulties in the coming three years, thus laying a solid foundation for China's accession to the World Trade Organization (WTO) in December 2001.

[15] Rongji Zhu, Further Open up a New Situation of Financial Reform, China Financial Publishing House in China, February 5, 2002. The People's Bank of China and CCCPC Party Literature Research Office (eds): *Selected Literature on Financial Work (1978–2005)*, China Financial Publishing House, 2007; p. 464.

1.5 Going Global and Joint-Stock System Reform

From 2002 to 2011, China's financial sector embarked on going global, carrying out the joint-stock system reform of financial institutions, and thereby fully integrating into the world economy and the international financial market.

1.5.1 WTO Accession Propelled Internationalization

Following China's accession to the WTO in December 2001, the Chinese government has been steadfastly pursuing the national strategy of opening China to the outside world and proactively fulfilling the country's relevant commitments to opening up its financial sector in a progressive manner according to the relevant conventions. In the meantime, efforts have been also making to push forward with the internationalization of the financial sector.

First, the Chinese government loosened restrictions on foreign capital's access to the financial sector. Restrictions on regions, customers, business scope and foreign shareholding ratio were liberalized. In 2002, the Chinese government successively introduced qualified domestic and overseas institutional investor systems (namely QFII and QDII), thereby allowing qualified domestic and foreign institutional investors to conduct the securities investment business at home and abroad and stimulating the two-way flow of domestic and foreign capital. In 2006, it also lifted the regional and customer restrictions on foreign banks' RMB business operations in China, as well as the restrictions on the establishment of branches and operation in business by foreign financial institutions in China.

Second, the Chinese government promoted international cooperation in the financial sector and participated in international financial governance. The Chinese government has proactively leveraged such mechanisms as China-US Strategic and Economic Dialogue, China-UK Economic and Finance Dialogue, China-Japan Executive Economic Dialogue, China-EU Central Bank Working Group, and China-Russia Financial Cooperation Sub-Committee, with a view to promoting bilateral pragmatic economic and financial cooperation, and encouraging and supporting cross-border trade settlement in *renminbi*. By August 2011, cross-border trade settlement in *renminbi* had been up-scaled to the whole country.

From 2008 onwards, the PBoC officially joined in the Financial Stability Board, the Basel Committee on Banking Supervision, and the Committee on the Global Financial System, thoroughly participated in the formulation of international regulatory rules such as Basel Capital Accord III and Globally Systemically Important Financial Institutions (G-SIFIs), as well as got involved in the discussion of major issues like global economic and financial governance, international monetary system reform and financial regulation reform.

Third, the insurance industry was at the forefront of the opening up and internationalization of the financial sector. As of the end of 2001, there were a total of 29 foreign insurance companies established in China, including 16 Sino-foreign joint ventures. As of the end of 2004, China's insurance industry was the first to complete the transition of WTO accession and enter the stage of opening to the outside world. Specifically, 37 insurance companies from 14 countries and regions entered China's insurance market, earning a premium revenue of RMB9.8 billion, accounting for 2.3% of the total. As of the end of 2007, there were a total of 43 foreign insurance companies from 15 countries and regions that had set up 134 business outlets in China.[16]

At the end of November 2015, there were a total of 147 life insurance companies (excluding group companies, reinsurance companies, asset management companies, etc.) in China, including 50 foreign-funded insurance companies. Out of 72 property insurance companies in China, 22 were foreign-funded companies; and among 75 personal insurance companies, 28 were foreign funded companies. By the end of 2016, insurance companies from 16 countries and regions had set up 56 foreign-funded insurance institutions in China, while 12 Chinese insurance companies had established 38 insurance business outlets abroad, effecting two-way opening up.

Fourth, the Chinese government relaxed the control over capital accounts and liberalized capital accounts in a progressive manner. The Chinese government promoted cross-border settlement in RMB, and progressively upscaled cross-border RMB settlement business under current accounts to some capital accounts. At the end of June 2012, the RMB settlement business conducted by banks under current accounts totaled RMB3.2 trillion. As of the end of 2012, China's foreign exchange reserve balance stood at US$3.31 trillion.

From 2002 onwards, China's financial sector has seized the opportunity of joining in the WTO and taken the initiative to align itself with international practices in a bid to expedite the process of going global, step up market opening-up, progressively integrate into economic and financial globalization, and comprehensively promote the development of China's financial sector.

1.5.2 Joint-Stock System Reform of State-Owned Banks and Insurance Companies

In the recent 10 years since its accession to the WTO, the Chinese government has attached importance to a joint-stock system reform of wholly state-owned commercial banks and non-banking financial institutions, as well as the commercialized reform of the national investment system and the rural financial system, with a view to enhancing the international competitiveness of the financial sector.

First, the reform in the joint-stock system of state-owned commercial banks and policy banks was initiated. By upholding the spirit of the Second National Conference on the Financial Work in 2002, the Third National Conference on the

[16] Sun Rong and Yang Fu, Thirty Years of Reform and Opening up: The Transitional and Evolutionary Trajectory of China's Insurance Industry, *Insurance Studies*, Issue 8, 2008.

Financial Work in 2007 and the Third Plenary Session of the Sixteenth CPC Central Committee, the Chinese government decided on a reform strategy of reorganizing wholly state-owned commercial banks into state-controlled joint-stock commercial banks, aiming to transform banks into true modern financial enterprises and allow qualified banks to go public to raise funds at home and abroad.

From 2004 to 2010, state-owned commercial banks including the BOC, BCM, CCB, ICBC and ABC were the first to complete joint-stock system restructuring, and they successively got listed in Hong Kong and Shanghai. During this period, great strides were also made in the reform in the joint-stock system of policy banks. In December 2008, China Development Bank Co., Ltd. also successfully went public.

Second, the reform in the stock system of insurance institutions was carried out. From March 18 to 20, 1999, the People's Insurance Company of China, China Life Insurance Company Ltd. and China Reinsurance Group were successively established in Beijing. On July 19, 2003, the People's Insurance Company of China was renamed the People's Insurance Company (Group) of China Ltd., which initiated the establishment of PICC Property and Casualty Insurance Co., Ltd. and PICC Asset Management Company Limited. On November 6, 2003, PICC Property and Casualty Insurance Co., Ltd. successfully made its IPO in Hong Kong, becoming China's first financial enterprise to get listed overseas. In February 2004, the People's Insurance Company (Group) of China Ltd., China Life Insurance (Group) Company and China Re Group all successfully completed the restructuring of their joint-stock system, of which the People's Insurance Company (Group) of China Ltd. and China Life Insurance (Group) Company both went public abroad.

Third, the reform in the joint-stock system of other financial institutions was rolled out. On March 20, 2007, the Postal Savings Bank of China was established by China Post Group Co., Ltd. in Beijing. On May 14, 2011, the State Council approved China Export and Credit Insurance Corporation for implementing the Overall Reform implementing Plan and the Draft for Articles of Association (Revised Version) and reiterated its orientation as a policy-oriented financial institution, while substantially sinking its capita in preparations for its reform in the joint-stock system. In June 2011, Central Huijin Investment Co., Ltd. injected RMB20 billion into it.

1.5.3 Commercialized Restructuring of State-Owned Financial Institutions

First, the commercialized reorganization of financial asset management companies was initiated. At the time of their establishment in 1999, financial asset management companies were established to dispose of the non-performing assets of state-owned commercial banks, and the MoF specified their ten years of business operation period. By the end of 2003, the four financial asset management companies had disposed of non-performing assets totaling RMB806.16 billion since their establishment, completing the bulk of their asset disposal tasks. What would be their orientation in the future?

According to the Request for Instructions on Issues Concerning the Reform and Development of Financial Asset Management Companies submitted by the MoF to the State Council in March 2003, upon the expiry of the ten-year operation period, the development orientation of financial asset management companies and relevant supporting policies were clarified, including establishing an asset disposal and recovery target assessment system for asset management companies; allowing asset management companies with a prompt asset disposal capacity to engage in commercially entrusted and commercialized acquisition and disposal of non-performing assets; allowing asset management companies to use capital funds to invest in treasury bonds; and allowing asset management companies to be reorganized into commercial financial institutions following their completion of asset disposal tasks.

In 2004, the four financial asset management companies commenced to reorganize themselves into commercial financial institutions and progressively got involved in financial services beyond the scope of the non-performing asset disposal business. From 2007 onwards, their reorganization gathered pace. Specifically, China Cinda Asset Management Co., Ltd. and China Huarong Asset Management Co., Ltd. took the initiatives to bring in strategic investors and carry out a joint-stock system reform. Besides, the two companies both successfully went public on the main board trading market of the Hong Kong Exchanges and Clearing Limited, metamorphosing from policy-oriented financial institutions to commercial ones.

Second, the commercialized reform of state investment institutions was instituted. On December 16, 2003, Central Huijin Investment Ltd. was established as a wholly state-owned investment holding company with a registered capital of RMB372,465 million, subject to the approval of the State Council. Specifically, Central Huijin Investment Ltd was designated to exercise the rights and discharge the obligations of an investor of large state-owned financial enterprises on behalf of the state, and it was tasked with the efficient leverage, hedging and appreciation of foreign exchange reserves. In July 2004, the Chinese government granted autonomy to enterprises and established an investment decision-making accountability system in line with the principle of "whoever invests would make decisions and whoever reaps a profit would bear risks". On September 29, 2007, China Investment Corporation was set up as a state-owned investment company specializing in the foreign exchange investment business.

1.5.4 Optimization of the Capital Market and Its Management Regime

In 2004, the government decided to push forward with the reform and opening up of the capital market in a bid to ensure a stable development, reiterating the necessity to give full play to the important role of the financial market in optimizing resource allocation.

First, a market maker and centralized clearing and settlement system was established. In 2001, a market maker system was introduced in the interbank bond market. In January 2007, the PBoC stepped up its supporting policy for market makers and further optimized the framework of the market maker system, offering more opportunities for different types of financial institutions to get involved in the market maker business in the interbank bond market. Meanwhile, the PBoC was positioned to develop the OTC market and targeted institutional investors as main investors.

The Chinese government has progressively established a settlement agency and currency brokerage system and a sound bond trading, custody, clearing and settlement system, employed delivery versus payment (DVP), and conducted the netting settlement of spot transactions in the capital market. In November 2009, Shanghai Clearing House (SHCH) was established to provide the inter-bank market with comprehensive and centralized clearing and settlement services, with central counterparty as the core, improving settlement efficiency and bringing down settlement costs.

Second, a securities margin trading system was piloted. Securities margin trading refers to operations in business whereby in the securities transactions conducted on a stock exchange or other securities trading centers approved by the State Council, an investor purchases securities with borrowed money from a securities company, or sells securities borrowed from a securities company by providing collateral to the securities company.

In May 2008, the CSRC announced the official initiation of pilot securities margin trading. Eleven securities companies including CITIC Securities and Haitong Securities respectively conducted the network tests for securities margin trading twice on October 25 and November 8, 2008 respectively.

In line with the principle of "piloting first and progressively up-scaling", the CSRC selected six premium securities companies including Guotai Junan Securities and Guoxin Securities as the first batch of companies for piloting securities margin trading in January 2010. In April, 2010, securities margin trading was conducted in the market.

Third, restrictions on prohibiting insurance funds from being sunk into the securities market were lifted and a non-tradable share reform was instituted. On October 25, 2004, the China Insurance Regulatory Commission (CIRC) and the CSRC jointly lifted the restrictions on prohibiting insurance funds from being channeled to the securities market. The move was conducive to improving the structure and efficiency of insurance fund leverage in China, optimizing the structure of investors in the market, increasing stable and long-term money supply for the securities market, guiding a long-term value investment philosophy to take root, and promoting the stability and healthy development of the capital market.

On April 29, 2005, the CSRC officially piloted a non-tradable share reform of listed companies. As is widely known, the non-tradable share reform was conducive to shaping rational investment expectations, with a far-reaching impact on value judgments, governance regimes of listed companies, and investor behavior in China's capital markets.

Fourth, the original regulatory regime was reformed and the administration of the capital market was strengthened. On April 28, 2003, the China Banking Regulatory Commission (CBRC) was officially established and a regulatory regime of "one bank, three commissions and one administration" took shape.[17] In 2003, the National People's Congress deliberated and adopted the Securities Investment Fund Law to continuously overhaul the legal system for exercising capital market regulation. In June 2010, third-party payment was officially incorporated into the regulatory system, and a license management regime was also put into implementation. In the meantime, efforts were also made to strengthen the comprehensive governance of securities companies.

1.5.5 Response to Crises and Prevention of Financial Risks

From 2002 to 2010, the Chinese economy entered a period of phenomenal growth and low inflation. In recent ten years, annual average GDP growth has exceeded 10%. In 2002, China's GDP passed the RMB10 trillion mark, hitting RMB10,239.8 billion.[18] The sustained and healthy development of the Chinese economy has promoted the stability of economic operations and created a good external environment for maintaining financial stability. Nevertheless, the financial crisis that erupted in 2008 has had a huge impact on financial stability and national economic development.

With a view to responding to an unprecedented financial crisis in a century, the PBoC implemented a lax monetary policy. In 2008 alone, it cut down the deposit and loan interest rate five times in a row, bringing them down from 7.47 to 5.31% at the end of the year. Additionally, the deposit reserve requirement ratio was lowered for four times. Specifically, the deposit reserve requirement ratio for large financial institutions was reduced to 15.5%. The PBoC lifted credit loan quota restrictions on commercial banks, and offered proper window guidance on credit loans to be granted and on how to grant credit loans to commercial banks. Additionally, it also promptly instituted policies designed to sustain economic growth and bolster market confidence, and guided financial institutions to increase their credit lines. In the meantime, central bank bills issued in open market operations were curtailed to ensure money supply.

On November 5, 2008, the Chinese government rolled out a policy package of ten initiatives to promote an economic growth by stimulating domestic demand, which involved accelerating the construction of affordable houses, rural amenities, railways, highways, airports and other major infrastructures. In the following two years, the

[17] "One bank, three commissions and one administration" respectively stand for the PBoC, the CBRC, the CSRC and the CIRC and SAFE.

[18] The author's estimate based on the relevant data released by the National Bureau of Statistics from 2002 to 2012.

central government increased investment by RMB1.18 trillion, thereby initiating the country's RMB4 trillion worth of investment programmes.

In 2009, China's original prevalent economic growth downturn was reversed and there was a turnaround in China's economy due to a combination of emerging positive factors as a result from stimulus packages, with GDP hitting RMB3,353.5 million that year, up 8.7% from 2008. In other words, the rolling out of such stimulus packages was a contributor for maintaining the stability and security of the financial system. From 2010 onwards, China's economic growth fell all the way from 10.4 to 9.3% in 2011 and 7.8% in 2012, taking on a long-tailed "L" shape. So far, this downward trend has not been substantively reversed[19] and the underlying economic downturn has posed a huge challenge to the Chinese government's maintaining financial stability.

Another factor that posed a threat to China's financial stability was the domestic shadow banking system, which refers broadly to a network of financial institutions that serve as intermediaries to conduct unregulated financial activities outside the regulated commercial banking system, and the regulated bond and stock markets. Much of its debt was collateralized through the process called securitization instead of credit loans granted by traditional banks. As compared to traditional regulated banks, shadow financial institutions grew faster but they still escaped regulatory limits and laws imposed on the traditional banking system. Meanwhile, they also concurrently fell outside of the protective umbrella of lender of last resort in the regulated financial sector.

According to Financial Stability Board (FSB) estimates in 2012, China took a share of 1% or RMB 4 trillion of global shadow banking. According to a related study by the Bank for International Settlements in 2016, shadow banking instruments in the stage of lenders of last resort issued in China made up 71% of national GDP and 46% of bank deposits at the end of 2016. According to narrow-standard statistics, the value of shadow banking instruments traded in the stage of borrowers of last resort accounted for 32% of GDP and 23.9% of bank loans and the bond market,[20] posing a potential risk to financial stability.

Amidst a fully open competitive milieu, while facing increasing external economic risks and continued downward pressure on the domestic economy, how to effectively prevent systemic financial risks and maintain the stable, healthy and safe operation of the financial system will remain a long-term and arduous task.

---

[19] China Financial Stability Analysis Group, China Financial Stability Report 2013, China Financial Publishing House, 2014, p. 8.

[20] Torsten Ehlers, Steven Kong and Feng Zhu, *Mapping Shadow Banking in China: Structure and Dynamics*, BIS Working Papers No. 701, Monetary and Economic Department, February 2018, pp. 27, 29.

1.6 Encouraging Innovative Development and Deepening Reform

From 2012 to 2019, China's financial sector entered a period of encouraging an innovative development, deepening reform, and developing fintech.

1.6.1 Technology-Driven Financial Innovation and Its Impact

From 2012 onwards, China's real economy entered a period of low growth and underwent a transition to overcome widespread overcapacity and an unbalanced development. By contrast, the financial service industry emerged to become the mainstay of the national economy due to a combination of contributing factors such as technology, capital and demand. According to the statistics of the National Bureau of Statistics, there were 29,000 legal entities with 5,139,000 employees in the financial sector at the end of 2013, up 8.4% and 4.1% respectively from the end of 2008. In 2015, there were a total of 6.07 million practitioners engaging in the financial sector, and the cumulative contribution of the financial service industry to GDP was as high as 16.9% in 2015.

Various financial and non-financial institutions got involved in financial activities under the banner of technological and financial innovation, and even real economy enterprises joined in, managing to bring in more revenues and profits from the financial business Amidst the new round of innovation, Internet finance and fintech became new "invaders" into the financial sector.

The year 2013 is hailed as the Year of Internet finance in China, and the rapid development period of Internet finance was marked by the joint launch of "Yu'E Bao" by Alipay (China) Network Technology Co., Ltd. and Tianhong Asset Management Co., Ltd., with a momentum of rampant growth building up across the country. A swarm of Internet enterprises made foray into the financial sector through the channels of mobile payment, P2P online lending and crowd-funding. Internet finance continued to keep the irresistible momentum going, despite the incidents of some P2P platforms including "Fanya Metal Exchange" and "e Zu Bao" running away with their raised funds in the second half of 2015. As such, technology-driven financial innovation has diffused across the financial sector and become the mainstay in the financial sector.

When it came to mobile payment, financial innovation diffused widespread in the sectors of smart healthcare, smart transportation, mobile e-commerce, taxi software, municipal services and sharing economy. As of 2019, Alipay was available for people to pay bus fares and highway tolls in most medium-sized and big cities across China. It was worth mentioning that people could use Alipay to pay utility bills, register at hospitals, and enquire about social security and provident fund in more than 300 cities.

In 2005, the government commenced to tighten up the regulation of Internet finance. By leveraging technology and capital, efforts were made to remove the "label" of Internet finance as a negative factor militating against the development of the financial sector. In 2016, Internet finance quickly switched to a fintech development stage. Driven by technology, new "hot" spots emerged, such as big data, cloud computing, digital currency, robo-advisor and blockchain, attracting a large number of investors. Actually, fintech fever outpaced Internet finance fever. In the process, ANT Financial Services Group, Ping An Group, WeChat Pay, Baidu Group and Jingdong Finance all have developed into a top-notched enterprise in the industry.

On the one hand, fintech has stimulated the demand and market of "the long dormant financial consumers" to effectively remedy the weaknesses of China's financial sector by innovating service models, and developing inclusive finance, micro finance and all kinds of special financial services. Nevertheless, rule violations and irregular operations still bubbled away in the financial sector from time to time due to loopholes in the regulatory system. Even more, the financial sector deviated from its mission to serve the real economy, resulting in financialization and the formation of economic bubbles.

On the other hand, fintech is likely to cause creative destruction to the existing financial system. In other words, it has shifted the balance of the original financial system and rebuilt a new financial eco-system, thus changing global financial patterns. Additionally, it has also promoted the development of inclusive finance and financial democratization, reshaped the infrastructure of the financial system, altered the nature of currency, and shook the foundation of central banks. For financial service users, it is undoubtedly a democratic revolution, which has broken from the long-standing norms in the financial sector.

Up to date, science and technology has diffused and coalesced with finance across the financial sector and we have entered a new era in which financial institutions are rather technology companies and vice versa.

1.6.2 Breaking Up Financial Monopoly by Establishing Private Banks

The development of private banks can be traced back to urban credit cooperatives and private financial institutions in the early 1980s. For instance, Fangxing Private Bank founded by Fang Peilin in Qianku town of Cangnan county, Zhejiang province on September 22, 1984 is viewed as the first private bank in the People's Republic of China.[21] From the twenty-first century onwards, private banks with the name "bank" have emerged. In 2002, Taizhou Commercial Bank Co., Ltd. was jointly established by eight financial institutions and it was renamed Taizhou Bank in September 2010.

---

[21] Wei Yutao, *The Rise and Fall of Fangxing Money House*, China Economic Times, August 14, 2013, the Third Edition.

True private banks originated from the government's policies for developing the non-public economy. For instance, the State Council issued a "36-point Policy for Developing the Non-public Economy" in January 2005 and the new "36-point Policy for Developing the Non-Public Economy" on May 1, 2010, both of which allowed private capital to be injected in the financial sector in support of the establishment of various private banking financial institutions, which played a positive role in breaking up financial monopoly, eliminating market access barriers to the private economic sector, and promoting the development of private banks.

In August, 2006, Zhejiang Wenling Urban Credit Cooperative and Taizhou Urban credit Cooperative were reorganized into Zhejiang Mintai Commercial Bank and Zhejiang Tailong Commercial Bank with approval respectively. In the meantime, Ningbo Donghai Bank and Zhejiang Congzhou Commercial Bank were also established.

From 2012 to 2013, the Chinese government and the CBRC rolled out multiple measures to encourage and guide private investments to be channeled to the banking industry, and they also approved the trial establishment of true private banks.

On June 19, 2013, the State Council proposed to explore the establishment of private banks which could bear risks on their own. At the Third Plenary Session of the Eighteenth CPC Central Committee, this policy was further deliberated and clarified, allowing qualified private investors to set up financial institutions including small and medium-sized banks, financial leasing companies and consumer finance companies according to the law. The move was initiated to further broaden the channels for earmarking private capital for the financial service industry.

On March 11, 2014, the CBRC finalized a pilot scheme for the first batch of private banks. On July 25, 2014, official approval was granted to the applications for setting up three private banks. On December 28, 2014, WeBank with Tencent as the biggest shareholder was established with approval. From January to May 2015, Shanghai Huarui Bank Co., Ltd., Wenzhou Minshang Bank, Zhejiang MYBank Co., Ltd. and Kincheng Bank of Tianjin Co., Ltd. won the approval for establishment.

In 2016, 40-odd private enterprises submitted applications for establishing private banks, of which 13 private banks including Bank of Sanxiang Co., Ltd. in Hunan province, Chongqing Fumin Bank, Sichuan XW Bank Corp., Ltd., Zhongguancun Bank in Beijing city, Jiangsu Suning Bank Co., Ltd., Anhui Xin'an Bank Inc. and Jiangxi Yumin Bank Co., Ltd. were successively established with approval. As of the end of 2019, there were a total of 18 private banks that had won the approval for establishment, emerging as a new force of China's financial sector.

With the mission of "reforming finance through technological innovation and pursuing the strategy of financial inclusion", these newly established private banks are committed to serving small and micro enterprises and developing inclusive finance. By coalescing Internet finance and financial technology, private banks provided digital and inclusive finance with Chinese characteristics. Nevertheless, due to their relatively short history, private banks still need to stand the test of time in terms of their development model, competitive environment, risk control systems and competitiveness. There is still a long way for the private banking industry to go ahead.

1.6.3 Exploration of New Opening Mechanisms Through PFTZs

Following the Third Plenary Session of the Eighteenth CPC Central Committee, the government launched the major innovative initiative of setting up pilot free trade zones (PFTZs) as a "pilot scheme" for stepping up economic opening up, with a view to comprehensively deepening economic and financial reforms and expanding openness to the outside world.

The State Council officially granted the approval for the establishment of the China (Shanghai) PFTZ on August 22, 2013 and the official inauguration ceremony was held on September 29, 2013. On December 2, 2013, the PBoC issued the Opinions on Rendering Financial Support for the Construction of the China (Shanghai) Pilot Free Trade Zone, which set out the guidelines of serving the real economy and facilitating cross-border investment and trade, insisted on opening up, innovation and pilot schemes, explored on how to facilitate the inflow and outflow of investment capital, promoted the cross-border investment and finance settlement in RMB, steadily pushed forward with the market-oriented interest rate reform, deepened the reform of foreign exchange regulation regime, and strived to make breakthroughs in the financial reform of the Shanghai PFTZ.

The Shanghai FTZ is hailed as a model of China's FTZ as a result of efforts to provide financial support for constructing the FTZs, which has achieved remarkable results. According to the 2018 Shanghai Municipal Statistical Communiqué on National Economic and Social Development, three master plans (i.e. Version 1.0, Version 2.0 and Version 3.0) have been successively promulgated for implementation for five consecutive years since the establishment of the Shanghai FTZ. With the objectives of building a "comprehensive reform test zone" that integrates openness and innovation, a risk pressure test zone for the open economic system, a test zone for improving government governance, and a gateway to provision of supporting serves for implementing the 'Belt and Road' initiative and incentive for encouraging market participants to go global, the Shanghai FTZ has vigorously promoted institutional reforms in investment, trade, finance, and in-event and post-event regulation, and strived to create a law-based, internationalized and convenient business environment.

As far as the financial market system is concerned, the Shanghai PFTZ has basically carried out the unified management of the *renminbi* and foreign currencies. At the end of December 2018, there were 136,000 free trade accounts (FTA) opened in the pilot free trade zone, with cross-border RMB settlements totaling RMB 2,551,888 million, bringing about an increase of 83.9% over the previous year and accounting for 35.3% of the total in Shanghai; and cross-border two-way RMB pool income and expenditure amounted to RMB 482.6 billion in aggregate, up 180%.

Following the Bo'ao Forum for Asia in April 2018, the Chinese government decided to build the Hainan FTZ. In November 2019, the CPC Central Committee and the State Council held relevant conferences to study and discuss the policies and institutional system for building the Hainan FTZ. The year 2020 was hailed as the Year of Free Trade Port Construction in the Hainan Island in line with expectations.

1.6.4 Promotion of Inclusive Finance to Benefit Special Groups

Inclusive finance is universal access, at a reasonable cost, to a wide range of financial services, provided by a variety of sound and sustainable financial institutions. Inclusive finance strives to enhance access to financial services for both individuals and micro-, small and medium-sized enterprises, primarily targeting special groups such as SMEs, farmers, urban low-income people, the poor, the disabled and the elderly.

The CPC Central Committee and the State Council have made an important decision on vigorously developing Inclusive finance and establishing an inclusive finance system. In January 2016, the State Council formulated the Planning for Promoting the Development of Inclusive Finance (2016–2020), which has mapped out the implementing strategy for inclusive finance at the national level for the first time. Subsequently, different government departments including the PBoC rolled out a series of policies to push forward with the development of inclusive finance.

At the end of 2016, ten ministries and commissions including the PBoC officially approved the Master Plan for Piloting the Lankao County Inclusive Finance Reform Zone in Henan Province, setting up the first national pilot inclusive finance reform zone in China. On May 26, 2017, the CBRC encouraged medium-sized and big banks to set up inclusive finance business divisions to focus on serving micro and small enterprises, agriculture, farmers and the countryside, entrepreneurial and innovative enterprises, and poverty alleviation. As of the end of 2018, there were 1,616 township and village banks engaging in inclusive finance business in China, covering 31 provinces. Loans granted to farmers and micro and small enterprises accounted for more than 92% of the total, and therefore farmers and micro and small enterprises became the main beneficiaries of inclusive financial services.

1.6.5 Developing Green Finance to Support the Green Economy

Green finance refers to any structured financial activity, which has been created to improve environment, address climate changes, and efficiently conserve and leverage resources, i.e. financial services provided for the investment, financing, operation, and risk management of projects in the areas of environmental protection, energy conservation, clean energy, green transportation and green buildings.

The Chinese government's attaching importance to environmental protection and enacting relevant laws and regulations is a prerequisite for supporting China's green finance. In September 2015, the State Council issued the Master Reform Plan for Overhauling the Ecological Civilization System, which explicitly called for establishing a green finance system for the first time and formulated a green finance development strategy based on a top-down design. In December of the same year, seven ministries and commissions including the PBoC issued the Guiding Opinions on Establishing a Green Finance System to impose thirty-five specific measures for the development of green finance, which were viewed as the "fundamental law" of China's green finance system, kicking off the initiation of building a holistic green finance system in the country.

In the Thirteen Five-Year Development Plan issued in 2016, the Chinese government explicitly called for developing green credit loans, green bonds, green funds and green rating systems, supporting the financing for ecological and environmental protection projects, and incorporating green finance into China's national strategy. At the Executive Meeting of the State Council held in June 2017, Premier Keqiang Li announced that some regions in Zhejiang province, Jiangxi province, Guangdong province, Guizhou province and Xinjiang Uyghur autonomous region had been selected as pilot regions for building pilot green finance reform and innovation zones with their respective key green finance reform and innovation projects and characteristics.

In terms of institutional system building, the Chinese government has set up a working group on green finance to improve the top-down design of the green finance system, and encourage the study on the framework of international green finance systems. In June 2018, the PBoC decided to amend the issuance rules and regulations on its medium-term lending facility (MLF) to include green bonds and green loans in the scope of collaterals. Meanwhile, it also officially established a green credit loan statistics system.

Green finance was rolled out in the credit loan, bonds, industry funds and insurance sectors. In 2016, China was top of green bond issued across the world. In 2017, there were 118 green bonds issued with a total value of RMB251,214 million in the country. In 2019, there were 214 domestic and overseas green bonds issued valued at RMB339,062 million, bringing about an increase of 26% and 48% from 2018 respectively and accounting for 21.3% of the global green bonds over the same period.

In February 2016, Shanghai Pudong Development Bank and Industrial Bank Co., Ltd. successfully issued RMB30 billion of green finance bonds in the inter-bank bond market. Meanwhile, the Chinese government proactively realized the securitization of green credit assets and encouraged enterprises to issue green financing instruments to raise funds. Specifically speaking, Industrial Bank Co., Ltd. issued RMB2.65 billion of green credit asset-backed securities, and green-related enterprises issued debt financing instruments worth RMB2.2 trillion. As of June 2018, Industrial Bank's outstanding green financing balance stood at RMB758.9 billion, and its supporting projects could save 29.51 million tons of coal equivalent, reduce 83,906,200 tons of carbon dioxide emissions, and conserve 408,908,400 tons of water per year in China.

As a move for achieving a green development of the economy and a key task of supply-side structural reform in the financial sector, green finance was complementary to the strategy for accelerating the reform of the ecological civilization system, promoting green development, and building a beautiful China as proposed in the Work Report of the Nineteenth CPC National Congress.

1.6.6 Construction and Strengthening of Financial Infrastructure

The infrastructure of the financial system was composed of sound legal and regulatory systems, accounting and information disclosure standards, independent and credible credit rating agencies, and efficient and reliable settlement systems.

First, the Chinese government established a regulatory regime and developed a legal infrastructure system. In 2003, the Chinese government established a regulatory system consisting of the PBoC, CBRC, CSRC, CIRC and SAFE and China's financial regulatory system progressively took shape. Meanwhile, it was committed to constantly revising and amending its laws and statutes on financial regulation. Over the years, it has enacted and amended the Law on Negotiable Instruments, the Insurance Law, the Securities Law, the Trust Law, the Law on Securities Investment Fund and the Law on the Regulation of Banks.

Second, the Chinese government accelerated the establishment of a social credit system based on the PBoC's national centralized commercial and consumer credit reporting system, as well as a credit system for small, medium and micro enterprises jointly supported by the central and local governments, basically succeeding in creating a national centralized commercial and consumer credit reporting system database. For instance, the commercial credit reporting system database originated from PBoC's national centralized commercial and consumer credit reporting system in 1997, which has developed into a national system and it was nationwide networked in 2006. As of the end of June 2012, there were 639 and 617 financial institutions that were connected to the national centralized commercial and consumer credit reporting systems respectively, and credit files were opened for 18.33 million enterprises and other organizations, as well as more than 814 million natural persons. As of the end of 2016, efforts were made to furnish data on 2,611,400 micro, small and medium-sized enterprises which had not applied to banks for any loan yet, and credit files were also opened for 172 million rural households as well.

Third, the Chinese government established an efficient cross-border settlement and online payment system. In 2012, the PBoC launched the construction of the Cross-Border Inter-Bank Payment System (CIPS). In March 2014, it decided to build the CIPS in two phases. In the first phase, the PBOC would apply the CIPS to cross-border trade in goods and services, cross-border direct investment, cross-border financing, cross-border personal remittances and other business settlements.

In the second phase, the CIPS would adopt a more liquidity-saving hybrid calculation method to support the settlement of cross-border and offshore RMB business.

On October 8, 2015, the CIPS was successfully put into operation in Shanghai, involving 19 direct participants and 185 indirect participants from 50 countries and regions across 6 continents. In the whole year of 2015, the CIPS processed 86,703 payment transactions with a total value of RMB 480,898 million. With its successful completion and operation, the system helped to improve the efficiency of cross-border settlement in RMB, support the development of the real economy and international trade, and promote cross-border settlement in RMB worldwide, rendering better support for the imposition of the "Go Global" strategy and the Belt and Road Initiative.

The PBoC commenced to establish China's Non-bank Payment Organization Internet Payments and Clearing Platform (NetsUnion) for non-banking payment institutions in October 2016, and launched a trial operation at the end of March 2017. As of the end of 2017, there were a total of 248 banks and 65 payment institutions which were connected to the NetsUnion. From June 30, 2018 onwards, all the online payment business conducted by payment institutions has been cleared and settled through the NetsUnion.

The efficiency of the financial infrastructure is the upper limit of that of the financial system services, and the safe operation of the financial infrastructure is the fundamental guarantee for China's financial security.

In the past seventy years, the financial sector developed and complemented with China's real economy and manufacturing industry, witnessing a historical transition from the first three decades of a planned economy to the second four decades of reform and opening up. Specifically speaking, funds were raised from the financial sector to support socialist revolution and construction in the first three decades; the second four decades saw a period of prosperity and development as a result of the ongoing reform of the financial system, which has greatly unleashed the vitality and potential of the financial sector.

Chapter 2
Historical Evolutionary Trajectory of Financial Institutions in China

In the past 70 years, China's financial organizations showed an unprecedented expansion tendency by developing a diversified institutional system and spawning multiple sub-sectors, forming the backbone of China's financial sector, and becoming major participants in the financial market.

2.1 The System and Main Types of Financial Institutions

Alongside monetary and regulatory authorities,[1] China's financial institutional system also consisted of banking financial institutions, securities financial institutions, insurance financial institutions and other non-banking financial institutions, among others.

2.1.1 The Banking Financial Institutional System

Banking financial institutions refer to depository and non-depository intermediaries, which primarily engage in the financing business.

Depository banking institutions refer to large state-owned commercial banks, national joint-stock commercial banks, urban commercial banks, development and policy banks, private banks, rural credit cooperatives (including rural credit unions), rural commercial banks, and foreign-invested banks and their branches.

By the end of 2018, there had been a total of 4,588 depository banking institutions in China, including 1 development financial institution, 2 policy banks, 6 large

[1] The monetary authorities refer to the PBoC and SAFE while the regulatory authorities include the CBRC, CSRC and CIRC, of which the CBRC and CIRC merged into the CBIRC in April 2018.

Y. Wu, *A Financial History of China (1949–2019)*, Research Series on the Chinese Dream and China's Development Path,
https://doi.org/10.1007/978-981-99-6571-7_2

state-owned commercial banks, 12 national joint-stock commercial banks, 134 urban commercial banks, 41 foreign-invested banks as a legal entity, 1,427 rural commercial banks, 71 rural cooperative banks, 812 rural credit cooperatives, 1 housing savings bank, 1,616 village and township banks, 45 rural mutual fund cooperatives, 13 loan companies, and 17 private banks. Altogether, these depository banking institutions held assets totaling RMB268.24 trillion, up 6.27% year on year, and took on liabilities totaling RMB246.58 trillion, a year-on-year increase of 5.89%.

Non-depository banking institutions refer to trust companies, asset management companies, financial companies affiliated to enterprise groups, financial leasing companies, auto finance companies, money brokerage companies, consumer finance companies, and representative offices of overseas non-banking institutions in China established with the approval of the CBRC. The bulk of financial institutions of this sort raised funds by issuing stocks and bonds, establishing trust, taking out insurance or otherwise, and leveraged raised funds to make long-term investments.

Among non-depository banking institutions in China at the end of 2019, there were a total of 68 trust companies, 4 state-owned asset management companies, 54 local asset management companies, and hundreds of asset management companies; 73 financial leasing companies; 253 financial companies affiliated to enterprise groups; 25 auto finance companies; 5 money brokerage companies; and 23 consumer finance companies.

2.1.2 Securities Intermediaries

Securities institutions refer to financial institutions which are regulated by the CSRC and mainly engage in the investment service business, including stock exchanges, securities companies (investment banks), securities investment fund management companies, futures companies, investment consulting companies, securities clearing corporations, credit rating companies, credit reference companies, among others.

Nowadays, there are three national exchanges in China, namely Shanghai Stock Exchange, Shenzhen Stock Exchange, and the National Equities Exchange and Quotations (NEEQ or New Three Board) established in September 2012. On November 5, 2018, the Sci-Tech Innovation Board (SSE STAR Market) was set up for piloting a registration system. Besides, there are also four other futures exchanges, namely Shanghai Futures Exchange, Zhengzhou Commodity Exchange, Dalian Commodity Exchange, and China Financial Futures Exchange.

As of the end of 2018, there were 131 securities companies (investment banks), 120 securities investment fund management companies, 149 futures companies, 9 credit rating companies, and 19 QFII custodian banks established in China.

As of the end of 2019, there were a total of 4,419 financial institutions which had joined the Asset Management Association of China (AMAC) as members, including self-regulated fund management companies and their subsidiaries, securities companies and their subsidiaries, futures companies and their subsidiaries, private funds; and asset managers, among others.

2.1.3 Insurance Intermediaries

Insurance institutions refer to financial intermediaries, including insurance companies and social security agencies, which were regulated by the former CIRC and mainly engage in the insurance service business.

Shanghai Insurance Exchange (SHIE) was established with approval in November 2015, and it officially opened for business on June 12, 2016. With its registered address in the Shanghai Free Trade Zone and directly under the administration by the CBIRC, the SHIE mainly provided a trading platform for insurance, reinsurance and insurance assets, which was supported by an integrated one-stop service system integrating account management, fund settlement, information disclosure, market consulting, operational system, and data management.

As of the end of 2018, China's insurance industry held assets totaling RMB18.33 trillion, including RMB2.35 trillion for property insurance companies, RMB14.61 trillion for personal insurance companies, and RMB364,979 million for reinsurance companies. Insurance density and penetration stood at RMB2, 724 and 4.22% respectively, which were far below the world average level over the same period.[2]

As of the end of June 2019, there were a total of 236 insurance companies in China, including 12 insurance groups, 1 export credit insurance company, 87 property insurance companies, 81 life insurance companies, 8 endowment insurance companies, 7 health insurance companies, 11 reinsurance companies, 26 asset management companies, and 3 other companies (rural mutual insurance cooperatives). Besides, there were also 2,652 specialized insurance intermediaries, including 5 insurance intermediary groups, 1,769 specialized insurance agencies, 497 insurance brokerage companies, and 381 insurance surveyors and adjusters companies.

As of the end of October 2019, foreign companies set up 59 foreign-funded insurance companies, 131 representative offices and 18 specialized insurance intermediaries in China.

2.1.4 Other Non-banking Institutions

Non-banking financial intermediaries included securities depository and clearing institutions, financial holding companies, private fund management companies, investment consulting companies, among others.

National quasi-securities depository and clearing institutions in China included China Central Depository and Clearing Co., Ltd. (1996, "CCDC"), China Securities Depository and Clearing Co., Ltd. (2001, "CSDC"), and the SHCH established with approval in 2009.

Financial holding companies (FHC) refer to financial institutions that invest in and have holding subsidiaries in two or more industries (e.g. banking, securities, and

[2] Financial Stability Analysis Group of the PBoC: China Financial Stability Report 2018, China Financial Publishing House, 2019, p. 42.

insurance), without conducting the financial business themselves. There were mainly six types of FHCs including central financial holding companies or other financial holding companies.

First, financial holding groups, which were established with the approval of the State Council to support the opening up and economic development of the country, with large non-financial enterprise groups acting as controlling shareholders. Examples of such financial holding groups included CITIC International Financial Holdings Limited, China Galaxy Financial Holding Co. Ltd. and China Everbright Financial Holding Company affiliated to CITIC Group, Central Huijin Investment Ltd. or China Everbright Group respectively.

Second, asset management companies, which were set up by parent companies of central enterprise groups to specialize in managing the financial business of these groups. Examples of such asset management companies included China Merchants Finance Holding Co., Ltd., State Grid Yingda International Holdings Group Co., Ltd., and Huaneng Capital Service Co., Ltd. set up by China Merchants Group, State Grid Corporation of China, and China Huaneng Group Co., Ltd.

Third, financial institutions with finance as their main business are classified into wholly-owned or joint-venture financial holding companies, including BOC International Holdings Co., Ltd., China International Capital Corporation Limited, Industrial and Commercial East Asia Finance Holdings Ltd, and Ping An Insurance Company.

Fourth, financial holding companies established by private enterprises and listed companies, including large financial holding groups set up by Tomorrow Holding Co., Ltd., Anbound Group, Fosun International Limited, HNA Group, and Evergrande Group.

Fifth, integrated asset investment and management companies which were established with the approval of local governments to co-control local financial institutions such as banks, securities companies and insurance companies, including Tianjin Teda Group Co., Ltd., Shanghai International Group, and Beijing Financial Holdings Group.

Sixth, financial holding groups set up by Internet giants such as Alibaba, Tencent, Suning Commerce Group Co., Ltd. (today's Suning.com), and Jingdong Group Co., Ltd. after they invested in the financial sector.

In recent years, private funds in China have kept the irresistible momentum going. As of the end of 2018, there were a total of 24,448 private investment fund managers, and 74,629 private investment funds with RMB12.71 trillion of assets registered with the AMAC.

As of the end of 2019, there were a total of 84 securities investment consulting companies, and 9 securities rating companies and credit rating companies in the country.

2.2 Depository Banking Institutions: The Mainstay of Financial Markets

After seventy years of development, there had been a total of 4,588 depository banking institutions established in China as major participants in China's financial market by the end of 2019. Through operating in different sub-sectors and catering for different customers' demand, they constituted a sophisticated monetary and indirect financing system.

2.2.1 State-Owned Commercial Banks: Restructuring and Metamorphosis

From 1949 to 1978, there was no commercial financial institution in a real sense in China's financial industry. In a monolithic financial system, the PBoC concurrently performed dual functions and it both served as savings institution and financial regulator.

After the PBoC commenced to exercise its functions as China's central bank in 1983, the ICBC, ABC, BOC and CCB were designated as state-owned specialized banks for providing financial services for state-owned enterprises. In 1995, state-owned specialized banks in China were called upon to reorganize themselves into wholly state-owned commercial banks, marking the initiation of their corporate, commercialized and market-oriented reform and restructuring. In this way, existing maladies such as serious capital shortage, high non-performing loan ratio, and unsound internal management system had been basically resolved by 2001.

From 2002 to 2010, wholly state-owned commercial banks embarked on carrying out a joint-stock system reform and going public, with the BOC and CCB being designated as banks for pilot joint-stock reform. By the end of 2004, the BOC and CCB had basically completed their joint-stock reforms, with their capital adequacy ratios rising to 10.04% and 11.9% respectively, and both banks had established a relatively standardized corporate governance structure.[3]

On October 27, 2005, the CCB issued H shares for trading in Hong Kong. On September 25, 2007, it got listed for trading A shares on the Shanghai Stock Exchange. In June and July 2006, the BOC successively issued stocks for trading on the Hong Kong Exchanges and Clearing Limited and the Shanghai Stock Exchange in the form of H+ A shares.

In 2004, the BOCOM brought in overseas strategic investors. In June 2005, it went public on the Hong Kong Exchanges and Clearing Limited, becoming the first commercial bank from China to publicly issue shares overseas. In May 2007, the BOCOM successfully got listed on the Shanghai Stock Exchange (A-share).

[3] Office of the Leading Group on the Pilot Joint-Stock System Reform of Wholly State-Owned Commercial Banks: Accelerating the Joint Stock Reform of Wholly State-owned Commercial Banks, *China Finance*, Issue 24, 2004.

In October 2005, the ICBC won approval for concurrently getting listed in Shanghai and Hong Kong in the form of "A + H" shares. On October 28, 2005, it officially made IPO.

In October 2008, the ABC was given the sanction for carrying out a joint-stock system reform. In January, 2009, the Agricultural Bank of China Co., Ltd. was officially inaugurated, and it successively got listed on the Shanghai Stock Exchange (A share) on July 15, 2010 and on the Hong Kong Exchanges and Clearing Limited (H share) on July 16, 2010.

By the end of 2010, all the large five wholly state-owned commercial banks in China all had gone public for trading and they had constituted a state-holding publicly listed banking sector in the stock market. From 2014 onwards, state-owned commercial banks commenced to explore a mixed ownership reform.

Through joint-stock system reform and restructuring, state-owned commercial banks have metamorphosed from problematic banks on the brink of technical bankruptcy into modern commercial banks with growing international influence and competitiveness, becoming the backbone in the global banking industry. Most notably, 136 Chinese banks were on the shortlist of Global Top 1,000 Banks 2019, with the ICBC, CCB, ABC and BOC ranking in the top four.

2.2.2 *Joint-Stock Commercial Banks: Characteristic Financial Institutions*

National joint-stock commercial banks constituted an important part of depository banking institutions in China. From 1986 to 2012, there were a total of twelve national joint-stock banks successively established with approval, including the BOCOM established in 1986; China Merchants Bank, CITIC Industrial Bank, Yantai Housing Savings Bank (renamed Hengfeng Bank in 2003), and Shenzhen Development Bank (renamed Ping An Bank Co., Ltd. in 2012) established in 1987; Fujian Industrial Bank[4] and Guangdong Development Bank (renamed China Guangfa Bank in 2011) established in 1988; China Everbright Bank, Huaxia Bank, and Shanghai Pudong Development Bank established in 1992; Zhejiang Commercial Bank (renamed China Zheshang Bank in 2004) established in 1993, and China Minsheng Bank established in 1996; and China Bohai Bank Co., Ltd. which was established in Tianjin with approval in December 2005 and officially operated in business in February 2006.

National joint-stock commercial banks are a product of China's market economy reform and financial enterprises' joint-stock system restructuring. For example, China Merchants Bank, CITIC Industrial Bank, and China Everbright Bank are the first three joint-stock banks set up by state-owned enterprises in the country. As the first commercial bank to go public in China, Shenzhen Development Bank made its initial public offering of common shares denominated in RMB to the public through

[4] In 2003, Fujian Industrial bank was renamed Industrial Bank. On February 5, 2007, it was officially listed for trading on the Shanghai Stock Exchange.

free subscriptions on May 10, 1987, and it officially announced its establishment on December 22, 1987. On September 22, 2006, China Merchants Bank got listed on the Hong Kong Exchanges and Clearing Limited. In January 1997, China Everbright Bank completed its joint-stock system reform and got listed for trading A shares on the Shanghai Stock Exchange on August 19, 2010.

There are many examples of joint-stock system reform banks. As China's first commercial bank set up by an industrial company, Huaxia Bank completed a joint-stock system reform on April 10, 1996 and it officially went public in the A-share market on July 21, 2003, becoming the fifth listed commercial bank in China. Another example is Shanghai Pudong Development Bank Co., Ltd., which officially made IPO in the A-share market in September 1999.

Here we will give other examples, China Zheshang Bank, a privately owned Sino-foreign joint venture, has twenty-one private enterprises among its twenty-two shareholders, and 85.71% of its capital comes from private resources. Founded in 1996, China Minsheng Bank is China's first joint-stock commercial bank established mainly by non-state-owned private enterprises under the auspice of the All-China Federation of Industry and Commerce, reforming the original equity shareholdings of commercial banks. Subsequently, it was officially listed in the A-share market on December 19, 2000 and in the Hong Kong H-share market on November 26, 2009.

By centering around China's national development strategies, twelve national joint-stock commercial banks were poised to serve the private sector, micro, small and medium-sized enterprises, as well as agriculture, rural areas and farmers in support of the development of the real economy. With a view to pursuing a differentiated, personalized and specialized development policy, they were committed to innovating and developing green finance, consumer finance, industrial chain finance and fintech, striving to grow into retail banks with their respective characteristics. Specifically, Bohai Bank continued to intensify the support for green, circular and low-carbon economies, and proactively penetrated into advanced manufacturing industry, strategically emerging industries, modern service industry, cultural and creative industries and other emerging credit loan markets. Besides, industrial chain finance provided by China Minsheng Bank, platform finance provided by Huaxia Bank, and integrated financial services provided by Ping An Bank all had their own distinctive characteristics.

2.2.3 Urban Commercial Banks: Citizens' Banks and Enterprise-Run Banks

The predecessor of urban commercial banks is urban credit cooperative which emerged in China in the late 1970s at first. In the 1980s, urban credit cooperatives were established in cities across China and they grew into specialized financial institutions for tackling "the difficulties in account opening, settlement, deposit and borrowing" facing local enterprises at the sub-district level, especially individual businesses. According to incomplete statistics, there were more than 3,409 urban credit cooperatives established in the country. In the 1990s, urban credit cooperatives were booming. As of the end of 1995, the number of urban commercial banks increased to more than 5,200 in the country.

During their business operations, urban credit cooperatives were nevertheless run as small local commercial banks due to their evading regulation, and deviating from the basic principles of the cooperative system. With an average asset size of RMB61 million, the bulk of urban credit cooperatives were controlled by local governments, and they faced various operational problems and risks such as too low capital ratio, low non-performing loan ratio, insufficient liquidity, and rigid operational mechanisms. All these maladies made it imperative to overhaul and reform urban credit cooperatives.

In 1994, the Chinese government decided to reorganize existing urban credit cooperatives into urban cooperative banks. The scheme was roughly formulated as follows: To take the city as a basic unit, and merge all the commercialized urban credit cooperatives in a city into a commercial bank to serve for promoting local economic development. In 1995, the urban credit cooperative reorganization work was up-scaled nationwide.

Urban credit cooperatives in five cities such as Beijing, Tianjin and Shanghai were selected for pilot reorganization into urban cooperative banks. In July 1995, Shenzhen Municipality took the initiative to set up the first urban cooperative commercial bank in China. By the end of 1997, the schemes for establishing cooperative banks in 152 cities had been approved by the State Council, with 71 of the banks wining the approval for opening for business operation and 15 for going ahead with the preparation for establishment.

In 1998, all the urban cooperative banks in China were renamed urban commercial banks, followed by their capital restructuring, transformation and consolidation work. From 1999 to 2001, the Bank of Shanghai, the Bank of Nanjing and the Bank of Beijing successively brought in overseas strategic investors. In July 2001, Shanghai Pudong Development Bank announced its successful acquisition of Zhejiang Wenzhou Ruifeng Urban Credit Cooperative; and Fujian Industrial Bank successfully acquired 20-odd business outlets affiliated to Foshan Urban Commercial Bank and reorganized all of them into its own branches.

As of the end of 2002, there were a total of 112 urban commercial banks in China, with the assets totaling RMB1, 302.94 billion and a deposit balance of RMB652, 391 million. However, their outstanding non-performing loan balance reached RMB107, 811 million, with a non-performing loan ratio of 16.53%. Additionally, cumulative losses in the whole industry stood at RMB5, 597 million, with fifty banks sustaining losses over the years, accounting for 44% of all the urban commercial banks in the country.

From 2004 to 2006, urban commercial banks carried out reform around privatization and cross-regional operation. In August 2004, Zhejiang Commercial Bank was founded, with capital contributions mainly from private resources. Thirteen in its fifteen shareholders were well-known private enterprises in Zhejiang province, and altogether they made up 85% of shareholders' equity. Nanhua Bank, Jiangyin

Commercial Bank, Shenzhen Minhua Bank, Bank of Ruifeng, and Great Wall Bank in Xi'an city all realized their privatization as urban commercial banks by bringing in private capital.

After the reform and reorganization, urban commercial banks were allowed to carry out cross-regional operations in September 2004. After a merger between six urban commercial banks and seven urban credit cooperatives in Anhui province, Huishang Bank was established in December 2005, setting a precedent for establishing provincial-level regional banks through the reform and reorganization of urban commercial banks. At the end of 2010, Huishang Bank saw its asset size reach RMB208, 976 million, with branches set up across Anhui province.

Urban commercial banks also explored new models for reforming local banking corporations. In January 2007, ten commercial banks in Jiangsu province merged into the Bank of Jiangsu. In the same year, the Bank of Ningbo, the Bank of Nanjing, and the Bank of Beijing went public in the A-share market. Following the 2008 financial crisis, urban commercial banks were called upon to cease going public through a joint-stock system reform. It was not until 2016 that relevant lax policies were imposed.

In 2009, urban commercial banks made a new attempt to carry out the reform for integrating industry and finance. In April, 2009, Karamay City Commercial Bank was renamed the Bank of Kunlun, and reorganized into a urban commercial bank characterized by industry-finance integration by using funds from China National Petroleum Corporation. In 2010, its total assets jumped to RMB82, 604 million, setting what was known as the "Kunlun big leap pace model" among urban commercial banks.

Following their reform and reorganization, urban commercial banks were well positioned to serve for supporting local economic development, small and medium-sized enterprises, and citizens, and develop into cross-regional citizen banks and banks run by small and medium-sized enterprises, albeit with their own characteristics. For instance, micro and small credit loans made up more than 90% of the lending business of Tailong Urban Commercial Bank, Mintai Urban Commercial Bank and Taizhou Urban Commercial Bank in Taizhou city of Jiangsu province, and such loans carried a risk weight of 75%. In this way, such banks created a model of micro and small financial services. By employing a microcredit loan business development model, Harbin Commercial Bank was hailed as "China's Yunus" in the industry. In 2011, it granted loans totaling RMB14.5 billion to 7,000 small enterprises.

As of the end of 2019, there were a total of 134 urban commercial banks in China. With diversified equity structures, these banks generally established a modern financial enterprise system and operated in line with market-oriented and commercialized business philosophy, providing convenient financial services in support of local economic development, especially the development of small and medium-sized enterprises in cities.

2.2.4 Rural Finance: Connecting Urban and Rural Areas and Serving Agriculture, Rural Areas and Farmers

Likewise China's dual economic structure, a dual structure also existed in the financial sector. A financial system mainly consisting of the ABC, rural credit cooperatives, and village and township banks was established to connect urban and rural areas, and serve for agriculture, rural areas and farmers.

First, the ABC, with the Agricultural Cooperative Bank of China established in 1951 as its predecessor, which was oriented towards "agriculture, rural areas and farmers" and undertook a mission of serving urban and rural areas. Following its dissolution twice, the ABC was restored in 1955 and 1963 respectively and merged into the PBoC twice in 1957 and 1965. On February 23, 1979, the ABC was restored again as a national specialized bank in charge of leading and regulating national rural credit cooperatives.

In December 1993, the ABC commenced its reorganization into a state-owned commercial bank. In April 1994, it handed over its major policy functions to the newly established Agricultural Development Bank of China. In August 1996, it discontinued its administrative relationship with rural credit cooperatives and ceased its related leadership and administration. In July 1999, it divested its non-performing assets to the newly established China Great Wall Asset Management Co., Ltd. in preparation for carrying out a commercialized and joint-stock system reform.

From 2004 to 2010, the ABC underwent six years of joint-stock system reform in preparation for its IPO. It was not until July 15 and 16, 2010 when it finally got listed in Shanghai and Hong Kong in the form of A + H shares, in what was the then biggest size of IPO in the world.

For five consecutive years starting from 2014, the FSB included the ABC in the List of Global Systematically Important Banks (G-SIBs).[5] In 2019, the ABC rose to the third place on the G-SIBs list. Despite all its great strides in comprehensive commercial operations, the ABC has persistently put serving rural revitalization and poverty alleviation at the top agenda of all its work. Additionally, it has made constant efforts to provide financial services in support of the county economy and render its services in a more inclusive and specialized manner.

Second, rural credit cooperatives, which gained a firm foothold in rural areas. Generally speaking, there were two kinds of rural credit cooperatives in China. One is rural credit cooperatives which stemmed from the PBoC's reorganization of business outlets in rural areas in the early 1950s. Prior to 1979, rural credit cooperatives were basically administered by the PBoC. After a spell of administration by the ABC, they came under the administration of the PBoC again in 1996.

The other is rural credit cooperatives newly established in the 1980s. In the mid-1980s, there were more than 50,000 newly established rural credit cooperatives of this sort in China.[6] Nevertheless, this kind of rural credit cooperatives departed from

[5] The Agricultural Bank of China 2016 Annual Report [R], December 31, 2018, p. 1.

[6] Li Yang, Wang Guoguang et al.: *Thirty Years of Financial Reform and Opening up in China*, Economy and Management Publishing House, 2008, pp. 1–2.

their original purpose of serving agricultural production and improving farmers' livelihoods due to their galloping ahead. Instead of being attuned to the needs of developing the rural commodity economy, they increasingly aligned themselves with a bank business pattern in terms of personnel, business scope and financial management, and progressively developed into "government-run" financial institutions. In the end, they have lost their edge as financial cooperative organizations.

From the 1980s to 2005, the regulatory authorities rolled out three major reforms, and launched restructuring campaigns against rural credit cooperatives.

From 1983 to 1987, the first reform was spearheaded by the ABC, with a focus on reforming the business management systems of rural credit cooperatives and reorganizing them into cooperative financial organizations to serve the masses. In 1983, a pilot reform was carried out among 8,755 selected rural credit cooperatives across China. In August 1984, the reform was up-scaled nationwide. As such, the reform has achieved the desired effect by coordinating the relationships between the ABC and rural credit cooperatives, and providing financial services for the masses in a more democratic and flexible manner.

From 1996 to 1999, the second reform was carried out to further coordinate the relationships between the ABC and rural credit cooperatives, and optimize the business management system of rural credit cooperatives. Following the reform, the ABC no longer administered rural credit cooperatives, and therefore this reform was also renowned as "decoupling reform". From September 1996 onwards, there were more than 50,000 rural credit cooperatives and 2,400 county rural credit unions which had been decoupled from the ABC, while the PBoC reinforced its regulation over rural credit cooperatives. From 1999 onwards, the PBoC progressively established prefectural (urban) rural credit unions to administer county rural credit unions.

Despite accomplishments achieved by the two reforms, rural credit cooperatives have still put in poor performance. From 1994 to 2003, they sustained losses for ten consecutive years, running such a huge deficit of RMB5.8 billion in 2002 alone, and their historical losses amounted to RMB150 billion. At the end of 2002, rural credit cooperatives slipped into an overall deficit of RMB330 billion nationwide and the capital adequacy ratio equaled to −8.45%, with non-performing loans accounting for 36.93% of the total.[7]

From 2003 to 2005, the government initiated the reform of rural credit cooperatives for the third time to effectuate corporate reorganization, commercialized restructuring, and management system optimization. Specifically speaking, pilot reform was carried out for the first time in eight provinces and cities such as Jilin province, Shandong province, Jiangxi province, Zhejiang province, Jiangsu province, Shaanxi province, Guizhou province and Chongqing city, and such a reform was up-scaled to 29 provinces, autonomous regions, and municipalities directly under the central government in 2005. As such, supporting policies have been progressively pursued, and substantial headways have been made in relieving and lifting historical burdens.

[7] *A Chronicle of Major Events in China's Financial Reform and Opening up*, China Financial Publishing House, 2008, p. 860.

In 2003, the PBoC decided to disband prefectural (urban) rural credit unions in a bid to hand over rural credit cooperatives to the provincial governments for administration. In this way, local governments' administrative functions were preliminarily defined.[8] In other words, the provincial governments successively set up provincial-level rural credit unions to administer county rural credit unions in a hierarchical manner.

The reform has achieved considerable accomplishments. For the first time, rural credit cooperatives in the country realized profits as a whole in 2004. Altogether, there were 26,245 rural credit cooperatives that had reaped profits.[9] In June 2005, the capital adequacy ratio of rural credit cooperatives reached 5.89%, while their actual non-performing loan ratio fell to 21.23%. As of the end of 2005, the PBoC arranged for the issuance of special bills totaling RMB159.9 billion in eight tranches in 2,263 counties (cities) in exchange for the non-performing loans and historical deficits of rural credit cooperatives. According to related statistics, it established a total of 72 rural banking financial institutions and 519 county (urban) financial institutions as a unitary legal entity, notching up a success in reforming the property right system and shifting the business model and the management mechanism.

Third, newly established rural commercial banks. Following the aforementioned decoupling reform, rural credit cooperatives were allowed to be reorganized into different legal entities which were positioned as local joint-stock financial institutions, including rural commercial banks, rural cooperative banks and rural credit cooperatives. It is noteworthy that the bulk of rural commercial banks were derived from rural credit unions in economically developed counties and cities and they became the mainstay of rural finance in developed regions.

In July 2000, the Jiangsu Provincial Government won the approval for reforming its rural credit cooperatives and piloting the establishment of rural commercial banks in Jiangyin city, Changshu city, and Zhangjiagang city. On November 28, 2001, Changshu Rural Commercial Bank and Zhangjiagang Rural Commercial Bank were established. On December 6, 2001, Jiangyin Rural Commercial Bank was officially inaugurated. The administrative powers of rural credit cooperatives and rural commercial banks were conferred on a provincial credit unions set up by the Jiangsu Provincial Government.

In 2004, the pilot reform was rolled out in more regions in China. On May 24, 2004, Guizhou Huaxi Rural Cooperative Bank was established with approval, becoming China's first rural cooperative bank established following the joint-stock system reform of rural credit cooperatives. On August 17, 2004, the pilot scheme for establishing rural cooperative banks was up-scaled from 8 to 29 provinces, cities or autonomous regions (excluding Hainan and Xizang), covering the bulk of regions in the country. At the end of 2005, there were a total of twelve rural commercial banks

---

[8] The Financial Stability Analysis Group of the PBoC: *China Financial Stability Report 2016*, China Financial Publishing House, 2007, p. 4.

[9] Wu Xiaoling (eds): *A Chronicle of Major Events in China's Financial Reform and Opening up*, China Financial Publishing House, 2008, p. 766.

established in China. As of the end of 2016, there were 1,114 rural commercial banks with a total asset of RMB20.3 trillion in China.

Among newly established rural commercial banks, Changshu Rural Commercial Bank, Zhangjiagang Rural Commercial Bank, and Jiangyin Rural Commercial Bank were operated on a large scale with an irresistible development momentum.

In 2019, China's rural financial institution system for connecting urban and rural areas to serve agriculture, rural areas and farmers basically took shape, involving 1,427 rural commercial banks, 71 rural cooperative banks, 812 rural credit cooperatives, 1,616 village and township banks, and 45 rural mutual fund cooperatives.

2.2.5 Policy-Oriented Financial Institutions: Supporting National Strategies

From 1949 to 1978, the PBoC dealt in major policy financial business. It is worth noting that such policy financial business operations were mainly conducted by the ICBC, ABC, BOC and CCB from 1978 to 1993.

In 1994, three policy financial institutions including China Development Bank, the Export–Import Bank of China, and the Agricultural Development Bank of China were successively set up to conduct the policy financial business operations which were previously undertaken by specialized banks. In this way, maladies such as non-separation of policy and commercial finance and dual functions performed by state-owned specialized banks have been tackled, and a regulatory regime of state-owned specialized banks characterized by integration of administrative functions with enterprise has been shifted.

On March 17, 1994, China Development Bank was established with approval in Beijing. As a legal entity with a registered capital of RMB50 billion, China Development Bank was discharged with the tasks of supporting the development of the national economy and improving the livelihood of the people. In the early stages, China Development Bank mainly conducted the loan and subsidized loan business for state key policy construction projects (including infrastructure and technological transformation projects), as well as administered the CCB, and regulated national investment and other business.

In December 2008, China Development Bank was reorganized into China Development Bank Co., Ltd., completing its restructuring from a policy financial institution to a joint-stock bank. In March 2015, it was oriented towards a development financial institution with an independent legal entity status. With a mission of "enhancing comprehensive national competitiveness and improving people's livelihood", China Development Bank was committed to rendering support for the development of key and backward sectors in the Chinese economy.

As of the end of 2018, China Development Bank held assets totaling RMB16.2 trillion, had an outstanding loan balance of RMB 11.68 trillion, and reaped a net profit of RMB112.1 billion, with a capital adequacy ratio of 11.81%. The outstanding loan balance was expressed as a proportion in different industries as follows: Railway construction occupied 7.28%; highway construction 16.14%; electric power 8.23%; public infrastructure 11.36%; shanty area renovation 27.4%; strategically emerging industries 10.13%; and other sectors19.47%.[10]

The Export–Import Bank of China was established with approval in Beijing on July 1, 1994. With a registered capital of RMB3.3 billion invested by the state, it is a state-owned policy bank with an independent legal entity status and directly under the leadership of the State Council. The Export–Import Bank of China is committed to promoting international economic cooperation, supporting China's economic development, and facilitating the construction of a harmonious international community.

The Export–Import Bank of China mainly engaged in cross-border financing for the import and export of large mechanical and electrical equipment, and its funds mainly came from special fiscal funds, financial bonds issued to financial institutions, and other resources. Backed by the credit of the Chinese government, the bank played a proactive role in stabilizing growth, adjusting structure, supporting the development of foreign trade, and pursuing the "going global" strategy.

As of the end of 2018, the Export–Import Bank of China held assets totaling RMB4, 193.7 billion, and granted foreign trade loans of RMB1, 076,528 million and cross-border investment loans of RMB272, 565 million. Besides, it also granted RMB 886,178 million in loans for supporting international cooperation and RMB1, 139,899 million in loans for supporting China's opening to the outside world.[11]

On November 8, 1994, the Agricultural Development Bank of China (ADBC) was established with approval in Beijing. With a registered capital of RMB57 billion, it was the sole agricultural policy bank with an independent legal entity status and directly under the leadership of the State Council in China, taking over the agricultural policy lending business which was previously conducted by the ABC and ICBC. The ADBC was discharged with tasks such as raising funds from the market on government credit to support agriculture, concentrating funds on supporting the development of agriculture, rural areas and farmers, and playing a supporting role in pursuing national strategies.

In 1998, the ADBC mainly specialized in granting policy loans for agricultural development, national grain, cotton and oil reserves and the contractual purchase of agricultural by-products. Meanwhile, it also acted as an agency in charge of the appropriation and oversight of agriculture-supporting fiscal funds.

In 2010, the ADBC developed a "three-pronged" development structure by providing credit facilities for purchasing grain, cotton and oil as main business, supplemented by loans for agricultural industrialization and agricultural and rural medium- and long-term credit loans. In 2011, it commenced to explore diversified

---

10 China Development Bank Co., Ltd.: 2018 Annual Report, December 31, 2017, p. 7.

11 Import-Export Bank of China Co., Ltd.: 2018 Annual Report [R], December 31, 2018. pp. 8–9 and 17.

operations and decided to make policy investments in agriculture, thus progressively establishing a commercialized and integrated business model.

The ADBC has persistently pursued national strategies, energetically served for agriculture, rural areas and farmers, and proactively followed the laws of banking business management. All in a word, it has spared no efforts to render serves in support of food safety, poverty alleviation, agricultural modernization, and integrated urban and rural development, as well as key national development strategies. As of the end of 2017, the ADBC held assets totaling RMB6, 221,499 million, had an outstanding loan balance of RMB4, 556.04 billion, and reaped a net profit of RMB17, 118 million.

All the aforesaid three development and policy banks were in a position to provide banking services in support of China's national strategies for promoting economic development in different sectors.

2.3 Non-depository Banking Institutions: Specializing in the Ancillary Business

Non-depository banking institutions refer to trust companies, asset management companies, financial companies affiliated to enterprise groups, financial leasing companies, auto finance companies, money brokerage companies, consumer finance companies, and other financial institutions, which constitute an part of the financial institutional system. In the different financial sectors, they are committed to serving and catering for diversified customer needs.

2.3.1 Trust Companies: Entrusted to Manage Wealth for Customers

Nowadays, the trust industry is China's second largest financial sector following the banking sector. From 1949 to the late 1950s, China's trust industry underwent the twists and turns of takeover, transformation and suspension. Until 1978, there was no any trust institution in the country at all. At the proposal of Yiren Rong, China International Trust and Investment Corporation was officially established with approval in October 1979.

Trust and investment companies emerged as a result of the demand stimulation and thrust of entrepreneurs and the encouragement and support of the government. As of the end of 1982, there were a total of more than 620 trust institutions in China, of which 568 were trust divisions or companies established within the banking system, including 186 set up by the PBoC, 266 by the CCB, 96 by the BOC, and 20-odd by the ABC. Altogether, they made up about 90% of all the trust and investment companies in the country in those days.

Due to demand stimulation and governmental support, the trust industry was on a rampant growth throughout the 1980s and its disorderly development disrupted the normal financial order, prompting the regulatory authorities to launch three major campaigns to overhaul the industry. Nevertheless, these campaigns, far from achieving the desired effect, have only attained the basic targets of "separating banks from trust business operations".

After Xiaoping Deng delivered his reform speech during his South China Tour in 1992, economical "overheating" re-surfaced across the country, offering new development opportunities to trust and investment companies and further fueling an already "overheated" economy. In 1993, the PBoC decided to launch the campaign to overhaul the trust industry for the fourth time, with the emphasis placed on "separating banks from trust business operations" and "dissolving and consolidating trust and investment companies".

In line with the business philosophy of separating banks from trust business operations as set forth in the Commercial Bank Law promulgated in 1995, the PBoC introduced and operated an exit mechanism, and preliminarily decoupled the ICBC and CCB from their trust companies. Meanwhile, it also called upon other banks to decouple themselves from all of their trust and investment companies, or reorganized them into their branches which were only allowed to engage in the banking business.

In October 1995, the PBoC temporarily took over the insolvent Bank of China Group Trust and Investment Co., Ltd. for illegal operation reasons, which was eventually acquired by Guangdong Development Bank. As of the end of 1996, the number of trust and investment companies with an independent legal entity status in China was reduced to 244. In 1997, the PBoC shut down China Rural Development Trust Investment Company and China New Technology Venture Capital Company, and closed and disposed of Guangdong International Trust Investment Company in accordance with market-oriented principles and legal procedures.

Following the overhaul of "separating banks from trust business operations", the remaining trust companies all suffered from such maladies as poor asset quality and payment difficulty, and they were prone to trigger systematic risks in the whole trust industry.

In February 1999, the PBoC decided to launch the fifth and the longest campaign to overhaul the trust industry, with a focus on "separating trust companies from securities operations". With the aim of resuming the original functions of the trust industry, the PBoC designated trust and investment companies to act as an agent or trustee to provide a wide range of services related to investment and asset management on behalf of a trust and it also defined their three main business of fund trust, property trust, and real estate trust. These efforts were reinforced to reflect the characteristics of the trust industry such as "managing wealth for customers" and all the trust companies were required to cease operating in the securities brokerage and stock underwriting business.

During the overhaul campaign, trust and investment companies set up by asset management companies such as China Huarong Asset Management Co., Ltd., China Great Wall Asset Management Co., Ltd., China Orient Asset Management Co., Ltd.

and China Cinda Asset Management Co., Ltd. were dissolved with approval. Meanwhile, China Electric Power Finance Co., Ltd. and China Economic Development Trust and Investment Corporation completed reorganization while a good number of well-managed trust and investment companies were retained for re-registration.

Also known as "One Law and Two Measures", China's Trust Law was promulgated in April 2001, the Measures for the Administration of Trust and Investment Companies and the Measures for the Administration of the Fund Trust of Trust and Investment Companies were issued by the PBoC in June 2001 to explicitly define the legal relationship, legal status, and business scope of the trust in China. It was only after the "One Law and Two Measures" took effect that the trust industry has progressively completed its reshaping institutional system according to the law by establishing a standardized corporate system and resuming its original missions of "managing wealth for customers". Thereafter, a modern trust industry emerged in China.

According to "One Law and Two Measures", the regulatory authorities launched the sixth campaign to overhaul the trust industry from 2001 to 2005, with a focus on "separating banks from securities and trust operations". Specifically, trust and investment companies were required to verify their assets and capital and overhaul their business operations according to the law. Among them, some were either disbanded or shut down due to their grave maladies, while those retained or merged must re-register with the PBoC. Meanwhile, trust and investment companies were called upon to reinforce their information disclosure systems and tighten up self-regulation.

The trust industry had eventually completed the separation of "banks from securities and trust operations", and carried out separate operations by the end of 2005 to showcase the specialized nature of the trust industry. In 2006, multiple trust models took shape in China's trust market, including securities investment, equity investment, loan-granting, asset quasi-securitization, trust beneficiary rights, and lease trust.

In 2007, the CBRC launched the seventh campaign to overhaul the trust industry, with a focus on the implementation of a "new trust policy", which explicitly ordered to delete "investment" from the title of trust and Investment Company and alter its title into "trust company" in a unified manner.

The "new trust policy" required all trust companies to complete recapitalization and re-registration. In April 2008, there were a total of 34 trust companies awarded a new license. Following this overhaul, the trust industry was booming, basically resuming its original business of wealth management and proactively switching to the asset management business. As of the end of 2009, there were a total of 54 trust companies in China, which posted an overall revenue of RMB20, 675 million, including RMB9, 065 million or 43.84% from the trust business.

The year 2011 marked another watershed in the development of the trust industry. Prior to 2011, extensive business cooperation between banks and trust companies provided a positive stimulus for promoting the development of the trust industry. From 2011 onwards, the trust industry placed a premium on three more specialized, differentiated and targeted business models, namely individual trusts for conducting the non- bank-trust wealth management cooperation business with high-end financial institutions as core large customers, joint trusts with mid-end qualified individual investors as target customers, and individual trusts for conducting the bank-trust wealth management cooperation business with low-end bank wealth management clients as targeted customers.

As of the end of 2012, there were a total of 66 trust companies in China that managed RMB7.47 trillion of trust assets, and reaped a gross profit of RMB44.14 billion. For the first time, the trust industry outperformed the insurance industry with a total asset of RMB7.35 trillion and became the second largest financial sector in the country, second only to the banking industry.

In 2013, the trust industry switched from specialized service provision to integrated service provision. For instance, CITIC Trust became the largest integrated trust company in China, while China Foreign Economy and Trade Trust Co., Ltd. (FOTIC) and Ping An Trust emerged as typical quasi-integrated trust institutions. From 2015 onwards, trust companies made bold to pioneer in innovating the land and family trust business. For instance, CITIC Trust ventured to conduct the land trust business and has preliminarily accumulated valuable experience in the process. In 2016, trust assets in China passed the RMB20 trillion mark, ushering in a new era.

The year 2017 was hailed as the year of imposing the most rigorous financial regulation in China, with the entire asset management industry coming under unified regulation. Amidst such a backdrop, trust companies leveraged their institutional advantages of acting as a financial institution specializing in the entrusted wealth management business, and proactively reverted to their original functions of providing wealth management products and services for institutional customers and high-end individual customers. By launching diversified trust business to be attuned to the fundamental needs of the real economy, the trust industry has achieved a sustainable and healthy development. By the end of 2018, 68 trust companies in China had managed trust assets totaling RMB22.72 trillion, with an average asset size of RMB333, 842 million per company, 11.14 times the size of that in 2008.

By launching several overhaul campaigns following reform and opening up, China's trust industry has finally metamorphosed from chaos to well-governance, and trust companies have also grown into a kind of well-regulated non-depository banking financial institutions.

2.3.2 Asset Management Companies: Accomplishing Missions and Effecting Transformation

As state-owned commercial banks pressed ahead with their reform and disposed of non-performing assets in 1999, the Chinese government decided to establish asset management companies to undertake three major missions, namely to resolve financial risks, to promote the reform and development of state-owned enterprises, and to preserve state-owned assets to the maximum extent possible.

On April 20, 1999, China Cinda Asset Management Co., Ltd. was established with approval as the first asset management company for disposing of the non-performing assets of the CCB. With a registered capital of RMB40 billion and an operational period of ten years, China Huarong Asset Management Corporation, China Great Wall Asset Management Corporation, China Orient Asset Management Company were subsequently established in succession to acquire, manage and dispose of the nearly RMB1.4 trillion of non-performing assets stripped from the ICBC, ABC, BOC and CDB.

By way of acquisition, the four asset management companies stripped RMB1.4 trillion worth of non-performing assets from four large state-owned commercial banks based on their book value from 1999 to 2000. The acquisition funds mainly came from RMB570 billion worth of loans granted by the PBoC to financial institutions, and RMB820 billion of funds raised from the issuance of financial bonds. As required by the PBoC, the four state-owned commercial banks must lower their average non-performing asset ratio to 15% by 2005, with an annual reduction of 3–5%.

To accomplish this daunting task, asset management companies actively explored ways to effectively dispose of non-performing assets (such as debt restructuring, asset restructuring, corporate restructuring, litigation, asset auctions, etc.) and maximize the recovery of non-performing assets. In view of the characteristics of non-performing assets which had been taken over, China Great Wall Asset Management Corporation piloted the injection of private capital into the non-performing asset disposal market in Dalian city in 2000. Specifically, it disposed of non-performing assets with a book value of more than RMB200 million by way of sales by lease in a pilot manner, with 90% of the investment coming from private capital. Meanwhile, it also initiated a cross-sectoral and cross-regional strategic non-performing asset restructuring scheme, involving more than 440 projects topping RMB10 billion. At the end of 2001, China Great Wall Asset Management Corporation launched the biggest non-performing asset auction week campaign in history, in which 60% of the auctioned projects were taken over by private investors, reshaping the ownership structure of enterprises.

However, the non-performing loan ratio of the four large state-owned commercial banks was still as high as 25.4% at the end of 2001, with nearly RMB1 trillion of non-performing assets in urgent need of disposal.

On November 13, 2002, China Orient Asset Management Company assigned RMB4.47 billion worth of creditor's rights it had in 90 projects and 100 enterprises in Shunde district of Foshan city, Guangdong province to domestic investors by way of invitation to treat and open bidding. By exploring a new way to dispose of assets, this assignment was reputed to be No.1 creditor's right assignment in the one-off disposal of non-performing assets by asset management companies in China.

As of the end of 2003, the four asset management companies disposed of RMB509.37 billion of non-performing assets (excluding policy debt-to-equity swaps), recovering a cumulative amount of RMB99.4 billion in cash, with a cash recovery rate of 19.52%.

From 2003 to 2004, the Chinese government established a target assessment accountability system for asset management companies to dispose of non-performing assets, and nudged them in their right commercialized development orientation. Meanwhile, it also granted an approval for adopting various commercial means for disposing of non-performing assets, including allowing asset management companies to use their own capital to invest in treasury bonds, engaging in commercially entrusted and commercial acquisition and disposal of non-performing assets, and conducting securities and other investment banking business. In March 2004, the MoF gave its official sanction for the four asset management companies to conduct three types of new business: commercial acquisition, investment, and agency by agreement. In 2004, the above four asset management companies commenced to acquire the non-performing assets of the BOC, CCB and BOCOM by way of submitting a tender or bidding. In 2005, the ICBC's non-performing assets were disposed of in line with the business philosophy of separation of wholesale and retail.

By the end of 2005, the four asset management companies had disposed of RMB839.75 billion of non-performing assets in aggregate and recovered RMB176.6 billion in cash, with a cash recovery ratio of 21.03%. The remaining non-performing loans of RMB1, 313.36 billion were slated to be disposed of within three years as specified by the government.

In 2006, the four asset management companies made good headways in disposing of non-performing assets by policy-based and market-oriented means. First, they took over RMB1, 393.9 billion of policy-related non-performing loans stripped from four large state-owned commercial banks and China Development Bank, involving more than 2 million enterprises burdened with debts. As such, it attained the cash recovery rate and expenditure rate targets set by the MoF ahead of schedule. Second, they made policy-based debt-to-equity swaps for 1,095 enterprises. Third, they were entrusted with the task of disposing of RMB442.9 billion of non-performing loss loans divested by the BOC, ICBC and CCB. Fourth, they were designated to deal with 22 high-risk financial institutions. Fifth, they made commercial acquisitions of RMB830.5 billion of non-performing doubtful loans granted by the CCB, ICBC, BOC and BOCOM. Sixth, they proactively conducted the commercial investment banking business and delivered a good business performance.[12]

In 2009, the four asset management companies basically fulfilled their non-performing financial asset disposal tasks. In total, they acquired more than RMB2 trillion of non-performing assets stripped from four large state-owned commercial banks, and made debt-to-equity swaps valued at more than RMB300 billion for over 500 medium-sized and large state-owned enterprises. In this way, they have maximized the recovery of state-owned assets, and defused the huge risks in the financial system, making a contribution to promoting banking reform, social stability, extrication of state-owned enterprises from deficits, and local economic development.

---

[12] Luo Weizhong: Explore Development Pathways of Asset Management Companies with Chinese Characteristics, Financial News, June 23, 2008, p. 8.

With the approaching deadline for the final disposal of non-performing debts and the full liberalization of the financial sector, it was imperative for asset management companies to chart way ahead for a sustainable development. In this regard, there were three options available for them, namely, business model shifts, long-term sustainable operations, and an integrated business model of financial holding company. As early as 2007, asset management companies commenced to explore on how to successfully shift their original business model by making forays into financial services other than non-performing asset disposal.

Firstly, asset management companies shifted their business philosophies and models by proactively seeking business opportunities instead of passively awaiting business allocation as before. Secondly, they took the initiative to shift from the original "wholesale" model of non-performing asset disposal to "refined" means to improve the competitiveness and professionalism of non-performing asset disposal, and strived to maximize the recovery of non-performing assets. Thirdly, they proactively restructured into a financial holding company to maintain their main business of non-performing asset disposal while also operating an investment banking business. In this way, they have grown into an asset management company in a real sense.

China Cinda Asset Management Co., Ltd., China Huarong Asset Management Corporation, China Great Wall Asset Management Corporation, China Orient Asset Management Company all expedited their business model shifts and market-oriented reform. In 2010, China Cinda Asset Management Co., Ltd. won an approval for comprehensively carrying out a joint-stock system reform. Subsequently, it was given the sanction for getting listed on the Hong Kong Exchanges and Clearing Limited in December 2013. In September 2012, Huarong Asset Management Corporation was approved to reorganize itself into a joint-stock limited company and it went public on the Hong Kong Exchanges and Clearing Limited in October 2015. In 2016, China Orient Asset Management Company and China Great Wall Asset Management Corporation both won the approval for reorganizing themselves into a joint-stock limited company respectively. As such, all the four asset management companies have metamorphosed from policy financial institutions to commercial financial institutions by switching from a single specialized business model to a diversified business operation model.

Apart from the aforementioned four state-owned asset management companies, the MoF and the CBRC promulgated relevant provisions in February 2012, allowing each provincial government to establish or authorize a local asset management company to participate in the bulk acquisition and disposal of non-performing assets of financial enterprises in their respective provinces. By October 2014, eight provincial governments and municipalities in Jiangsu province, Zhejiang province, Guangdong povince, Shanghai, Anhui province, Tianjin city, Fujian province and Beijing city all had completed the work of setting up or authorizing a local asset management company in succession. Meanwhile, the provincial governments in other provinces like Shanxi province and Shandong province also had undertaken to set up their respective local asset management companies.

As of the end of 2019, apart from the four state-owned asset management companies, there were also fifty-four local asset management companies and hundreds of other types of asset management companies in China. In a new era, asset management companies may serve as a financial stabilizer, resource optimizer and economic booster.

2.3.3 Financial Companies Affiliated to Enterprise Group: Serving for Enterprises and the Real Economy

Financial companies affiliated to enterprise groups in China emerged in the 1980s as a new means of financing and investment. The first finance company was established in the Shenzhen Special Economic Zone in 1984.

With a view to alleviating fund shortages in the enterprise development, and pursuing the strategy of "large companies and large groups", the PBoC proposed to set up non-banking institutions for serving enterprise groups. In 1987, China Dongfeng Motor Industry Financial Company was established with approval. In the same year, six financial companies affiliated to enterprise group such as Shenzhen Special Economic Zone Development Financial Company and China International Financial Co., Ltd. were set up in the Shenzhen Special Economic Zone. Subsequently, the number of financial companies affiliated to enterprise group increased from 7 to 17, and their total assets rose from RMB1.6 billion to RMB13.4 billion.

In the absence of relevant regulatory regulations promulgated and imposed in those days, there was no any sound existing regulatory regime for regulating the deposits and loans, settlement, bills, guarantee, financial leasing, investment and foreign exchange business operations of financial companies affiliated to enterprise group. Therefore, operations beyond the business scope, serious fund shortage and other maladies occurred from time to time.

In June 1990, the PBoC decided to overhaul financial companies affiliated to enterprise groups, with a focus on addressing such maladies as administrative departments running financial companies affiliated to enterprise group in disguise, financial companies affiliated to enterprise group taking deposits from outside of their enterprise groups, granting loans to external customers and hiking interest rates without authorization, as well as poor management. The approval for establishing new financial companies affiliated to enterprise group were no longer granted until 1991.

In 1991, the State Council decided to select a batch of large enterprise groups to pilot in the establishment of financial companies affiliated to enterprise group, stipulating that the main business of financial companies affiliated to enterprise group was to obtain internal finance for their own enterprise groups. In December, fifty-five qualified large enterprise groups were approved to set up financial companies affiliated to enterprise group in a pilot manner in 10-odd sectors, covering automobile manufacturing, non-ferrous metals, civil aviation, hotel management, steel, energy, textile, electronics, and medicine.

In September 1994, the China National Association of Finance Companies was established as a self-regulatory industry organization for financial companies affiliated to enterprise groups. Meanwhile, the PBoC formulated related administrative measures.

With the support of the government, financial companies affiliated to enterprise group were flourishing. In 1996, the number of financial companies affiliated to enterprise group nationwide increased to sixty-six from fifty-five in 1992, and their assets and gross profits grew to RMB122.56 billion and RMB2, 392 million respectively. In 2000, there was also an increase from seventy-five from sixty-six in 1996, with their assets growing to RMB519.77 billion.

The CBRC was responsible for regulating financial companies affiliated to enterprise group and mandating them to perform centralized fund management and provide financial management services for affiliates of enterprise groups. Meanwhile, it included financial companies affiliated to enterprise group in Class-V assets for regulation, allowing them to carry out the asset securitization business and issue financial bonds. In 2009, the PBoC allowed financial companies affiliated to enterprise group to connect to the national electronic commercial draft system, and selected financial companies affiliated to enterprise group such as Haier Group, SAIC Motor, China Minmetals Corporation and China Power Investment Corporation for piloting online business operations.

In 2011, there were a total of 127 enterprise groups that had set up affiliated financial companies in sectors including petrochemical, electricity, military engineering, automobile, coal, transportation, electronics and electrical appliances, iron and steel, machinery manufacturing, non-ferrous metals, building materials and trade across China, involving state-owned, collective, private and foreign-invested enterprises. As of the end of 2015, the number of financial companies affiliated to enterprise group in China increased to 224. It is noteworthy that they held on- and off-balance sheet assets totaling RMB6.5 trillion, had an annual operating revenue of RMB98, 149 million, and reaped a gross profit of RMB75, 776 million. In practice, financial companies affiliated to enterprise groups are a kind of quasi-banking institutions which mainly serve for enterprise groups, industrial chains, and the real economy. In 2018, financial companies affiliated to enterprise group succeeded in supporting the development of the real economy. In the whole year, they granted loans totaling RMB4.55 trillion, up 13.03% year-on-year, far outpacing the economic growth rate of the country at the time. Specifically speaking, forty-three financial companies affiliated to enterprise group provided consumer credit facilities and buyer credit facilities and conducted the group product financial leasing business for downstream enterprises of industrial chain, benefiting 4, 756 micro, small and medium-sized enterprises. Meanwhile, fifty-four financial companies conducted the industry chain discounting and industry chain factoring business totaling RMB131.8 billion per year for upstream enterprises of the industrial chain, involving 5,287 micro, small and medium-sized enterprises.

As of the end of 2018, there were 253 corporate financial companies affiliated to enterprise group in China, with on- and off- balance sheet assets totaling RMB9.50 trillion, net operating revenues of RMB141.3 billion, and net profits of RMB79, 034 million. Although risk incidents occurred on few financial companies affiliated to enterprise group, the industry still kept the robust momentum going. At the end of 2018, there were 214 or 85% of financial companies affiliated to enterprise group without non-performing assets, with an average non-performing asset ratio and a non-performing loan ratio being 0.46% and 0.96% respectively. Meanwhile, the average capital adequacy ratio of the industry stood at 20.48%, the core tier-1 capital adequacy ratio reached 19.49%, and the provision coverage rate was 292.85%. The average industry-wide capital concentration of financial companies affiliated to enterprise group reached 49.48%,[13] showcasing their strong capacity to pool and control funds.

2.3.4 Financial Leasing Companies: Equipment Financing Providers

Financial leasing companies are a product of China's opening to the outside world and bringing in foreign capital. As China's major portal for utilizing foreign capital in the late 1970s, the CITIC is the first company to conduct the international leasing business, and effectively opened up a new channel for leveraging foreign capital.

In the early 1980s, financial leasing was introduced into China as a channel for leveraging foreign capital. The first leasing company is China Orient Leasing Co., Ltd. jointly set up by the CITIC, Beijing Electromechanical Equipment Co., Ltd. and Japan Orient Leasing Co., Ltd. in February 1981. In July 1981, China Leasing Co., Ltd. was established with approval, heralding an emergence of a modern financial leasing industry in China.

With various leasing institutions being set up one after another, the leasing industry was flourishing, their business scope was expanded, and customers came from various industries all over the country in the 1990s. Hit by the 1997 Asian financial crisis, China's financial leasing industry underwent its first crisis, and financial leasing business was slack due to ballooning bank debts in 1999.

In 2000, the financial leasing industry was allowed to raise private capital, which set off a new round of industry-wide merger, reorganization and integration. Founded in 1994, Sichuan Financial Leasing Co., Ltd. (CFL) was successfully reorganized into a compliant financial leasing company in 2000 by using the funds injected by private enterprises including Ningbo Tuopu Group Co., Ltd., Chengdu Commercial Bank and PKU Founder Group. Following the reorganization, the CFL saw its capital increase to RMB500 million.

---

[13] http://www.cnafc.org/cnafc/front/detail.action?id=234B1082FE4C4D87B21D7B0DECE381D1. China National Association of Financial Company: China Enterprise Group Financial Company Industry Development Report (2019) [EB/OL], August 1, 2019, http://www.cnafc.org/cnafc/front/detail.action?id=234B1082FE4C4D87B21D7B0DECE381D1.

In terms of their approval and administrative departments, financial leasing companies roughly fall into the following categories: finance lease companies (there were about 13 of them) which are approved and administered by the PBoC, operating lease companies which are approved and administered by the Ministry of Foreign Trade and Economic Cooperation, and operating lease companies which are approved and administered by the former Ministry of Domestic Trade and other relevant departments. As regards the nature of their leasing business, financial leasing companies can be divided into financial leasing companies and Sino-foreign joint venture leasing companies that mainly specialize in the finance lease business, and other leasing companies which mainly conduct the operating lease business.

Financial leasing companies refer to non-banking institutions which specialize in providing investment and financing services, subject to the approval and regulation of the CBRC. In 2007, the CBRC granted the approval for banks to have stakes in financial leasing companies. From 2007 to 2008, five financial leasing companies were established by banks. In 2014, the CBRC gave sanctions for financial leasing companies to set up their specialized subsidiaries, so that they could better give full play their characteristics and advantages of combined financing of funds and assets.

As of February 2019, forty-eight in seventy financial leasing companies in China were controlled or held by state-owned banks, joint-stock banks, urban commercial banks and rural commercial banks. Generally speaking, the bulk of them conducted the business in the sectors of urban utilities, large equipment, aviation and shipment, healthcare, rail transit, motor transportation, engineering machinery, green energy, and education and culture, as well as agriculture, rural areas and farmers.

2.3.5 Other Financial Institutions: Catering for the Needs of the Niche Market

Other non-depository financial institutions refers to auto finance companies, money brokerage companies, consumer finance companies, small credit loan companies and pawnshops, which mainly specialize in catering for the needs of the niche market and provide services for different targeted customer groups.

Auto finance companies refer to non-depository banking institutions which are established with the approval of the CBRC to provide financial services for automobile buyers and sellers in China.

In August 2004, SAIC-GMAC was the first auto finance company jointly set up by General Motors Acceptance Corporation (GMAC), SAIC Motors and SAIC Finance with approval. By the end of 2012, the company had up-scaled its business operations to more than 300 cities in 30 provinces and regions in China, providing one-stop auto finance services for more than one million automobile consumers. In 2017, the company saw its retail loan contracts pass the 1 million mark for the first time, becoming the first auto finance company that hit 1 million worth of contract price in China.

In September 2004, wholly foreign-owned Volkswagen Finance China Co., Ltd. was established with approval. From 2005 onwards, some wholly foreign-owned or Sino-foreign joint venture auto finance companies (e.g. Toyota Motor Finance (China) Co., Ltd.) were set up. From 2010 onwards, Chinese auto finance companies emerged. As of the end of 2019, there were twenty-five auto finance companies established in China and the bulk of them were foreign-owned companies or Sino-foreign joint ventures.

Money brokerage companies refer to non-depository banking institutions which are incorporated within the territory of China that specialize in promoting inter-financing, foreign exchange transactions and other brokerage services among financial institutions by employing electronic technology or other means, and charge commissions on services.

In December 2005, Shanghai Tullett Prebon SITICO (China) Ltd. operated in business with approval. From 2007 to 2012, Shanghai CFETS-NEX International Money Brokerage Company (2007), Ping An Tradition International Money Brokerage Company (2008), China Credit BGC Money Brokerage Company Limited (2010), and CITIC Central Tanshi Money Brokering Company Limited (2012) were established. As of the end of 2019, there were merely five money brokerage companies in China.

Money brokerage companies were allowed to operate in the four markets, namely money, bond, foreign exchange, and derivatives. By improving the efficiency of interbank market trading, and market liquidity, they effectively made up for deficiencies facing small and medium-sized financial institutions, including limited information access channels, weak bargaining power, and difficulty in finding business partners in the market. Through their services, money brokerage companies could help to achieve market fairness and ensure transparency.

Consumer finance companies refer to non-depository banking institutions which are established with approval in China to grant loans to individual residents for the consumption purposes on a small-sum and diversified basis without taking public deposits.

In January 2010, the first batch of three consumer finance companies, namely the Bank of Beijing Consumer Finance Company, *BOC Consumer Finance* Co., Ltd., and Sichuan Jincheng Consumer Finance Co., Ltd. (a Sino-foreign joint venture) set up by the BOC, Bank of Beijing, and Bank of Chengdu respectively were approved to conduct pilot business operations. In November 2010, Home Credit *Consumer Finance* Co., Ltd. was established with approval in Tianjin city, becoming the first wholly foreign-owned consumer finance company in China.

As of the end of October 2012, the above four consumer finance companies which were established in Beijing, Shanghai, Chengdu and Tianjin respectively held assets totaling RMB4, 016 million, had an outstanding loan balance of RMB3, 709 million and served more than 190,000 customers in total. In 2013, the pilot scheme for consumer finance companies was up-scaled, bringing about a sharp increase in the number of consumer finance companies and a rapid development of the industry. In early 2017, twenty-two consumer finance companies were established with approval, including twenty set up by banks, and largely by small and medium-sized banks. In

2018, the net profit of licensed Merchants Union Consumer Finance Company and Home Credit Consumer Finance Company passed the RMB1 billion mark for the first time in China.

By the end of 2019, twenty-six companies had obtained a consumer finance license. More than 3/4 of them were consumer finance companies established by banks, and the rest were established by industrial enterprises, listed companies and retail enterprises, including Mashang Consumer Finance Co., Ltd., *Haier Consumer Finance* Co. Ltd, *Suning Consumer Finance* Co., Ltd., and Huarong Consumer Finance Corporation.

Small loan companies emerged in China in 2006. On February 13, the first batch of private small loan companies (e.g. Shanxi Pingyao County Rishenglong Small Loan Co., Ltd., Shanxi Pingyao County Jinyuantai Small Loan Co., Ltd. and Shanxi Pingyao County Weiliansheng Small Loan Co., Ltd.) were approved to operate in business in Pingyao city of Shanxi province. In 2008, the three small loan companies saw their total capital rise to RMB112, 966,000, with an average annual growth rate of 63.9%.[14]

In May 2008, the CBRC approved the pilot scheme for establishing and developing small loan companies. In July, the Zhejiang Provincial Government pioneered in launching pilot small loan companies. As the Chinese government has legalized private finance, small loan companies galloped ahead. As of March 2009, there were a total of 583 small loan companies established in China.

As an important "last mile" financing channel for serving agriculture, rural areas, farmers and small and micro enterprises, small loan companies played an active role in promoting inclusive finance. However, small size, poor management and irregular operations were common problems prevalent in small loan companies. In March 2013, Jinhua Guangliheng Small Loan Company in Zhejiang province was dissolved due to poor risk prevention, becoming the first dissolved small loan company in Zhejiang province since the pilot scheme was launched in 2008.

As an economic downturn continued and P2P online lending emerged in 2018, small loan companies were confronted with a series of development bottlenecks, including a lack of premium customers, shrinking profits due to market-oriented interest rate, mounting bad debts, and intensified competition. As such, their pace of development has been slowed down.

As of the end of June 2019, there were a total of 7,797 small loan companies in China, with a combined outstanding loan balance of RMB924.1 billion, dropping by RMB30.4 billion in the first half of the year.[15]

Small loan companies are characterized by small size and scattered distribution. To achieve a stable development, they must provide specialized and differentiated premium services, operate according to the law, effectively prevent financial

[14] Ju Jinwen: Study on Non-State-owned Economies Entering Monopolistic Industries, Economy and Management Publishing House, 2009, p174.

[15] PBoC: Small Loan Company Statistics Report for the First Half of 2017, July 25, 2017; Microfinance Company Statistics Report for the First Half of 2019, July 25, 2019.

risks, concentrate on supporting agriculture and small businesses, and serve the real economy.

Pawnshops were once a kind of conventional financial institutions in China. As a special niche subsector of the financial sector, pawn brokerage is viewed as an auxiliary means of financing. The whole industry was phased out in 1949, and pawnshops re-emerged in China in December 1987 when Huamao Pawnshop in Chengdu opened for business.

In 1988, pawnshops emerged in Zhejiang province, Shenyang, Shanxi province, Guangdong province, Shanghai, Fujian province, Hainan province, Jilin province, and Guizhou province. In the 1990s, the pawn brokerage industry kept a rapid momentum going. In 1996, there were a total of 3,013 pawnshops operating in business across China.

During its rapid development, the pawn brokerage industry encountered numerous problems due to a lack of corresponding laws and regulations, and existing regulatory loopholes. For instance, there were numerous illegal financial institutions conducting the pawn brokerage business, and some pawnshops operated in business illegally or beyond their business scope; some pawnshops illegally raised funds and hiked interest rates to attract deposits; few pawnshops colluded with social evil forces to take or dispose of stolen goods, granted loans for exorbitant profits, and forced pawnor to redeem collateral, which have disrupted the normal economic and financial order, and created adverse social impacts.

From 1996 to 2001, the PBoC decided to overhaul the pawn brokerage industry. Specifically speaking, all the pawnshops were handed over to the State Economic and Trade Commission for unified administration, and illegal pawnshops were dissolved or banned. In November 2001, the number of pawnshops in China fell to 1,180 from 3,013 in 1996. In April 2018, all the pawnshops were brought under the administration of the CBIRC.

From 2005 onwards, legal pawnshops flourished. As of the end of 2013, there were 6,833 pawnshops operating in business across the whole country, with a registered capital of RMB121.7 billion in aggregate and an outstanding pawn brokerage balance of RMB86.6 billion. Under the pawn brokerage business structure, real estate accounted for 52% of the total, movable property 29%, and property rights 19%. Generally speaking, the pawn brokerage industry mainly served micro and small enterprises and individual businesses, playing a role of filling up gaps and opening up an ancillary financing channel in the financial system.

As of the end of February 2018, there were a total of 8,532 pawn brokerage enterprises and 950 branches in China, with a registered capital of RMB173.13 billion in aggregate. Specifially, movable property, real estate and property rights pawnshops accounted for 30.88%, 52.89% and 16.23% of the total respectively.[16]

---

[16] http://pawn.cbrc.gov.cn/pawn_monitor/_news/html/2018/3/20/1521533556464.html. National Pawn Brokerage Industry Regulation Information System: The Business Performance of National Pawn Brokerage Industry in January to February 2018, [EB/OL], March 19, 2018, the official website of the National Pawn brokerage Industry Regulation Information System:

2.4 Securities Financial Institutions: Constituting a Chinese-Style Investment Banking System

The capital market that emerged in the regime of the Republic of China from 1949 onwards was phased out during the economic recovery and overhaul campaigns in the early 1950s, and it was not until 1990 when a new capital market was re-incubated and developed. Securities companies, securities investment fund management companies and futures companies constituted an investment banking system with Chinese characteristics.

2.4.1 Securities Companies: Forming the Core of the Investment Banking System

Securities companies, also known as securities brokers, originated from the issuance of treasury bonds and the joint-stock system reform of state-owned enterprises in China in the early 1980s, forging a bond between listed companies and investors.

During the "stock fever" of the 1980s, a large number of securities companies were established with approval, including Shenzhen Special Economic Zone Securities Co., Ltd. (1987),[17] Shanghai Wanguo Securities Co., Ltd. (1988),[18] Shenyang Securities Co., Ltd., Wuhan Securities Co, Ltd. and Shanghai Shenyin Securities Co., Ltd.. At the end of 1988, there were a total of thirty-three securities companies established with approval in China.

From 1992 onwards, the securities industry ushered in a period of rapid development. A good number of securities companies were established, while many trust and investment companies also invested in the securities sector. Securities companies and securities business offices of trust and investment companies sprang up like mushrooms across China. For instance, Zhenhua Road in Shenzhen is hailed as "Securities Street" because it is crammed with securities companies. At the end of 1992, sixty-seven securities companies were established with approval nationwide. Besides, there were also 913 business offices and 5,384 operating agencies which concurrently operated in securities business.[19]

---

[17] In 2001, Shenzhen Special Economic Zone Securities Co., Ltd. developed into a comprehensive securities company. In 2002, it was rename Jutian Securities Co., Ltd… Due to its illegal operations, Jutian Securities Co., Ltd. was taken over by China Merchants Securities on October 13, 2006, making a gloomy exit from the market.

[18] On July 16, 1996, Shanghai Shenyin Securities Co., Ltd. and Shanghai Wanguo Securities Co., Ltd. merged to form Shanghai Shenyin and Wanguo Securities Co., Ltd.

[19] The Master Plan of the State Commission for Economic Restructuring for Deeping the Economic System Reform in 1988, the People's Bank of China and the CCCPC Party Literature Research Office (eds): *Selected Literature on Financial Work (1978-2005)*, China Financial Publishing House, 2007; p. 126.

In the midst of rapid development, various maladies occurred and lingered on securities companies, involving small size, numerous institutions, vicious competition, law and rule violations, and even shell securities companies. From 1993 to 1996, the regulatory authorities commenced to overhaul securities brokers in a centralized manner.

The regulatory authorities set forth the following provisions: Securities companies must specialize in securities investment rather than engaging in the business other than securities investment; securities companies that are engaging in trading in the primary market and the secondary market, as well as proprietary business and agency business of securities companies must be clearly defined and clarified; trust and investment companies established by banks must not engage in securities investment to ensure "separation of banks and securities companies" and securities brokers must operate separately from commercial banks; raise the market entry thresholds for securities companies, and tighten up the controls on securities broker qualifications.

After the overhaul campaign, all of commercial banks have exited the securities industry, while a small number of securities companies with a huge registered capital and high competitiveness have been newly set up, including United Securities, Orient Trust Securities and China International Capital Corporation Limited (CICC). The existing securities companies were progressively committed to enhancing regulated management and operation, which led to the formation of six types of securities companies.

First, securities companies with a legal entity status which were set up by banking syndicates and the government to specialize in the integrated securities business of investment banks and showed their strong competitiveness (e.g. Guotai Securities Company, Huaxia Securities and Everbright Securities). Second, large provincial securities companies backed by local governments and the financial authorities (e.g. Shenwan Securities, SEZ Securities, Beijing Securities, and Guangdong Securities), the bulk of which were distributed in economically developed regions, special economic zones, and medium-sized and large cities in the coastal regions. Third, large joint-stock securities brokers established and wholly-owned by local commercial banks (e.g. China Merchants Securities, GF Securities, and Fujian Industrial Securities). Fourth, securities companies or business divisions established and wholly-owned by insurance and trust investment companies (e.g. PICC Securities, CITIC Securities, Ping An Securities, and Shenzhen Guosen Securities). Fifth, joint-stock securities companies like Junan Securities, China Eagle Securities, Orient Securities and Great Wall Securities set up by using the industrial capital of other national financial institutions or large state-owned enterprises, which were mainly concentrated in the Shenzhen Special Economic Zone and the Shanghai Pudong New Area. Sixth, trust and investment companies, financial companies affiliated to enterprise group, and financial leasing companies that concurrently engaged in single or multiple securities business in the form of a non-legal entity business division or wholly-owned financial institution with a legal entity status.

As of the end of 1996, securities institutions included 2 national stock exchanges, 30 securities trading centers, 96 specialized securities companies, 6 accounting firms, approximately 100 asset appraisal agencies, 2 securities rating agencies, and

200 securities business outlets. Therefore, a securities-broker-centered Chinese-style investment banking system has taken shape.

Nevertheless, securities companies still had some maladies in urgent need of addressing. First, small size and insufficient capacity. In 1996, the market capitalization of ninety-six securities companies merely totaled RMB159, 053 million, with an average of only RMB1, 657 million per company. Nevertheless, there were merely ten securities companies with a market capitalization of approximate RMB 1 billion. Second, low-end business. The bulk of securities companies mainly engaged in the brokerage and proprietary business whereas they seldom conducted the investment banking business such as recapitalization of state-owned enterprises, and merger and acquisition and capital operation of enterprises. Third, a lack of effective solutions for financing. All in a word, securities companies were still far from being an investment bank in a real sense. Fourth, repeated violations committed by some securities brokers. For example, Shenzhen Junan Securities was closed down in 1997 due to violations involving management buyout (MBO) and transfer of huge capital to speculate in H-share, and it was taken over by Guotai Securities Company in 1998, restructuring into today's Guotai Junan Securities.

With a view to solving financing maladies facing securities companies, the CSRC and the PBoC granted the approval for qualified securities companies to invest in the interbank lending market on August 19, 1999, and seven securities companies including Guotong Securities Co. Ltd., Guosen Securities Co., Ltd., Xiangcai Securities Co., Ltd., China Eagle Securities Co., Ltd., *Everbright* Securities Company Limited, CITIC Securities Company Limited and GF Securities Co., Ltd. won the approval for establishment. In November 1999, several more securities companies were also allowed to invest in the interbank lending market and financed more than RMB3 billion.

In the second half of 2001, China's stock market dropped from 2,245.43 points to 1,339.20 points, plunging the capital market into a downturn and severely affecting the business performance of 118 securities in the country. From 2001 to 2002, the securities industry which suffered a loss and had zero capital was viewed as facing technical bankruptcy.

In 2002, the securities industry carried out structural reform. In addition to conventional investment banking and brokerage business, securities companies were also allowed to explore on the asset management business. As of June 2002, more than fifty securities companies applied for the license for conducting the asset management business. Meanwhile, securities companies were allowed to set up subsidiaries to operate in investment banking, securities brokerage, online securities brokerage, investment consulting, asset management and other types of business.

In July 2005, the CSRC launched a special overhaul, reorganization and system building campaign against problematic securities companies. In this campaign, eight securities companies such as Galaxy Securities, ShenYin and WanGuo Securities, Guotai Junan Securities, Huaxia Securities, and Beijing Securities were reorganized, while a third-party custody system for trading and clearing funds of customers was operated among reorganized securities companies at first. Meanwhile, problematic securities companies were promptly dealt with. The CSRC handled 7 high-risk securities companies in 2004 and 13 high-risk securities companies in 2005.

As of the end of 2006, there were a total of 130 qualified securities companies and more than 3,000 business offices engaging in different securities business following the overhaul campaign. It is noteworthy that they basically operated in a paperless manner throughout the process of issuing, trading and settling securities. However, the four traditional business of investment banking, brokerage, wealth management and proprietary business remained the main business of securities companies until 2011, while innovative business such as funds, financial advisory and mergers and acquisitions were newly launched on a limited scale. Meanwhile, the emerging international derivatives business such as options, futures and asset securitization have not yet taken root in China at all, and Chinese securities brokers were still far from being modern investment banks.

In 2014, the CSRC put forward 15 proposals concerning building modern investment banks, supporting business and product innovation, and shifting regulatory models, and this move played an important role in guiding the specialized and regulated operation of securities companies in the country. In 2018, the government rolled out multiple policies to support emerging enterprises in piloting in the issuance of stocks or depository receipts in the domestic market. In response, securities companies commenced to upgrade and transform their systems to embrace more business opportunities.

Securities companies went global in the 1980s. In 1992, the Shanghai Stock Exchange set up a B-share market for foreign investors.[20] As the first Sino-foreign joint venture, China International Capital Corporation Limited (CICC) was officially established with approval in August 1995. In 2001, securities companies expedited the process of going global and brought in foreign strategic investors. In 2002, the first Sino-foreign joint venture securities company was established. In 2006, the government launched a number of opening-up initiatives in 2006 to provide policy support for foreign strategic investors and help them enter the Chinese securities market.

After the 19th National Congress of the Communist Party of China was held, the Chinese government decided to significantly liberalize market access threshold for securities companies in the financial sector, allowing foreign investors to hold up to a 51% stake in joint ventures, without imposing shareholding ratio ceiling three years later. As of April 2019, there were thirteen foreign securities companies in China, including BOCI Securities Limited (2002), Goldman Sachs Gaohua Securities (2004), UBS Securities (2006), Morgan Stanley Huaxin Securities Company Limited (2010), and HSBC Qianhai Securities (2017).

Following the specialized, regulated and internationalized development, reform and overhaul campaign, there were a total of 131 securities companies with Chinese

[20] Prior to February 19, 2001, the B-share market was restricted to foreign investors. From February 19, 2001 onwards, the B-share market was opened to domestic investors and it is noteworthy that B-share investors were mainly institutional investors.

investment banks being mainstay at the end of 2019, including 35 listed securities companies.

2.4.2 Securities Investment Funds: Growing and Thriving According to the Law

Securities investment funds (hereinafter referred to as "Fund Companies") emerged in the 1980s, and have grown into major financial institutions in the securities industry. Tracing their development trajectory in the past 30 years, they have switched from spontaneous growth to regulated operation according to the law, with fund products and markets preceding fund management companies. With 1997 as a watershed year, two different types of funds, namely "old funds" and "new funds", were spawned at two different development stages in the fund industry.

"Old funds" refer to all the funds and business which were established and conducted prior to 1997. For example, the BOC and CITIC were the first to conduct the fund investment business in China in 1987, which symbolized the emergence of investment funds and the fund market in the country. In May 1989, Sun Hung Kai Capital Partners (SHKCP) launched the first China concept fund "Sun Hung Kai China Development Fund". Thereafter, investment funds flourished rapidly in the mainland securities market.

From 1990 to 1991, a number of funds were established in China, including closed-end China concept fund "Shanghai Fund" established by Amundi China in 1990, as well as the Sino-Foreign joint venture China Real Estate Fund, closed-end Zhuxin Fund, Wuhan Securities Investment Fund and Shenzhen Nanshan Venture Capital Fund, all of which were established in 1991.

As the first regulated closed-end corporate investment fund in China, Shandong Zibo Township Enterprise Investment Fund was established with approval in November 1992, and all the funds raised were used to support the development of township enterprises in Zibo city of Shandong province. In August 1993, Zibo Fund won the approval for getting listed on the Shanghai Stock Exchange, becoming the first fund to get listed in China. In addition, thirty-seven other funds were also established with approval in 1992, including China concept funds "Shenzhen Jingtai Fund" and "China Investment Development Fund".

In 1993, Shenzhen Blue Sky Fund, China Enterprise Development Fund and Central China Real Estate Fund were established. As of the end of 1993, there were a total of more than sixty investment funds established, with a total asset of more than RMB8 billion. Among them, fifty-six were domestic funds and more than 90% of them were initiated to be set up by finance institutions, with thirty-three getting listed on the Shanghai Stock Exchange.

Securities investment funds in China displayed a down-top development characteristics, with spontaneity playing a role behind the scenes. Many problems also surfaced in the course of their operation, including lax approval for funds and a lack of uniformity in entry thresholds across the country; irregularities such as irregular organizational structure, irregular operational management and irregular risk monitoring occurring from the outset in relation to some financing instruments launched for trading in the financial market in the name of funds; and funds functioning as a disguise means of raising capital at the early extensive developing stage.

In May 1993, the PBoC's head office commenced to overhaul the fund market. Specifically, it required all branches to cease the irregular issuance of funds and income bonds in a timely manner, to encourage the development of fund companies, to prohibit from approving the establishment of new funds, and to strictly regulate the operation of established funds, and the issuance of approved funds.

These efforts to overhaul securities investment funds have produced results. As of the end of 1994, a nationwide fund trading market took shape. It included 73 securities investment funds with a total asset of about RMB 8 billion, of which 51 were listed on either the Shanghai or Shenzhen Stock Exchange, or one of the regional securities trading centers.

"New funds" refer to funds which were established in accordance with the Interim Measures for the Administration of Securities Investment Funds issued by the CSRC in November 1997. These funds are contractual closed-end funds characterized by separate operation and they are regarded as specialized, regulated and true investment funds. The year 1998 saw the launch of the first batch of five new closed-end funds to the market, which were operated by five fund management companies respectively. Thereafter, investment fund companies and the fund market have progressively entered a law-based development stage.

The Securities Law (1999) provided for that only funds were allowed to operate in the investment fund business, while trust and investment companies and securities brokerage companies must progressively exit from the investment fund market and discontinue the securities investment business. By the end of 1999, 20-odd securities investment funds had been issued in China, all of which were established in the form of contractual closed-end funds.

In 2000, open-end securities investment funds became mainstream funds. In September 2001, the first open-end fund "Hua An Innovations Fund" was issued, marking a switch from closed-end to open-end funds. Closed-end funds ceased to be issued in China from August 2002 onwards.

In accordance with the relevant provisions of the Securities Investment Fund Law (2004), the fund industry entered a regulated and rapid development period. As of the end of 2004, there were a total of 161 funds, of which 54 were closed-end funds and 107 were open-end funds. Besides, 45 fund management companies were established, with a total asset of 243,667 million under management.

In 2005, the fund business entered a new phase of mixed operation. Most notably, commercial banks were allowed to set up fund companies and the ICBC, CCB and BOC became the first three pilot banks for setting up fund companies. In 2007, the regulators expanded the scope of pilot banks. As of the end of 2012, there were eight commercial bank-controlled fund management companies with total assets of nearly RMB500 billion. In a new era of asset management and wealth management, fund management companies stepped up their business model shift to become major financial institutions specializing in modern wealth management from 2013 onwards.

Private funds refer to investment funds that are not publicly offered to raise funds from a limited pool of investors. The Securities Investment Fund Law revised in December 2012 accorded the legal status of private funds. According to the Law, the establishment of private fund management companies and the issuance of private funds were not subject to administrative approval. The CSRC was responsible for regulating the business activities of private funds, while the AMAC took charge of their registration and self-regulation.

In 2014, the AMAC imposed a private fund registration and filing regulatory regime. All the private fund management companies registered with the AMAC were allowed to set up private securities investment funds as managers; private funds registered with the AMAC were allowed to open accounts at the CSDC and invest in stocks, bonds and other financial derivatives traded on exchanges. As of the end of 2014, there were 1,471 registered private equity fund managers in China. In 2015, the number soared, hitting 10,921 at the end of the year.

The imposition of relevant legislation and regulatory regime has put an end to the spontaneous growth of private equity funds and investment companies. By shifting to "sunshine private funds" governed by laws and regulations, private equity investment funds have become major institutional investors in the securities market. As of the end of 2018, private funds invested in 50,300 SME projects, and 24,700 high-tech enterprise projects. Among the first batch of the twenty-five enterprises listed on the SSE STAR Market, twenty-three listed enterprises were backed by private funds.[21] Due to a combination of aggravating factors such as a short development history, a lack of sound legal norms and lax regulation, there still existed maladies like illicit fundraising, illegal investment operations and irregular regulation in the private fund industry.

As of the end of 2018, there were 120 fund management companies, 24,448 private fund managers registered with the AMAC, and 74,642 registered funds with a total asset of RMB12.78 trillion in China.[22]

2.4.3 *Futures Trading Institutions: Indispensable Financial Organizations*

As a late comer, futures trading institutions emerged in the 1990s, and have developed into indispensable financial organizations in the securities market, mainly including futures exchanges, futures companies, and futures brokerage companies, among others.

---

[21] The Financial Stability Analysis Group of the PBoC: China Financial Stability Report 2018, China Financial Publishing House, 2019, pp. 69–70.

[22] The Financial Stability Analysis Group of the PBoC: China Financial Stability Report 2018, China Financial Publishing House, 2019, pp49-50.

On October 12, 1990, the Zhengzhou Grain Wholesale Market which took the initiative to operate the futures trading mechanism in China was officially opened for business operations. From 1992 to 1995, Shenzhen Nonferrous Metals Exchange, Shanghai Metals Exchange,[23] Zhengzhou Commodity Exchange, Dalian Commodity Exchange and Shanghai Futures Exchange were established and opened for trading. As such, China's futures market has taken shape from scratch.

From 1991 to 1992, a number of futures brokerage companies such as Jinpeng International Futures Brokerage Co., Ltd. and China International Futures Company Limited were established with approval and opened for business operations. As of the end of 1992, there were a total of nearly 300 futures brokerage companies established across China, including more than fifty Sino-foreign joint venture futures brokerage companies.

During its initial blind development stage from 1993 to 1999, the futures market was riddled with many maladies, including an overabundance of futures exchanges and brokers operating in an irregular manner, whose offshore futures trading operations were mostly speculative in nature, and some of which even more have caused serious losses to the country; violations such as employing various unscrupulous tactics to defraud domestic clients by some Sino-foreign joint venture or pseudo-joint venture futures brokers, incurring massive foreign exchange losses; rampant illegal underground futures trading; and disruptive market order with manipulative operations occurring from time to time.

From 1993 to 1999, government regulators launched a lengthy overhaul and regulation campaign against the futures trading market and futures companies.

First, a legal status of futures brokerage companies was clarified. On April 28, 1993, the State Administration for Industry and Commerce issued the first administrative measures for regulating the futures market to clarify the status of futures brokerage companies and set forth their codes of organization and conducts. Measures were also taken to curb the blind development tendency of the futures market.

Second, a correlation and coordination mechanism involving multiple regulatory authorities was established. In December 1993, the CSRC set up the Department of Futures Supervision to tighten up targeted regulation. Meanwhile, the CSC, the Ministry of Domestic Trade, the State Administration for Industry and Commerce and the PBoC all constituted part of the futures market regulatory regime.

Third, exchanges, trading business and trading institutions were all overhauled and closed down. As of the end of 1993, more than fifty existing exchanges were overhauled and closed down, while only fifteen pilot exchanges such as Shanghai Commodity Exchange were retained. All the exchanges were required to reform their membership systems and amend their articles of association and trading rules and regulations. In April 1994, the CSC banned the futures trading of

[23] In 1999, Shanghai Metal Futures Exchange, Shanghai Grain and Oil Commodity Exchange and Shanghai Commodity Exchange merged to form Shanghai Futures Exchange. At of the end of 2019, it had 198 members, of which futures company members accounted for nearly 75percent of the total.

steel, sugar and coal. From September 1994 to February 1995, the futures trading of japonica rice, rapeseed and soybean oil was suspended, and futures trading activities in the name of conducting medium- and long-term forward sugar contract trading were banned.

In October 1994, a futures companies licensing regulatory regime was imposed. In 1995, there were 330 futures brokers subjected to re-examined and re-approval, all types of futures brokers were subjected to stringent approval, joint venture futures brokers were closed down, illegal foreign exchange futures trading was cracked down on, and illegal futures brokage activities were investigated and dealt with. In November 1995, the relevant authorities commenced to re-examine the license for engaging in futures brokerage business by non-futures brokerage companies. As of the end of 1995, there were 326 futures brokers that had registered and applied to the CSRC for approval.

Fourth, excessive speculative operations were rigorously regulated in the futures market. In February 1996, the CSRC stipulated that state-owned enterprises were not allowed to engage in the speculative trading in futures, that all types of financial institutions were not allowed to engage in the proprietary and agency business in commodity futures, and that all of futures brokers were not allowed to engage in the proprietary business. Additionally, state-owned enterprises and state-holding institutions or public institutions and enterprises were only allowed to engage in hedging transactions in commodity futures associated with their manufacturing and operations rather than conducting speculative transactions, let alone vicious publicity stunt. No financial institution was allowed to engage in the proprietary or agency business of commodity futures and a market debarment regime has been therefore established.

Through the implementation of an annual inspection system, the CSRC overhauled and closed down futures brokerage companies. In 1996, thirty-three brokerage companies were inspected and closed down, followed by nineteen brokerage companies in 1997. In 1998, sixty-five brokerage companies failed to pass annual inspection. The CSRC raised the market access threshold for futures brokerage companies in 1999, requiring a minimum registered capital of not less than RMB30 million.

Fifth, the futures market was further overhauled and regulated. In August 1998, government regulators retained only three futures exchanges, namely Shanghai, Zhengzhou and Dalian futures exchanges, and placed them under the direct administration and regulation of the CSRC. The number of commodities for futures trading was reduced from 35 to 12. Meanwhile, they also closed down financial institutions that concurrently operated in the futures business and disqualified all the non-futures broker members from futures brokage trading. No futures broker was allowed to engage in the proprietary business, and stringent control was imposed on offshore futures trading.

Sixth, law-based regulatory rules and regulations were laid down for the futures market. In addition to documents and regulations governing futures brokerage contracts and futures transactions, the CSRC also successively issued the

Measures for the Administration of Futures Exchanges, the Measures for the Administration of Futures Brokers, and the Measures for the Administration of Qualifications of Futures Practitioners and Senior Managers of Futures Brokers from May to December 1999. With the implementation of these measures and regulations, the futures market has basically entered a regulated development period, while the large-scale overhaul of the futures market has also been temporally suspended.

Following years of close-down and overhaul, the futures market has been on the wane and progressively plunged into a low ebb. In other words, some futures brokerage companies have been meted out penalties for illegal business operations, and poorly managed futures brokers have been shut down, merged or reorganized into other types of businesses. As of the end of 2000, there were only 185 remaining futures brokerage companies in China. It was not until the end of 2003 when the number rose to 190, and there were about 6,270 futures practitioners registered with the China Futures Association.

In 2006, the futures market effected a turnaround. In March and April 2006, two batches of domestic futures companies were allowed to set up branches in Hong Kong. On September 8, 2006, China Financial Futures Exchange (CFFE) was officially inaugurated in Shanghai. As a corporate exchange specialized in the trading and settlement of financial futures, options and other financial derivatives, the CFFE had great significance for improving the trading systems of the securities market.

In May 2012, the government introduced relevant policies to encourage and guide private investors to hold a stake in futures companies by way of capital increase, merger and reorganization, or other means, and to support qualified private holding futures companies in joining the innovative futures business pilot scheme.

On November 6, 2013, the Shanghai International Energy Exchange Co., Ltd. (INE) was approved for registration and inauguration in the Shanghai Free Trade Zone (FTZ), which is an international trading venue initiated to be set up by the Shanghai Futures Exchange and opened to futures market participants for business operations.

As of the end of 2018, there were a total of 149 futures companies in China, which set up 79 risk management subsidiaries and 10 asset management subsidiaries, and held assets totaling around RMB540 billion. Additionally, there were 61 futures and option products traded in the market, including 51 commodity futures products, 6 financial futures products, 3 commodity options products, and 1 financial options products. The futures industry expedited the process of going global, bringing in foreign traders to deal in iron ore futures and PTA futures in May and November 2018 respectively.[24]

[24] The Financial Stability Analysis Group of the PBoC: China Financial Stability Report 2019, China Financial Publishing House, 2019, p. 50.

2.5 Insurance Institutions: Commercial Financial InstitutionsWere Committed to Ensuring Security

As a financial institution continuing in business in China in the past seventy years, insurance institutions were not only major participants in the financial market, but also constituted an important part of China's social security system.

2.5.1 Government-Mandated Compulsory Insurance in the Early Period

From 1949 to 1952, China's insurance industry was in embryo. As the first national insurance company and a state-owned financial enterprise in China, the People's Insurance Company of China (PICC) was officially established in Beijing on October 20, 1949, with a registered capital of 60 billion denominated in old RMB.[25] In June 1950, the PICC set up 5 major regional subsidiaries and 31 branches, with 2,263 employees across the country. In 1950, the PICC suspended domestic reinsurance business, yet still carried on the reinsurance business in its overseas insurance operations in the London insurance market. Additionally, it also entered into reinsurance contracts with insurance companies in the Soviet Union, Poland, Czechoslovakia, Bulgaria and Hungary.

In February 1951, the Chinese government mandated compulsory insurance for state organs, state enterprises, cooperatives' property, travelers and property and it stipulated that the PICC must provide compulsory insurance against property, shipment, railway transportation, motor vehicle, accidental injury of passengers in air, rail, road and sea transit. Therefore, the bulk of enterprises and state organs have purchased insurance. Besides, the PICC also offered livestock insurance, crop insurance, and import and export cargo insurance as well.

In the early 1950s, the compulsory insurance policy introduced by the Chinese government provided major economic security for the newly liberated Chinese society.

2.5.2 Discontinuation of Insurance Provision and Social Security Provided by Insurance

From 1953 to 1978, a combination factors such as overall political situations, political movements and common misconceptions in those days militated against the development of the insurance industry. Some people even argued that as long as socialist

[25] From 1949 to 1984, the People's Insurance Company of China (PICC) was affiliated to the PBoC internally, but was known as the PICC externally.

reform had completed and a socialist public ownership economy had been built in China, all the expenditure in the people's birth, illness and death, as well as property losses should all be financed by state revenues, and thus social security provided by insurance was no longer needed at all. Misled by such common misconceptions that there was no need to arrange for and take out insurance, the Chinese government has discontinued insurance provision and social security provided by insurance.

Amidst this background, the PICC comprehensively suspended its compulsory insurance business in the sectors of iron, grain, geology, posts and telecommunications, water conservancy, and transportation. Additionally, it discontinued all the domestic insurance business and disbanded the related staff. From April 1964 onwards, the PICC successively suspended ocean vessel insurance, motor vehicle third party liability insurance, and insurance against strike-incurred import and export losses. Meanwhile, the number of countries maintaining a reinsurance relationship with the PICC fell from 32 to 17.

In the 1960s and 1970s, the people had no guarantee for their social security and life and property security provided by insurance due to the crippling or even disbanding of the insurance industry,

2.5.3 Restoration and Establishment of the Economic Compensation System

It was not until February 1979 that the domestic insurance business of the PICC was resumed, and its domestic insurance business, which had been suspended for more than 20 years, was fully resumed in 1980, including enterprise property insurance, family property insurance and automobile insurance, and covering nearly 100,000 enterprises, more than 900,000 households and 130,000 automobiles, with a total value of RMB 200 billion. Of these, state-owned enterprise property was valued at RMB193.5 billion, accounting for approximately 23% of the fixed assets and working capital of the above enterprises.

As of October 1981, there were a total of 477 specialized insurance institutions and 803 banking agency outlets established in large and medium-sized cities and a few counties of 28 provinces, cities and autonomous regions (excluding Xizang), with more than 5,700 insurance specialists employed. The payouts topped RMB148 million in aggregate, accounting for 46.8% of gross insurance premium revenue.

As a state-owned specialized insurance company, the PICC further expanded its business scope to include property insurance, life insurance, liability insurance, credit insurance and agricultural insurance, as well as reinsurance, etc. in December 1982. In 1983, it became a bureau directly under the State Council, and it was officially separated from the PBoC on January 1, 1984 yet still operated under the leadership, administration, coordination, supervision and audit of the PBoC at that time. In July 1987, the PICC established a branch in the Xizang Autonomous Region. Henceforth, it has set up branches in all provinces and regions in China.

Through business restoration and institutional restructuring, the PICC rapidly expanded its business operations. As of the end of 1993, the PICC had over 4,000 branches, over 100,000 employees and over 200,000 agents in China. Additionally, it set up over 60 overseas branches across the country, with over 800 recruited employees. As such, PICC has established an overseas insurance network with Hong Kong and Macao as the mainstay, alongside Britain, Singapore, the United States, Germany, Canada and Central America as key business regions.

During the period of recovery and development in the 1980s, the insurance industry played a proactive role. Specifically, it not only served as a channel for pooling domestic construction funds, but also helped to establish China's economic compensation system, effectively providing a security network for ensuring the normal production and operation of enterprises, protecting people's livelihood, and reducing social wealth losses.

2.5.4 Reform of Institutional Mechanism and Commercialized Operation

Insurance institutions refer to financial institutions which provide social security and concurrently engage in commercialized operations. As a kind of commercial enterprises, insurance companies must operate in business. Prior to 1995, China's insurance industry operated a mixed operation system in which property insurance and life insurance were concurrently conducted. Nevertheless, the system of this sort was not conducive to control of insurance risks. Meanwhile, it also stunted the balanced development of insurance products. With the implementation of financial system reform in 1995, it was imperative for the insurance industry to comprehensively carry out reform in its operating regime in six aspects as well.

First, separating administrative functions from enterprises, and carrying out separate operations. It was imperative to separate social insurance from commercial insurance, separate life insurance from non-life insurance, and separately account for policy insurance and commercial insurance. Insurance companies must operate as genuine insurance enterprises and realize equal and orderly competition. Second, building a multi-tier insurance institution system (e.g. national, regional and specialized insurance companies). Third, establishing reinsurance companies. Fourth, progressively developing rural insurance in various forms. Fifth, duly increasing the scope and autonomy of insurance enterprises in the use of funds, and appropriately raising the insurance reserve requirement ratio. Sixth, establishing insurance associations, and tightening self-regulation.

According to China's Insurance Law (1995), the business philosophy of separating operations in property insurance and life insurance was set forth. In July 1996, the PICC took the initiative to carry out reform in its business model system. After it renamed the People's Insurance Company (Group) of China Limited, it carried out separate operation. Meanwhile, the PICC set up the PICC Property and Causality

Co., Ltd., the PICC Life Insurance Co., Ltd., and the PICC Reinsurance Co., Ltd., while its overseas branches were still under the administration of the head office.

Other domestic insurance companies successively initiated separate operation reform. In 2002, the former Xinjiang Construction Corps Insurance Company, Ping An Insurance Company and China Pacific Insurance Company Limited all completed their reform for separating property insurance from life insurance.

In the meantime, insurance institutions were reformed and restructured to specialize in their operations, starting with the separation of property insurance from life insurance. Subsequently, endowment insurance, health insurance and agricultural insurance were also separately operated by newly established specialized insurance companies as well.

In 2004, specialized endowment insurance companies such as Ping An Endowment Insurance Co., Ltd., China Pacific Insurance Aging Industry Investment Management Co., Ltd., China Life Pension Company Limited, Changjiang Pension Insurance Co., Ltd., and Taikang Pension and Insurance Co., Ltd. were successively established with approval in tandem with specialized agricultural insurance companies including China Pacific Anxin Agriculture Insurance Co., Ltd., Anhua Agricultural Insurance Co.,Ltd., and Sunlight Agricultural Mutual Insurance Company. In 2008, there were four specialized health insurance companies engaging in business operations in China's personal insurance market, namely PICC Health Insurance Company Limited., the Ping An Health Insurance Company of China, Ltd., Reward Health Insurance Company Ltd. and Kunlun Health Insurance Co., Ltd.

Through the above separate operation reform, the insurance industry has progressively established a diversified institutional system, and it has constantly expanded business scope. In 2005, insurance companies researched and developed more than 200 liability insurance products, which played an active role in maintaining social stability. Additionally, insurance companies were allowed to set up securities investment fund companies. As of the end of November 2005, RMB106 billion of insurance funds were indirectly injected in the securities market, and RMB13.57 billion of insurance funds were directly invested in the securities market. As of the end of 2005, insurance companies became the second largest institutional investor in the bond market, with their direct investment in stocks hitting RMB15, 888 million. Additionally, some insurance companies also piloted in integrated cross-business operations by setting up subsidiaries, and banking and insurance industries also promoted their cooperation by switching a loose business alliance to a capital alliance.[26] In March 2008, insurance companies saw assets under management hit RMB12.25 billion.

In addition to their business management system reform, insurance institutions have also reshaped their institutional framework. In February 2002, the joint-stock system reform entered a substantive implementation stage in the insurance industry. In November 2003, the PICC became the first domestic financial enterprise to go public abroad, taking the lead in completing its joint-stock system reform. In

[26] Financial Stability Analysis Group of the PBoC: China Financial Stability Report 2006, China Financial Publishing House, 2007, p. 5.

December 2003, the China Life Insurance Company set a new financing record for its first IPO in the international capital market that year.

In June, 2004, Ping An Insurance (Group) Company of China, Ltd. became the first Chinese financial company to go public overseas in the form of a group corporation. Following the establishment of China United Insurance Group Company Limited in 2006, wholly state-owned insurance companies have completely exited from the market, marking the full completion of joint-stock system reform of all state-owned insurance companies. As of 2007, there were a total of six Chinese insurance companies going public at home or abroad.

Although the reform of the separate operation in the insurance industry achieved the desired effect prior to 2003, it ran counter to the development trends of the expanded opening up to the outside world in China's financial industry and financial globalization. To that end, insurance companies must switch from separate operation system to integrated operation by establishing financial holding companies. In 2004, Ping An Bank was established with Ping An Insurance (Group) Company of China, Ltd. as its controlling shareholder, which signified that Ping An Insurance (Group) Company of China, Ltd. had become a company group integrating diversified financial services.

From the twenty-first century onwards, the commercialized insurance industry was booming. As of 2005, there were a total of 93 legal entity institutions in the insurance industry, including 6 insurance groups and holding companies, 35 property insurance companies, 42 personal insurance companies, 5 reinsurance companies, and 5 insurance asset management companies. As a whole, the insurance industry reaped a premium revenue of RMB493, 128 million, with assets totaling RMB1, 529,869 million.

2.5.5 Bringing in Private Capital and Changing Shareholder Structure

The insurance industry is among the first batch of the financial industries which lifted the restrictions on private capital injection in China. In 2002, the private insurance industry emerged and private capital was injected into some newly established non-state-owned insurance companies or state holding companies through acquiring shareholdings. In 2002, Beijing Yuanxinhang Investment Consulting Company and Beijing Baohua Investment Company which were both controlled by natural person, acquired all the shares transferred by China Merchants Group, the former second largest shareholder of Ping An Insurance (Group) Company of China, Ltd.. In this way, they were among Top10 ten shareholders of Ping An Insurance (Group) Company of China, Ltd. and reorganized Ping An Insurance (Group) Company of China, Ltd. into an insurance company with a huge injection of private capital. After completing its reorganization from a state-owned holding company to a private holding company, SINOSAFE Insurance became China's first private property insurance company on May 27, 2003.

On June 28, 2003, Minsheng Life Insurance Co., Ltd. was established with approval, kicking off the official entry of private capital into China's insurance industry. This insurance company had over 80% of its capital coming from 10-odd private enterprises, including Wanxiang Group Corporation, East Hope Group, and New Hope Group Co., Ltd..

From 2004 to 2005, many private investors invested in the insurance industry and there was a sharp increase in the number of insurance companies with a large injection of private capital. In July 2004, eighteen Chinese insurance companies were newly approved for establishment, eleven of which opened for business operations in 2005. Among them, massive private capital was injected to the above insurance companies, including eight life insurance companies such as PICC Life Insurance Co., Ltd., Union Life Insurance Co., Ltd., Great Wall Life Insurance Co, Ltd. and Jiahe Life Insurance Co., Ltd.; seven property and casualty insurance companies such as Sunshine Property and Casualty Insurance Company Limited, Dubon Property and Casualty Insurance Co., Ltd., Bohai Property Insurance Company, Bank of China Insurance Company Limited and Sunlight Agricultural Mutual Insurance Company, as well as three health insurance companies including PICC Health Insurance Company Limited and Ping An Health Insurance Company of China, Ltd.. Most notably, Unionlife Insurance Co., Ltd. and Jiahe Life Insurance Co., Ltd. were both private insurance companies.

From 2005 onwards, the government progressively relaxed the policy restrictions on private capital's entry into the insurance industry. Therefore, private investors saw their shares of the insurance industry exceed 40%, which was far higher than that of other financial sectors. All the insurance companies which were established with approval from 2011 to 2012 all received a huge injection of private capital, including Li'an Life Insurance Company Limited, Foresea Life Insurance Co, Ltd., Urtrust Insurance Co., Ltd., and JinTai Property and Casualty Insurance Co., Ltd.

With a view to implementing the "New 36-point Policy for Non-Public Economies" issued by the State Council, the Chinese government intensified efforts to support the development of private insurance institutions by encouraging the injection of private capital into the insurance sector, and opening up a wider green channel[27]for private investors to invest in the insurance market in June 2012. As such, the shareholder structure of the insurance industry has been further reformed.

[27] Xiao Yang: Abolishing the 20percent Ceiling: Implementing Rules on How to Guide Private Capital to Grow in Maturity, July 4, 2012, p. 11.

2.5.6 Giving Priority for Risk Prevention and Control and Leveraging of the Insurance Security Functions

Following the Third Plenary Session of the 18th CPC Central Committee held in 2013, the insurance industry has received two major policy dividends. In August 2014, the State Council called for accelerating the development of the modern insurance service industry and this created historical opportunities for the insurance industry. Meanwhile, top-level decisions and designs were in place to promote the development of commercial health insurance, and the insurance industry was incorporated into China's overall strategic blueprint for economic and social development. According to the 13th Five-Year Plan for the Insurance Industry, the insurance industry shifted its focus to endowment insurance and health insurance, stressing that insurance must provide a basic means for the government, enterprises, and residents to carry out risk and wealth management.

On May 12, 2016, an earthquake catastrophe insurance system for protecting urban and rural dwellers was officially launched in the insurance industry. On June 12, 2016, the Shanghai Insurance Exchange was established to provide a business platform for bidding, tendering and special risk diversification for international reinsurance, international cargo insurance and bulk insurance projects. On June 26, 2016, the catastrophe insurance platform system with insurance and settlement functions was officially launched, aiming to provide earthquake catastrophe community with one-stop integrated services covering underwriting, claims, trading and settlement.

As of the end of 2018, the insurance industry held assets totaling RMB18.33 trillion, including RMB2.35 trillion for property insurance companies, RMB14.61 trillion for personal insurance companies, RMB364, 979 million for reinsurance companies, and RMB55, 734 million for asset management companies. Besides, the outstanding insurance fund balance stood at RMB16.41 trillion, while insurance density and insurance penetration were RMB2, 724 and 4.22% respectively. As compared to the global average insurance density and penetration over the same period, China still had a big gap to narrow.[28]

As of June 2019, there were 236 insurance institutions in China, including 12 insurance group companies, 87 property insurance companies, 82 life insurance companies, 25 insurance asset management companies, 11 reinsurance companies, 8 endowment insurance companies, 7 health insurance companies, 1 import and export insurance company, and 3 other financial institutions.[29] In addition, there were also 2,652 insurance intermediaries, insurance Surveyor and Adjusters companies, specialized insurance agencies, and insurance brokerage companies in the country.

---

[28] The Financial Stability Analysis Group of the PBoC: China Financial Stability Report 2019, China Financial Publishing House, 2019, p. 42.

[29] http://www.cbirc.gov.cn/cn/view/pages/ItemDetail.html?docId=875933&itemId=924&generaltype=1.

China Banking and Insurance Regulatory Commission (CBIRC): List of Legal Persons of Insurance Institutions (as of the end of June 2019), [EB/OL], CBIRC official website, October 10, 2019, accessed on February 17, 2020.

With its functions of economic compensation, risk assurance, capital financing and social management, the insurance industry provided a basic means for risk management of a market-oriented economy, and constituted an important part of the financial system and social security system. In the past seven decades, the insurance industry played an important role in promoting the coordinated development of the money, capital and insurance markets, establishing and improving a financial market system, optimizing the socialist market economy system, innovating social governance, public services and social security models, and exercising government administration in a more effective manner. In short, it is a microcosm of the development and reform trajectory of China's financial sector.

Chapter 3
Structure and Evolution of China's Financial Market System

In the past 70 years, China's financial market evolved through distinct development stages and spawned diverse structured financial transaction networks, thereby building a complex and integrated financial market system that played a unique role in successfully promoting the development of a socialist market economy with Chinese characteristics, and effectively allocating resources.

3.1 Four Development Stages of the Financial Market

From 1949 onwards, China's financial market has evolved through four stages: suspension and resumption (1949–1991), trial operation and expansion (1992–2001), opening up and integration (2002–2012), and regulation and innovation (2013–2019).

3.1.1 Suspension and Resumption of the Securities Market

Prior to 1949, Stock exchanges were established in cities such as Shanghai, Tianjin, Beijing, Wuhan and Qingdao. Nevertheless, they were bearing a brunt of closure one after another, and the securities market was phased out during the socialist transformation process in the early 1950s.

It was not until 1981, when the Chinese government resumed the issuance of treasury bonds, that a market for trading treasury bonds resurrected, with treasury bond issuance and underwriting as core business. Additionally, there were also a combination of factors such as issuance and trading of stocks, and pilot joint-stock system reform of state-owned enterprises that all had contributed to the recovery and development of the financial market.

Y. Wu, *A Financial History of China (1949–2019)*, Research Series on the Chinese Dream and China's Development Path,
https://doi.org/10.1007/978-981-99-6571-7_3

On July 8, 1983, *Shenzhen* Bao'an County United Investment Co., Ltd. issued shares to the public as the first "experimental shares" issued in the name of the county government after the founding of the People's Republic of China, thereby giving birth to China Bao'an Group Co., Ltd. (Shen Bao'an), the first joint-stock enterprise in China's mainland following the reform and opening up, and bringing about the reform of the shareholding system of state-owned enterprises. In August 1984, Beijing Tian Qiao Department Store Co., Ltd.[1] was established, the earliest joint-stock commercial enterprises in China. Through individual and collective subscription, Shanghai Feilo Electric-audio Equipment Co., Ltd. issued 10,000 shares at RMB 50 per share at its inauguration ceremony held on November 18, 1984, making it the first real share in China following the reform and opening up.

Meanwhile, the issuance of government bonds and shares has also spawned a market for trading securities. On August 5, 1986, Shenyang Trust and Investment Company commenced to conduct the over-the-counter (OTC) transfer business for negotiable securities for the first time. On September 26, 1986, the first securities OTC trading outlet was set up in Shanghai for the purposes of best efforts commitment and underwriting of the stocks of Shanghai Yanzhong Industrial Co., Ltd. and Shanghai Feilo Electric-audio Equipment Co., Ltd., thus officially initiating trading in the securities market. On November 26, 1986, Wanguo Securities Co., Ltd. was approved for establishment as the first securities company in Shanghai, so did Shenzhen Special Economic Zone Securities Company in Shenzhen in September 1987. By using November 2, 1987 as base period, Industrial and Commercial Bank of China Trust & Investment Co., Ltd. (Shanghai) compiled Shanghai Jing'an Stock Price Index as the first stock market index in China on November 2, 1987.

Jointly founded by nine national non-banking institutions in China on March 15, 1989, the Stock Exchange Executive Council (SEEC) got involved in the blueprint design of the Shanghai and Shenzhen Stock Exchanges, and it directly engaged in the design, creation and management of the Securities Trading Automated Quotations System (STAQ), among others.

On September 28, 1990, the first STAQ system was approved for establishment. Following its inauguration on November 26, 1990, the Shanghai Stock Exchange was officially opened for business on December 19, 1990. It was reported that the first batch of eight companies listed on the Shanghai Stock Exchange included Shanghai Feilo Electric-audio Equipment Co., Ltd., Shanghai Yanzhong Industrial Co., Ltd., Shanghai Ace Co., Ltd., Beijing Vacuum Electronic Technology Co., Ltd., Shanghai Shenhua Holdings Co, Ltd. Shanghai Feilo Acoustics Co.,Ltd, Yuyuan Inc., and Zhejiang Province Phoenix Chemical Co, Ltd., which were also known as "Eight Old Stocks". The Shanghai Stock Exchange is reputed to be the first stock exchange opened for business in China since 1949.

On November 26, 1990, the China Securities Depository and Clearing Corporation Limited Shenzhen Branch was put into trial operation as the first securities depository and clearing financial institution in China. On December 1, 1990, the

[1] The company initiated its joint-stock system reform in 1983. On May 24, 1993, it was among the first batch companies from Beijing to get listed on the Shanghai Stock Exchange.

Shenzhen Stock Exchange was officially opened for business as well. Nevertheless, only three companies, namely Shenzhen Development Bank, China Vanke Co., Ltd., and Gintian Industry (Group) Co., Ltd., which were also known as "Three Old Stocks", were traded on the Shenzhen Stock Exchange at the time. On December 5, 1990, the STAQ system was officially put in operation.

The Shanghai and Shenzhen stock exchanges, also known as China's main board A-share markets, primarily provide services for leading state-owned blue-chip companies. As such, a money market serving for different entities has also progressively taken shape. By the end of 1991, China's financial market had been preliminarily restored to a certain scale.

3.1.2 Trial Running of the Capital Market and Institutional Building

After Xiaoping Deng made his keynote speeches during his South China tour in the spring of 1992, a "securities fever" and a "stock fever" swept all over the country, thrusting China's securities market into a period of "trial operation" and institutional building.

First, enterprises were allowed to go public and issue shares both at home and abroad. In addition to the A-share common stock market which was established and opened to domestic investors in 1990, Shanghai Vacuum Electronic Devices Co., Ltd. issued special RMB-denominated shares (B share) on November 29, 1991. In 1992, the Shanghai Stock Exchange established a B-share trading market[2] for the subscriptions and trading in foreign currencies of RMB-denominated stocks issued on domestic stock exchanges.

In retrospect, there were 60-odd overseas securities companies that directly dealt in B-shares on the Shanghai Stock Exchange, and 20-odd foreign securities companies including Merrill Lynch, Nomura and Jardine Fleming all had their special seats on the Shanghai Stock Exchange. Most notably, Shanghai-listed companies riveted the attention of world renowned multinationals, and these multinational giants such as Ford, Mitsubishi, Sony, DuPont, and Siemens all invested in the companies listed on the Shanghai Stock Exchange. As of the end of 1992, there were a total of 18 B stocks listed in China.

On July 15, 1993, Qingdao Brewery was listed on the Hong Kong Exchanges and Clearing Limited, issuing shares denominated in Hong Kong dollars and getting listed

[2] Prior to February 19, 2001, the B-share market was only restricted to natural persons, legal entities and other investors from foreign countries, or natural persons, legal entities and other investors from China}s Hong Kong, Macao and Taiwan, or Chinese citizens permanently residing abroad, or other investors as specified by the CSRC. As of February 19, 2001, the B-share market was opened to domestic investors, yet mainly institutional investors.

in Hong Kong as a domestic Chinese enterprise (H shares). Subsequently, five state-owned enterprises got listed in Hong Kong as well, involving Sinopec Shanghai Petrochemical Company Limited (SPC), Beiren Printing Machinery Holding Limited., Maanshan Iron & Steel Company Ltd., Guangzhou Shipyard International Company Limited, and Shenji Group Kunming Machine Tool Company Limited. In 1994, Yangzhou Chemical Industry Parkin Yizheng city of Jiangsu province, Dongfang Electric Corporation, and Tianjin Bohai Chemical Industry Group Co., Ltd. also made their IPOs in Hong Kong. Altogether, there were nine state-owned heavy industry enterprises went public in the H-share market in 1994.

In 1994, Chinese companies issued US dollar-denominated shares (called N shares) for trading on the New York Exchange.

Huaneng Shandong Power Co., Ltd. and Huaneng Power International Inc. issued N-share for trading on the New York Stock Exchange (NYSE) for the first time in the form of direct listing by a state-owned joint-stock company. In contrast, some SOEs employed a roundabout tactic to issue securities on the NYSE. For instance, Brilliance Auto Group Co., Ltd.,Luoyang Northern EK Chor Motorcycle Co., Ltd and China Tire Enterprise Co., Ltd. were registered with Bermuda preceding their issuing shares in the United States in late 1992 and early 1993. Additionally, other state-owned enterprises issued American depository receipt (ADR) in the United States in 1995, including Sinopec Shanghai Petrochemical Company Limited (SPC), Sinopec Yizheng Chemical Fibre Limited Liability Company, Maanshan Iron & Steel Company Ltd., *Shanghai* Haixing Shipping Company. Ltd. and Harbin Power Equipment Company Limited. In particular, some companies that have issued depositary receipts on an A-share basis included *Shanghai* Tyre & Rubber Co., Ltd., Shanghai Erfangji Co., Ltd., Shanghai Chlor-Alkali Chemical Co., Ltd. and Shenzhen Special Economic Zone Real Estate & Properties (Group) Co., Ltd.

COSCO Corporation was the first Chinese company (S share) to go public on the Singapore Exchange (SGX) in 1994 and the Port of SHEKOU attempted the secondary listing of its B shares in Singapore (S share) in 1995. S shares refer to the shares of Chinese enterprises that are denominated in Singapore dollars and are issued for trade on the SGX. A number of companies have become listed S-share companies through a joint-stock reform for IPO, and through "reverse takeover" by acquiring stakes in Singapore companies. In 1999, Guangdong Foshan Eagle Brand Group was the first Chinese township enterprise that got S-share listed in Singapore. As of the end of 2001, there were a total of twenty-one Chinese companies that got S-share listed in Singapore, the bulk of which were high-tech private enterprises.

H shares, N shares, and S shares all provided important channels for Chinese enterprises to go public overseas. In 1996, twenty-six enterprises from China were listed abroad, three of which were listed in Hong Kong and New York, twenty-one in Hong Kong, and two in New York.[3] From April 6 to April 7, 2000, China Unicom successfully went public both in Hong Kong (H share) and New York (N share).

[3] Wu Xiaoling (ed): *A Chronicle of Major Events in China's Financial Reform and Opening up*, China Financial Publishing House, 2008, p. 389.

Second, the securities market was opened up and developed. In February 1992, Shanghai Shenyin Securities Company entered into an agreement with Shanghai United Textile Industry Co., Ltd. to float the first Sino-foreign joint venture stock in China. In May,1992, the Shanghai and Shenzhen stock exchanges successively relaxed stock price control, allowing on-exchange transactions. In October 1993, the Shanghai Stock Exchange conducted bond futures transactions for the public. In 1993 and 1995, China Textile Machinery Co., Ltd. and CSG Holding Co., Ltd. respectively issued convertible enterprise bonds in the Swiss securities market.

In 1997, the Chinese government pursued a newly listing policy of "imposing the control over the total number of newly issued shares and limiting the number of listed companies", prioritizing the support for infrastructure and high-tech industries. Though rein in development pace, the securities market progressively tended to be stabilized. As of the end of 1998, China had 800 listed companies, 30 of which were listed in Hong Kong through H shares and in New York through N shares.

Third, the model of issuing new stocks was constantly optimized. From 1991 to 1992, new stocks were mainly issued through limited selling subscription certificates. Following the "August 10 Purchase Rush" in Shenzhen in 1992, the model of limited selling subscription certificates was no longer used.

With the approval of the State Council, Shanghai Municipality took the initiative to switch to an unlimited selling subscription certificates plus lottery model for new share issue in 1992. This model has not been widely accepted in China due to a number of unfavorable factors such as an uncertainty of the number of subscriptions, huge subscription costs, the associated investment risks and a negative impact on the secondary market. On August 18, 1993, an unlimited selling deposit certificate-based applications plus lottery model for new share issues was proposed. However, this model has not been widely adopted because it tended to trigger speculative behaviors in the stock market. As of 1996, there were four models of IPO approved by the CSRC: Online quotation, online bidding, full prepayment and deposit certificate-based applications.

In August 1998, the CSRC stipulated that all new stocks with a public offering of more than 50million shares (inclusive) could be allotted to funds. In July 1999, it prescribed that companies with a market capitalization of less than RMB400 million shall still adopted original issuance models such as online quotation, full prepayment, or deposit certificate-based applications. However, companies with a market capitalization of more than RMB400 million were at liberty to issue shares through a combination of making online issuance to general investors and making allotment to legal entities. In April 2000, the restriction of over RMB400 million was lifted, and companies were allowed to directly allot shares to legal entities when issuing shares.

In February 2000, the CSRC adopted a new model of issuing new shares by piloting the allotment of new shares to investors in the secondary market. Under the new model, investors may voluntarily subscribe to new shares based on the market capitalization of the listed marketable securities they held and within the converted quota on voluntary application for purchase.

Fourth, stock price indexes were compiled and stock market data was released. On April 3, 1991, the Shenzhen Stock Exchange commenced to publish the Shenzhen Composite Stock Price Index by taking April 3 as base date and supposing the base value of the index is 100. On July 15, 1991, the Shanghai Stock Exchange published China Shanghai Composite Stock Market Index or Shanghai Composite Index for short, which would track the performance of all the stocks listed on the Shanghai Stock Exchange. When Shanghai Sock Composite Index was being compiled, eight stocks then traded in the market were chosen as constituent stocks and weighted by the total number of stocks issued by taking December 19, 1991 (the exchange's official opening date) as base period.

On May 3, 1993, the Shanghai Stock Exchange published five major sectoral stock indexes for the first time, which stand for industry, commerce, real estate, public utilities, and composite stock indexes respectively. On June 1, 1993, the Shanghai and Shenzhen stock exchanges jointly compiled what were known as "China Indices".

In terms of stock information disclosure, a national monolithic securities market data network basically took shape in China in 1994, which consisted of the Shanghai and Shenzhen stock exchanges, the STAQ system, the NET system, and three large national securities companies (i.e. Guotai Securities Company, Huaxia Securities and South Securities).

Fifth, a lead underwriter qualification regulation regime was installed. Lead underwriters refer to an investment bank or another financial organization, which play a key role in the issuance of shares by initiating to organize the establishment of an underwriting syndicate or solely underwriting a stock. The lead underwriter qualification regulation regime was installed to regulate the underwriting activities of securities operation institutions and protect the legitimate rights and interests of both investors and issuers. In 1996, the CSRC commenced to impose a lead underwriter qualification regulation regime. In May 2000, there were a total of 26 lead underwriters that had obtained the qualification from the CSRC, including Haitong Securities, GF Securities, Xiangcai securities, Everbright Securities, Beijing Securities, and Guotai Junan Securities.

The evolutionary trajectory of China's regulatory regime for the securities market can be traced back to the 1990s. Founded on August 28, 1991, the Securities Association of China served as the self-regulatory organization of the industry. The early regulators of the securities market included the Securities Administrative Office set up by the PBoC in May 1992, and CSC and the CSRC, both of which were established on October 12, 1992. After the CSC was disbanded in 1998, the CSRC became the sole securities regulator in China, with local offices set up across the country. In July 1999, the Securities Law was promulgated to prescribe the establishment of fundamental legal framework for financial market regulation.

After nearly 10 years of trial operation and evolution, China's financial market has progressively taken shape. Specifically speaking, three types of markets including national stock exchanges, regional securities trading centers and local OTC markets constituted the secondary trading market. Meanwhile, securities business outlets scattering throughout the country formed the decentralized trading market, involving integrated business banks, securities companies, trust and investment companies, securities investment consulting companies, credit cooperatives OTC markets, securities registration and transfer companies, and certified public accounting firms. As a result, a financial market system integrating centralized and decentralized trading business has taken shape.

3.1.3 Expediting the Process of Opening up and Going Global

Following China's accession to the WTO in 2001, the Chinese capital market expedited the process of two-way opening-up by way of "bringing in" and "going global". Through ongoing reform in the process of aligning itself with international practices, China's capital market has made new headways.

In April and December 2002, China Merchants Bank Co., Ltd. and CITIC Securities were successively approved for listing on the Shanghai Stock Exchange. In December 2003, the PICC and China Life Insurance Co, Ltd. both successively won the approval for issuing H shares in Hong Kong.

In June 2005, the BOCOM completed its restructuring, reorganization and financing, and took the initiative to make its IPO in Hong Kong. In October, 2005, the CCB issued H shares for trading in Hong Kong. In July 2007, it got listed for trading A shares on the Shanghai Stock Exchange. In June and October 2006, the BOC and the ICBC successively issued stocks for trading on the Hong Kong Exchanges and Clearing Limited and the Shanghai Stock Exchange in the form of H + A shares. In July 2010, the ABC went public in Shanghai and Hong Kong. Through leveraging domestic and overseas capital markets, state-owned commercial banks have established their diversified property right structures by adopting a mixed ownership model.

In August and November 2009, Everbright Securities and China Merchants Securities were successively approved for A-share listing on the Shanghai Stock Exchange. As of the end of 2009, there were eleven listed securities companies in China in total, including CITIC Securities, Everbright Securities, China Merchants Securities, Haitong Securities, and Pacific Securities.

Private enterprises also went public abroad as well. In Fujian province alone, more than twenty private enterprises had their S shares listed in Singapore in 2018. As of 2012, there were a total of 182 Chinese companies listed on the Singapore Exchange.[4]

In October 2002, the Shanghai Gold Exchange (SGE) was approved for establishment, which marked the opening up of China's gold market. In 2011, the RenminbiQualified Foreign Institutional Investors (RQFIIs) system was introduced. In

---

[4] As of 2017, twenty-four enterprises from Jiangsu Province in the shipbuilding, metallurgy, chemicals and other industries, were listed on the Singapore Stock Exchange, with 2 billion Singapore dollars raised.

December 2011, two batches of fund management companies and securities companies obtained RQFII qualification, including nine fund management companies such as HFT Investment Management Co., Ltd., HuaAn Fund Management Co., Ltd., Bosera Asset Management Co., Limited, China Southern Asset Management Co., Ltd., China Asset Management Co., Ltd., Harvest Fund Management Co., Ltd., Da Cheng Fund Management Co., Ltd. and China Universal Asset Management Co.,Ltd., and twelve securities companies such as Guoyuan Securities (Hong Kong) Limited.

3.1.4 Reduction of State-Owned Shares Through Non-tradable Share Reform

Due to unreasonable and irregular shareholding structure resulting from mismatched reform initiatives and limitations on institutional design in the newly established China's securities market, listed companies were ordered to hold non-tradable shares and tradable shares. What is more, non-tradable shareholders held a high proportion of shares, about two thirds, and had controlling stakes in a business, resulting in a dual-class share structure or even a weighted-voting right structure which have undermined the legitimate rights and interests of the shareholders of tradable shares, especially small and medium shareholders. The issue of state-owned non-tradable shares was evaded for a long period, thereby bringing forth a de facto pattern of coexistence of non-tradable and tradable shares.

The issue of non-tradable shares inevitably came to the fore when state-owned enterprises endeavored to raise funds in support of their reform and development by cashing in their state-owned shares. With a view to addressing this issue, an exploratory reform has been carried out to reduce state-owned shares since the 1990s. The reduction of state-owned shares is not just an issue of equity transfer we needed to address in history. In addition, it also involves theoretical and practical issues, such as state-owned shares, full tradability and loss of state-owned assets. As early as April 1994, Zhuhai Hengtong Group acquired a 35.5% stake of Shanghai Lengguang Industrial Co., Ltd., which was the first transfer of state-owned shares in China's securities market. Thereafter, enterprises took the initiative to explore their own ways to reduce state-owned shares.

In December 1999, a pilot proportional transfer scheme for state-owned shares was launched. The CSRC selected ten pilot enterprises such as *Tangshan* Jidong Cement Co., Ltd., Guangdong Huayi Investment Co., Ltd., Shenyang Huitian Thermal Power Co., Ltd., Shanghai Lujiazui Finance and Trade Zone Development Co., Ltd., China Jialing Industrial Co., Ltd. (Group), Port of Tianjin, and Taiji Group Co., Ltd. for operating the pilot scheme, instituting the reform for reducing state-owned non-tradable shares. In June 2001, the state-owned share reduction policy was officially put into implementation. A number of listed companies including Fiberhome Telecommunication Technologies Co., Ltd., *Guangxi* Beisheng Pharmaceutical Co., Ltd., Anhui

Jianghuai Automobile Group Co., Ltd., and Huafang Co., Ltd. transferred their state-owned shares which was equivalent to 10% of the amount raised in the listing at the price at which the IPO was conducted. However, the CSRC urgently suspended this pilot scheme in October 2001 on the ground that it fell short of market expectations.

In November 2001, the CSRC publicly solicited for the proposals for reducing the shareholdings of state-owned shares. However, it has failed to devise a workable solution that could both take into account the interests of all the stakeholders and won their unanimous acceptance for some certain reasons. On June 23, 2002, the State Council decided to cease the implementation of the relevant rules and regulations on the reduction of state-owned non-tradable shares in the securities market and prohibited the promulgation of relevant implementing measures (except for overseas listings).

In 2004, the non-tradable share reform was placed on the agenda once again as an institutional reform move for promoting the reform, opening up and stable development of the capital market. In April, 2004, the CSRC won the approval to institute the pilot reform to reduce non-tradable shares. As of the end of 2004, listed companies in China had a total of 714.9 billion shares, of which 454.3 billion shares were non-tradable, accounting for 63.55% of the total shares; and state-owned non-tradable shares made up 74% of the non-tradable shares and 47% of the total shares respectively.[5]

In April 2005, the pilot reform of non-tradable shares was officially launched. In May 2005, the CSRC designated Hebei Jinniu Energy Resources Co., Ltd., Sany Group, Tsinghua Tongfang Co., Ltd., and Zijiang Holdings as the first batch of pilot reform companies. Through consultation with various parties, the proportions of voting tradable shares of these four companies were set at 76.72%, 32.72%, 54.90% and 69.33% respectively. On June 19, 2005, the CSRC announced the second batch of 42 companies for the pilot reform, including 28 companies listed on the Shanghai Stock Exchange, 14 on the Shenzhen Stock Exchange, and 10 on the SME Board, which typified various enterprises in different sectors (e.g. large-scale central enterprises, local state-owned enterprises, private enterprises, and SMEs).

In September 2005, the reform of non-tradable shares was put into full implementation. Altogether, there were 40 joint-stock system companies which had been designated as pilot reform companies by the Shanghai and Shenzhen stock exchanges, including 12 companies listed on the Shanghai Stock Exchange, 8 companies on the Shenzhen Stock Exchange, and 20 companies on the SME Board. As of December 2005, there were 15 batches of 407 listed companies in total that had either completed the pilot reform or were pushing through with the non-tradable share reform.[6]In March 2006, the 23rd batch of 46 listed companies was announced as pilot reform companies, increasing the proportion of pilot reform companies to almost 50% of China's listed companies. As of December 31, 2006, there were a total of 1,303

[5] Wu Xiaoling (ed): *A Chronicle of Major Events in China's Financial Reform and Opening up*, China Financial Publishing House, 2008, p 825.

[6] Wu Xiaoling (ed): *A Chronicle of Major Events in China's Financial Reform and Opening up*, China Financial Publishing House, 2008, pp: 865–866.

companies that were pushing through with or had completed the non-tradable share reform, with a total market capitalization of around RMB6,050,447 million, accounting for approximately 98.55% of the total market capitalization of the A shares on the Shanghai and Shenzhen stock exchanges. All in a word, the reform has achieved considerable accomplishments.

The joint-stock reform was instituted to regulate the shareholding structure of listed companies subject to the requirements of the Company Law and the Securities Law, among others. Through the operation of a consultation mechanism designed for balancing the interests between shareholders of non-tradable shares and tradable shares, the non-tradable share reform was carried out to eradicate institutional disparity in the transfer of shares in the A-share market. As such, it was an institutional tactics for trading non-tradable shares in the market deployed in those days. Thereafter, non-tradable A-shares were unlocked to become tradable, and therefore majority and minority shareholders would have equal rights and interests. As a result, the original securities trading model has switched from government-guidance to market-orientation.

With respect to the solutions for reducing the non-tradable shares held by shareholders after the institution of the reform of non-tradable shares, the CSRC stipulated in April 2008 that shareholders holding outstanding shares to be unlocked for trading must transfer them through the block trading systems of stock exchanges provided that these unlocked outstanding shares to be traded by a company in the coming month were projected to exceed 1% of the total shares of the company.

After nearly a decade of opening up to the outside world, especially through long-term reform, exploration and regulation, China's financial market was flourishing and its functions and systems have been further optimized.

3.1.5 Innovative Development and Management Regime Reform

Through reform and transformation, China once again realized the "soft landing" of its economy in 2012, ushering the capital market into an era of innovative development and regulation regime reform.

First, new products were launched and the trading mechanism was innovated. As regards new products debuted into the market, silver futures contract product was traded on the Shanghai Futures Exchange in May 2012; treasury bond futures product was officially launched on the China Financial Futures Exchange, and oil asphalt futures contract product was approved for trading on the Shanghai Futures Exchange in September 2013; and iron ore futures contract product was traded on the Dalian Commodity Exchange in October 2013, marking the official launching of China's iron ore futures products. Additionally, the first transaction of thermal coal futures was closed in January 2014, and the China Agricultural Products Futures Index was officially released in March 2014.

In January 2012, the first batch of Renminbi Qualified Foreign Institutional Investor (RQFII) products was launched with approval, including Haitong China RMB Income Fund of Haitong International Securities Group Limited and the CUAM RMB Bond plus Fund of China Universal Asset Management Co., Ltd. listed in Hong Kong. In February, 2012, Hang Seng Bank launched the first RMB-denominated Exchange Traded Fund (ETF) for trading on the Hong Kong Exchanges and Clearing Limited. In June 2012, the first batch of funds was issued for cross-border trading with approval, including the China AMC Hang Seng ETF-QDII, the E Fund Hang Seng China Enterprises (QDII) ETF and the E Fund Hang Seng China Enterprises (QDII) ETF Feeder Fund. In February 2014, the CSOP China 5-YearTreasury Bd CNY ETF was listed on the Hong Kong Exchanges and Clearing Limited.

In 2012, the pilot securitization scheme for credit assets was re-initiated, with the first securitization product launched on September 7, 2012. In June 2013, PingAn Bank Co, Ltd debuted small-sum consumer loans ABS. In May 2015, new credit assets were newly increased by RMB 500 billion for pilot securitization. Meanwhile, banks were encouraged to work together with financial asset management companies to steadily expand the scope of the pilot securitization of non-performing assets, with a view to stepping up the disposal of non-performing financial assets.

On April 10, 2014, the Shanghai Stock Exchange and the Hong Kong Exchanges and Clearing Limited won approval to pilot the stock trading connect mechanism, also known as the "Shanghai-Hong Kong Stock Connect". On June 18, 2014, the first batch of financial institutions officially conducted the free trade (FT) account business in Shanghai, and five banks such as the BOC, ICBC, CCB Shanghai Branch, Shanghai Pudong Development Bank Shanghai Branch, and Bank of Shanghai were approved to open FT accounts.

Second, the IPO system was reformed and the registration system was operated on a pilot basis. From 2009 to 2010, the CSRC carried out two major reforms in the IPO system. With a focus on the quotation of new shares, the reforms were pushed through to optimize the quotation constraint mechanism for quotation inquiries and applications for purchase, liberalize government guidance and regulation, and impose a market-oriented quotation formation regime. With a view to better developing a multi-tier stock market, the government decided to implement a registration system for stock issuance for a period of two years according to the law in March 2016. In February 2018, it ordered to extend the registration system reform period for another two years up to February 29, 2020. In June 2019, the SSE STAR Market was officially launched to pilot a registration system for the issuance of new stocks.

As a market-oriented regime for stock issuance with information disclosure at the core, the registration system was imposed to improve the rules and regulations of information disclosure. Under the registration system, stock exchanges were in charge of examining and approving the applications for the registration of share issuance lodged by companies, and submitting qualified ones to the CSFC for mandatory registration. Market participants had the power to determine the timing, number, and quotation of stocks issued at their discretion. Investors were responsible for appraising the asset quality and investment value of issuers, and bearing investment risks. Regulators were mandated to tighten up in-event and post-event regulation, impose severe penalties on violations such as fraudulent issuance, and illegal and irregular information disclosure, and effectively safeguard the financial market order and the legitimate rights and interests of investors.

Third, ways for innovative enterprises to pilot the issuance of shares or depository receipts in China were constantly explored. In March 2018, With a view to supporting the issuance of shares for trading by innovative enterprises in China, the CSRC stipulated that innovative enterprises were allowed to issue stocks or Chinese depository receipts (CDRs) on a pilot basis in China provided that they had reached a certain business size, pursued national strategies, mastered core technologies, won widespread recognition in the market, and engaged in high-tech and strategically emerging industries (e.g. Internet, big data, cloud computing, AI, software, IC, high-end equipment manufacturing and biomedicine). To that end, it set up a special Science and Technology Innovation and Industrialization Advisory Committee to select pilot enterprises.

A Chinese Depositary Receipt (CDR) is a negotiable instrument traded on a Chinese stock exchange which represents a kind of securities, usually in the form of underlying equity interests, issued by a foreign publicly-listed company. In June 2018, the CSRC issued a number of documents to lay down the governing laws and fundamental regulatory provisions for depository receipts, and set forth the detailed implementing provisions for the issuance, listing, trading, and information disclosure systems of depository receipts. Meanwhile, the Shanghai and Shenzhen stock exchanges and the CSDC also notified securities companies of depository receipt mock tests. Thanks to these efforts, the underlying regime for CDRs[7] has been eventually established for implementation.

Fourth, a switch was made from management of state-owned financial assets to management of state-owned financial capital. In July 2018, the CPC Central Committee and the State Council issued the Guiding Opinions on Tightening up the Management of State-Owned Financial Capital, which classified financial institutions into four categories for management. Specifically, these financial institutions were classified as follows: (1) Development- and policy-oriented financial institutions, the nature of which still remained as wholly state-owned or wholly-owned financial institutions; (2) Financial infrastructure institutions that got involved in national financial security and had a strong spillover effect, over which the state maintained absolute control; (3) State-owned financial institutions with an important influence in the financial sector, in which state-owned financial capital played a controlling and leading role; and (4) Other state-owned financial institutions engaging in competitive sectors, which took the initiative to attract different types of capital, with state-owned financial capital taking absolute or relative control, or making an investment to hold a stake.

[7] A Chinese depositary receipt (CDR) refers to an investment certificate that a foreign company listed overseas (including China's Hong Kong) escrow some of its issued and listed shares with a local custodian bank and entrusts a depository bank in China to make issuance and conduct trading in the A-share market in China, which is cleared and settled in RMB, as well as traded by investors in China, so as to enable off-site trading of shares.

The above scientific classification of state-owned financial institutions reflects the top-level institutional design characteristic of the reform and evolution of China's securities market. As we can learn, the Chinese government has completed the transitions from managing assets to managing capital, and from state-owned financial assets to state-owned financial capital. This is an important milestone in the evolution and structural transition of the securities market since the 1990s, and it would have a profound impact on the future reform and development of China's capital market.

3.2 Establishing Multiple Money Market Systems

The multiple money market systems which had been established since the 1980s constituted the backbone of China's financial market. The short-term money market consisted of the interbank lending market, the interbank bond market, the short-term bill market, the central bank bill market, among others.

3.2.1 The Interbank Lending Market

The Interbank lending market is a market in which banks and financial institutions lend loans to one another for a specified term to maturity. In a narrow sense, it refers to the market for temporary cash position adjustment between financial institutions, and in a broader sense, it refers to the market for the financing of short-term funds. Generally speaking, interbank loans are for maturities of half a day to one day, seven days, one month, and four months. The interbank rate is the rate of interest charged on short term loans between banks and there are an array of published interbank rates, including the CHIBOR (China) and the LIBOR (UK). Interbank lending is a purely credit-based lending pattern without collaterals which is characterized by short maturities, non- collateral and a wide range of participants.

The evolutionary trajectory of China's national interbank lending market can be traced back to the 1980s. In 1981, the discount business of intra-city commercial acceptance bills and inter-city banker's acceptance bills (cross- province and city) was conducted on a pilot basis at first in Shanghai, and then nationwide. In 1987, there were a total of more than fifty large regional markets in China, building up a cross-regional and cross-system financing network. By breaking through the unified credit fund management and allocation system, the pattern of the longstanding sectoral segmentation and regional blockade in the financial market has been eventually overhauled.

In the 1990s, the PBoC expedited the unification and institutional building of the national interbank lending market. On April 18, 1994, the China Foreign Exchange Trade System (CFETS) and the National Interbank Funding Center was officially established to tighten up the regulation and improve the services for spot transactions and derivative product transactions in the interbank money, bond and foreign exchange markets.[8]

On January 3, 1996, the national interbank lending market trading system was put into trial operation in Shanghai. On January 4, 1996, the PBoC announced the first weighted average China interbank offered rate (Chibor), marking that a national monolithic interbank lending market has progressively taken shape in China. Specifically, 12 commercial bank headquarters and 15 financing centers conducted online transactions at first, and the number had respectively increased to 20 and 35 by the end of March 1996. As of the end of December, 1996, there were 20, 235 transactions completed, with a total lending amount of RMB587, 158million.[9]

In January 1997, the PBoC declared that the CFETS and the National Interbank Funding Center were two offices with the same personnel staffing, both coming directly under the administration of the PBoC.

From 1998 to 2000, the PBOC successively gave its official sanction that financial institutions such as foreign banks licensed to conduct the RMB business in the Pudong New Area of Shanghai, licensed branches of commercial banks, insurance companies, some rural credit unions, China Development Bank, the Export–Import Bank of China, securities companies and financial companies affiliated to enterprise group were allowed to join the interbank lending market. As of August 14, 2000, the cumulative turnover of transactions denominated in RMB passed the RMB1 trillion mark for the first timein the national interbank market, reaching RMB1,001.93 billion. In June 2002, a monolithic foreign currency interbank lending market was officially launched in China. As of the end of 2003, annual trading volume denominated in RMB and foreign currencies in the inter-bank market reached a new high, and the cumulative transaction turnover in the foreign exchange market hit US$151.13 billion.

On January 4, 2007, the Shanghai Interbank Offered Rate (Shibor) was officially published and applied. With the formation of a uniform market-oriented interbank benchmark lending interest rate dictated by market supply and demand, the interbank lending market entered a rapid and regulated development stage.

In July 2007, the PBoC designated fifteen major types of financial institutions as major participants in the interbank lending market, including policy banks, Chinese commercial banks, financial companies affiliated to enterprise groups, trust companies, and financial leasing companies. Additionally, it also imposed detailed requirements in terms of internal control systems, staffing, operations and penalties, as well as defined the due regulatory power for market access, maturity, quotas, registration, transparency and regulation of the interbank lending market, establishing a unified regulatory framework for the domestic interbank lending market.

---

[8] In this chapter, most data and materials related to the interbank lending market, the bond market and the foreign exchange market mainly source from the China Foreign Exchange Trade System and National Interbank Funding Center.

[9] Wu Xiaoling (ed): *A Chronicle of Major Events in China's Financial Reform and Opening up*, China Financial Publishing House, 2008, p 344.

From 2007 onwards, the interbank lending market regulatory regime has been constantly optimized. On November 26, 2009, the SHCH was approved for establishment. On September 25, 2010, a national interbank market loan transfer trading system was officially launched.

According to the statistics from the National Interbank Funding Center, there were a total of 2,234 members of the interbank lending market as of June 2020, which included 354 banks, 289 rural credit unions, 1,033 rural commercial banks and cooperative banks, 102 securities companies, 234 financial companies affiliated to enterprise group, 53 insurance companies, 4 asset management companies, 66 trust companies, 66 financial leasing companies, and 24 auto finance companies. By 2019, the cumulative interbank lending amount had reached RMB151.6 trillion, an increase of 8.9% year-on-year.

3.2.2 A Monolithic Interbank Bond Market

As an important constituent part of China's money and bond markets, the interbank bond market is a block trading market (wholesale market) for the trading and repurchase of bonds by financial institutions such as commercial banks, rural credit cooperatives, insurance companies and securities companies.

China's interbank bond market originated in the late 1990s. On June 5, 1997, the PBoC decided to conduct the interbank bond repo business in the national interbank lending market. On June 6, 1997, the first batch of twenty-seven commercial banks was granted membership of the market, marking the official establishment of the interbank bond market. On June 16, 1997, the National Interbank Funding Center commenced to conduct spot treasury bond transactions, and the interbank bond market was successfully put into trial operation, with trading products including treasury bond repo and spot transactions.

The bond products traded in the inter-bank bond market fall into two categories, namely coupon bonds and unsecured bonds. Generally Speaking, coupon bonds are basically issued by the state or financial institutions which are backed by the credit of the state and the central government, or have the same credit rating as the state, and they are believed to be free from credit risks. In contrast, the issuers of unsecured bonds are hardly backed by the credit of the state, and investors need to factor in credit risks when transacting with them. It can be inferred that there is a "credit spread" between coupon bonds and unsecured bonds.

The PBoC served as the main regulator of the interbank bond market. As the self-regulatory body and market access administrator of the market, the National Association of Financial Market Institutional Investors (NAFMII)[10] was responsible for the registration of the debt financing instruments of non-financial enterprises.

[10] The National Association of Financial Market Institutional Investors (NAFMII) is a non-profit self-regulatory organization where market participants voluntarily join, involvingparticipants from the inter-bank bond market, the inter-bank lending market, the foreign exchange market, the bill market and the gold market. NAFMII was established with approval on September 3, 2007.

The National Interbank Funding Centre took charge of effecting transactions in local and foreign currencies and their derivatives, which amounted to the Shanghai and Shenzhen stock exchanges in the stock market. The CCDC and the SHCH were the registration, custody and clearing agencies of the interbank bond market, with the former being responsible for coupon bonds and certain unsecured bonds, and the latter for unsecured bonds.

In 1999, the CCDC and Thomson Reuters jointly compiled the yield curve of China's interbank bond market, which is a milestone in the development trajectory of market-oriented interest rate in China. By October 24, 2000, annual repo transaction turnover had passed the RMB1 trillion mark in the interbank bond market. In 2001, the interbank bond market outperformed the bond exchange market in respect of the number of bonds issued, trading volume and custody size, becoming the largest bond market in China.

In April 2002, the PBoC applied a market access filing system for regulating financial institutions in the national interbank bond market. In the meantime, it was also mandatory that bonds were issued for trading in the national interbank bond market. On March 10, 2003, the daily value of bonds traded in the interbank bond market exceeded RMB10.22 billion.

In January 2006, the Straight-through Processing System (STP) was employed to operate in spot transactions, pledged repo and outright repo, as well as exercise pre-event control on forward bond transactions in the inter-bank bond market. In 2007, the NAFMII was established with approval to serve as a self-regulatory body of the market. In August, 2010, three types of financial institutions including offshore RMB clearing banks were allowed to invest in RMB in the interbank bond market on a pilot basis.

As of the end of 2016, there was a steady increase in the amount of bonds issued in the inter-bank bond market. The CCDC issued RMB3 trillion of treasury bonds, RMB 6 trillion of local government bonds, RMB3 trillion of policy bank bonds, RMB0.37 trillion of commercial bank bonds, and RMB0.35 trillion of credit asset-backed securities. Additionally, the SHCH issued RMB1 trillion of medium-term notes, RMB3 trillion of commercial papers (including super and short-term commercial papers), and RMB0.60trillion of private placement notes (PPN). Figure 3.1 shows the amount of different bonds issued as the proportion of the total in the interbank bond market.

As shown in Fig. 3.1, the volume of different bonds issued is expressed as the proportion of the interbank bond market: 31% of local government bonds; 17% of policy bank bonds; 14% of super and short-term commercial papers, 14% of treasury bonds; 7% of corporate bonds; and 6% of other bonds.

As of June 2020, there were 30 market makers, 54 trial market makers, and 49 settlement agents in the interbank bond market, including four large state-owned commercial banks, the BOCOM, the China Merchants Bank, the China Minsheng Bank, and the Everbright Bank of China.

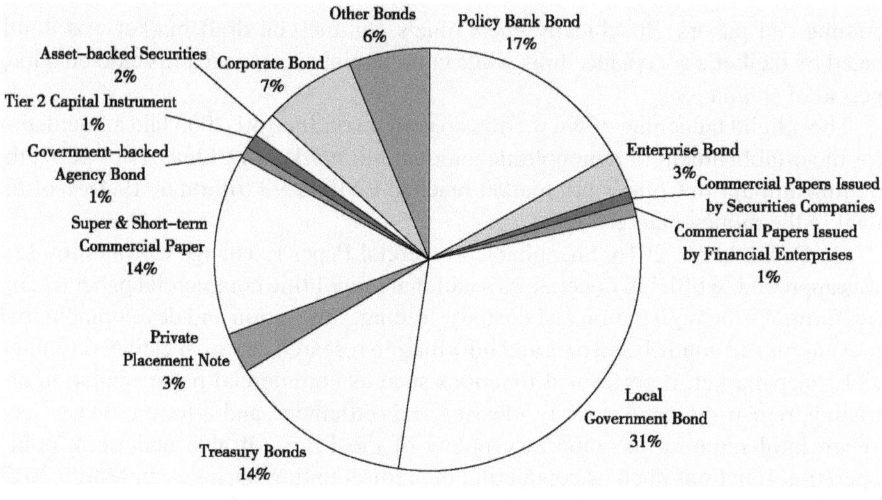

Fig. 3.1 The volume of different bonds issued as a proportion of the interbank bond market (2016). *Source* China Central Depository and Clearing Co., Ltd.: An Overview of China's Bond Market (2016), page 77, http://www.chinabond.com.cn/cb/cn/zqsc/jwtzzzl/scjs/20170405/146847902.shtml, Accessed on August 3, 2018

3.2.3 The Fund Shortage-Tackling Short-Term Bill Market

Commercial drafts and commercial papers were two major instrument products traded in the short-term bill market. According to the provisions of the PBoC, commercial drafts refer to bills issued to reflect the creditor's rights and liability relationships when deferred payment commodity transactions are conducted between the parties involved under purchase and sales contracts, and they are divided into banker's acceptance bill and commercial acceptance bill.

The first cross-provincial banker's acceptance bill discount business was conducted on a trial basis in Shanghai in October 1980, and then nationwide in 1985. It is noting that the Law of Negotiable Instruments promulgated in 1995 and the Administrative Provisions on Commercial Drafts issued by the PBoC in 1997 constituted a fundamental legal framework for regulating the commercial draft market.

In November 2000, the ICBC Bill Dealing Center was established in Shanghai with approval as the first specialized bill operation agency. Thereafter, the commercial paper business designed for providing financing services was booming, and almost all the commercial banks and some rural credit cooperatives were allowed to operate in the bill acceptance, discount and rediscount business. As such, a regional commercial bills market with central cities at the core has preliminarily taken shape. Nevertheless, there was an imbalance in the market shares of different types of commercial papers. Specifically, the China's commercial draft market was dominated by banker's acceptance bills while commercial acceptance bills entered a long period of stagnation.

The official launching of www.chinacp.com.cn on June 30, 2003 laid a foundation for the establishment of a monolithic national bill market in China. As of 2007, the trading amount in China's bill market reached RMB15.98 trillion or 19.48% of the total in the money market.

On December 8, 2016, Shanghai Commercial Paper Exchange Corporation Ltd. was approved to officially operate as a national monolithic commercial paper trading platform. As the registration and custody, trading, innovation and development, risk prevention and control, and data and information research centre of China's commercial paper market, it performed functions such as commercial paper quotation and trading, registration and custody, clearing and settlement, and information services. When implementing the monetary policy of the PBoC, it also undertook policy operation functions such as conducting the rediscounting business. In March 2017, the Shanghai Commercial Paper Exchange Corporation Ltd. was connected to the Electronic Commercial Draft System (ECDs) to function as a regulatory system for publishing rules and regulations on related trading, registration and custody business, and regulating the development of the commercial paper market.

As of the end of January 2020, the amount of banker's acceptance bills traded in China's short-term bill market reached RMB1,894,707.62 million, and that of commercial acceptance bills stood at RMB381,638.06 million; the amount of banker's acceptance bills discounted reached RMB1,348,595.83 million, and that of commercial acceptance bills discounted stood at RMB133,035.29 million; and the amount of banker's acceptance bills transfer discounted reached RMB2,985,695.70 million, and that of commercial acceptance bills stood at RMB403,048.16 million.[11] It was evident that the development imbalance between banker's acceptance bills and commercial acceptance bills had remained unchanged.

Commercial papers are negotiable securities which are issued for trading by non-financial enterprises with a legal entity status to tackle cash shortage, and purchased by domestic financial institutions with a maturity of up to one year for repaying principal and interest in the interbank bond market.

In November 1987, Shanghai Municipality was the first in the country to allow medium-sized and large state-owned enterprises suffering from a temporary or short-term liquidity shortage, and whose funding needs could not be met by banks to apply to issue commercial papers in the market to raise funds. This move shifted an existing business pattern in which enterprises were solely reliant on specialized banks for financing their short-term cash shortage, marking the onset of a new type of corporate financing instrument, namely, commercial paper. From 1987 to 1989, the PBoC approved the applications from twenty-nine enterprises for issuing commercial papers, with a total value of RMB655.7 million.

[11] Shanghai Commercial Paper Exchange Corporation Ltd.: Statistics onCommercial Paper Business in January 2020 [EB / OL], February 10, 2020,http://www.shcpe.com.cn/info_18_itemid_1838.html.

In 1988, enterprises piloted in issuing commercial papers across China. In 1989, the PBoC allowed enterprises to issue commercial papers nationwide. From 1993 to 1994, excessive bonds were issued in many regions of the country. In 1997, default on enterprise bonds and commercial papers surfaced in some regions. From 1992 to 1997, RMB 26 billion worth of corporate bonds were issued in Guangdong province, in which only RMB18.4 billion won the approval from the PBoC. Of the RMB6.7 billion of commercial papers issued, nearly RMB3 billion was defaulted at maturity, accounting for 18% of the balance of bonds outstanding that year.

Due to the illegal issuance of commercial papers, a campaign to crack down on "Three Irregularities" was launched to overhaul the financial market. From 1997 onwards, the PBoC no longer approved the issuance of commercial papers, and the business was thus phased out in the money market.

It was not until May 2005 that commercial papers were re-launched in the domestic money market. As a new means of direct financing for enterprises, the PBoC allowed eligible enterprises to issue commercial papers to qualified institutional investors in the inter-bank bond market. On May 26, 2005, five enterprises, including Huaneng Power International, Inc., Shanghai Zhenhua Heavy Industries Co., Ltd., Air China Limited, China Minmetals Corporation, and State Development and Investment Corporation, successfully issued seven commercial papers with a total face value of RMB10.9 billion to qualified institutional investors in the inter-bank bond market. In the meantime, securities companies were also allowed to issue commercial papers-Tranche 1 GuotaiJunan Securities Short-term Commercial Paper was approved for issuance with an amount of RMB600 million for a maturity of 91 days. The interest rate of commercial paper was mainly contingent on credit risks of issuing enterprises and supply and demand of funds in the market at the time. From 2007 onwards, an interest rate regime of Shibor plus basis point has been progressively installed.

As of December 2009, 450-odd enterprises issued 1,100 commercial papers totaling RMB1,640,415 million. In 2014, RMB2.15 trillion worth of commercial papers were issued in aggregate, on a small issuance scale, less than 10% of the total amount of commercial drafts issued that year.

In April 2018, the PBoC allowed eligible securities companies to issue commercial papers to qualified institutional investors in the interbank bond market. From January to February 2020, five enterprises, namely China Merchants Shekou Industrial Zone Holdings Co., Ltd., Tianjin Infrastructure Construction and Investment (Group) Co., Ltd., Zhuhai Huafa Group Co., Ltd., Sany Heavy Co., Ltd. and Shanghai Electric Power Co., Ltd. successively issued Super and Short-term Commercial Papers to raise funds to step up their epidemic prevention and control efforts, alleviate short-term fund shortage, and clear bad debts.

3.2.4 *The Central Bank Bill Market*

Central bank bills are short-term bonds and debt instruments (debt obligation facilities) issued by the PBoC to commercial banks (primary dealers) for the monetary policy purposes of adjusting the excess reserves of commercial banks, with maturities ranging from less than one year to three years.

The issuance of central bank bills is inextricably bound up with open market operations. In September 2002, the PBoC took the lead in issuing issuing central bank bills to mop up excess liquidity arising from the inflow of large amounts of foreign currencies. Thereafter, the central bank leveraged central bank bills to temporarily replace treasury bonds as the main instrument for open market operations transactions alongside statutory reserves.

Central bank bills are essentially short-term bonds issued by the PBoC as a supplementary monetary policy tool to adjust the excess reserves of commercial banks, control the amount of funds available for commercial banks to lend, and provide a benchmark interest rate for the market, thereby promoting the development of the money market.

From 2002 to 2011, central bank bills played an important role in mopping excess liquidity and gained the recognition from market participants as a short-term financial instrument in the market. As a result, central bank bills have become a major tool for central banks to conduct open market operations, and their issuance, market supply and secondary market trading volume have grown steadily. In 2008, the outstanding balance of central bank bills exceeded RMB4.5 trillion.

In 2009, the mounting inflationary pressures imposed more stringent requirements for the implementation of monetary policy and the options for instruments. In 2011, central bank bills progressively exited from the money market. From 2013 onwards, the PBoC temporarily ceased the issuance of central bank bills as a major means for conducting open market operation transactions.

With a view to putting into practice the policy outcomes of the Seventh China-UK Economic and Financial Dialogue, the PBoC successfully issued RMB 5 billion worth of central bank bills with a maturity of one year and a nominal interest rate of 3.1% in London on a book-building basis on October 20, 2015. This is the first time for China to issue RMB-denominated central bank bills overseas, which was of positive significance for diversifying offshore RMB financial products, promoting the development of the offshore RMB market, and facilitating cross-border trade and investment.

With a view to progressively establish a mechanism for issuing central bank bills in Hong Kong on a regular basis, the PBoC selected Hong Kong as the venue for rolling over central bank bills directly to offshore market participants from November 2018 onwards. As a result, central bank bills of 3-month, 6-month and 1-year maturity respectively have been issued in Hong Kong on a fixed schedule. It can be inferred that the re-issuance of central bank bills as a monetary policy tool would help facilitate the RMB internationalisation process.

On February 13, 2020, the PBoC successfully rolled over two tranches of central bank bills totaling RMB 30 billion in Hong Kong, with subscriptions from various types of offshore market investors including commercial banks, central banks, international financial organizations, and funds from different countries and regions (including Europe, the US and Asia).

3.3 Building a Multi-layer Capital Market System

China's capital market picked up in the 1980s. From the 1990s onwards, stock exchanges were formally established. Through these efforts, China has established a multi-layer capital market system.

3.3.1 Shanghai and Shenzhen A-share Main Board Markets

Established in 1990 and 1991 respectively, the Shanghai and Shenzhen stock exchanges provide the main venue for the issuance, listing and trading of shares in China, also known as the Main Board A-share market. The main board Shanghai stock code starts with 6 and the Shenzhen stock code starts with 0.

The A-share market regulator estalished relatively stringent criteria for listed companies. The bulk of the companies listed in the A-share market are large and mature companies with a high capital adequacy ratio and stable profitability. The stocks of listed companies are divided into common stock and preferred stock, of which preferred stock is divided into non-participating preferred stock, non-cumulative preferred stock, non-convertible preferred stock and convertible preferred stock. In addition, there are also state shares, legal person shares, individual A shares and RMB special B shares; as well as blue-chip, growth and speculative stocks.

Following the underlying logic of "top-down" establishment and construction, the A-share market was initially created to accommodate the reform and development needs of state-owned enterprises, and therefore it was a policy market from the outset, rather than a true market.

From its inception, only eight stocks and over 30 bond products were traded on the Shanghai Stock Exchange and five stocks on the Shenzhen Stock Exchange. In the past decade, the major A-share markets in Shanghai and Shenzhen were flourishing, as shown in Fig. 3.2.

As shown in Fig. 3.2, there were 3,584 listed companies on the Shanghai and Shenzhen exchanges in 2018, with a total market capitalization of RMB43.50 trillion and a free float market capitalization of RMB35.38 trillion respectively. Among them, the free float market capitalization accounted for 81.34% of the total market capitalization.

Nowadays, the Shanghai and Shenzhen A-share main board markets constitute an important part of the global financial market. Among them, the Shanghai Stock Exchange has developed into a stock exchange which established a relatively complete market structure and launched four kinds of securities products, namely stocks, bonds, funds and derivatives. In addition, new equity and stock exchange markets have been created on the basis of the Shanghai and Shenzhen A-share main board markets. In May 2013, the Shenzhen Qianhai Equity Exchange was officially opened for business, with 1,200 enterprises being listed for trading on the opening day.

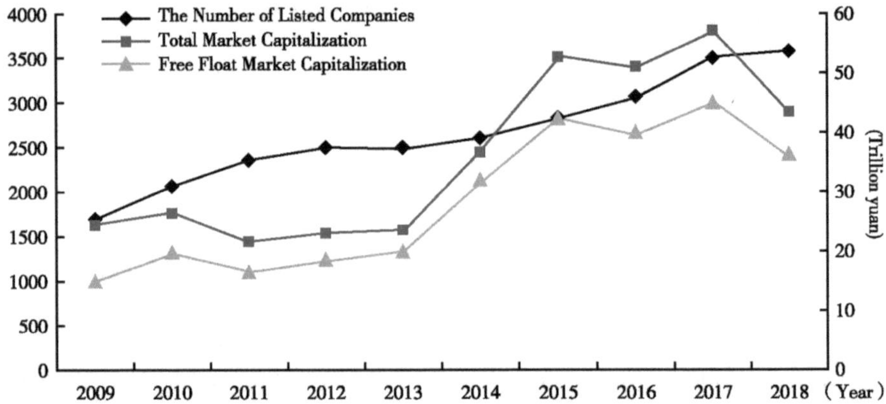

Fig. 3.2 Total market capitalization and free float market capitalization of listed companies on the Shanghai and Shenzhen Stock Exchanges (2009–2018). *Source* The Financial Stability Analysis Group of the PBoC: China Financial Stability Report 2019, China Finance Publishing House, 2019, p. 46

As of the end of 2019, there were a total of 1,572 companies listed on the Shanghai Stock Exchange, with a total market capitalization of RMB35.6 trillion. In 2019, the cumulative turnover of stocks for the year was RMB 54.4 trillion and the total amount of funds raised in the stock market was RMB 514.5 billion. Meanwhile, there were a total of 15,368 bonds traded in the bond market, with a cumulative turnover of RMB221.79 trillion; 292 funds in the fund market, with a cumulative value of assets traded hitting RMB6.9 trillion; and the cumulative value of derivatives traded in the derivatives market stood at RMB338.9 billion. It is learned that 24,398 investors opened accounts on the Shanghai Stock Exchange.[12]

As of the end of December 2019, there were a total of 2,205 companies listed on the Shenzhen Stock Exchange, including 471 on the main board, 943 on the SME board, and 791 on the GEM board, with a total market capitalization of RMB23.74 trillion. Meanwhile, there were 5,998 listed bonds, with a face value of RMB2.08 trillion in aggregate; and 530 listed funds, with a net asset value of RMB193.3 billion. In 2019, the total value of securities traded stood at RMB100.8 trillion, with RMB508.9 billion raised from stocks and RMB1.75 trillion raised from fixed-income products.[13]It is worth mentioning that some major indexes such as IPOs, the amount of equity financing and the turnover of stocks all came top in the world.

---

[12] Shanghai Stock Exchange: Profile of the Shanghai Stock Exchange, [EB/OL], http://www.sse.com.cn/aboutus/sseintroduction/introduction/.

[13] Shenzhen Stock Exchange: *Profile of the Shenzhen Stock Exchange*, [EB/OL], http://www.szse.cn/aboutus/sse/introduction/index.html.

3.3.2 The Shenzhen SME Board Market

The SME Board of the Shenzhen Stock Exchange refers to the Growth Enterprise Board Market for listing companies with a free float market capitalization of approximately up to RMB 100 million. For those companies that fall short of the requirements of the Main Board market, they were merely allowed to be listed on the SME Board market, which is a transition to the GEM market, with a stock code starting with 002.

In May 2004, the Shenzhen Stock Exchange was approved to set up a SME board in the main board market and officially launched the SME board market. The SME board was targeted at serving SMEs with main profitable business, sustainability and high technology, and the first batch of eight companies was approved for listing.

The SME board market was in a position to serve the strategy of China's committing to a manufacturing power, support SMEs in expanding their industrial chains, and specialize in different global industries worldwide. With a wide industrial coverage, it had nearly 40% of leading companies in their niche industries which were active in market-oriented M&A and reorganization, and epitomized the new economy under an upgrading industrial structure. The SME board market was among world markets that had succeeded in serving SMEs.

From 2004 and 2016, SME Board companies brought in a cumulative operating revenue of RMB14.25 trillion, with an average operating revenue growing from RMB651 million to RMB3,526 million at a compound average growth rate of 15.12%. In the past thirteen years since its opening for business, the cumulative net profit earned stood at RMB1 trillion, with an average net profit growing from RMB40 million to RMB264 million at a compound average growth rate of 17.03%; the total dividend reached RMB315,648 million, accounting for 32% of the total net profit earned. Some of the well-known companies have emerged in the SME market, including industry leaders such as Hangzhou Hikvision Digital Technology Co., Ltd., BYD Electronic (International) Co., Ltd., Suning Commercial Group Co., Ltd., Xinjiang Goldwind Science Technology Co., Ltd., IFLYTEK Co., Ltd., and Jiangsu Yanghe Brewery Joint-Stock Co., Ltd.[14]

As of February 28, 2020, there were a total of 946 companies listed on the SME board, with the total shares outstanding of 934.14 billion, a free float market capitalization of 731,212 million, a total turnover of RMB 302,744 million, and a total volume of shares traded of 27,504 million. Among them, the total value and volume of shares traded in the manufacturing industry were RMB 225,824 million and 19,464 million respectively. For information technology, they were RMB 37,301 million and 3,499 million respectively.[15] Undoubtedly, the SME board acted as a stimulus for promoting the development of the multi-layer capital market.

---

[14] Wu Shaolong: The 13th Anniversary of the SME Board: Making Strides While Maintaining Stability, and Leading SMEs to Forge ahead [N], *Securities Times*, May 26, 2017, Page A07.

[15] Shanghai Stock Exchange: Profile of the SME Board, [EB/OL], http://www.szse.cn/certificate/smeboard/.

3.3.3 Design and Launch of the GEM Market

As compared to the main board, the GEM board market, also known as the Second Board Market, is a securities market providing an alternative channel of financing for and promoting the growth of start-ups, SMEs and high-tech enterprises that have no way of temporarily going public on the Main Board. Its stock code starts with 300.

The GEM market in China originated from a proposal submitted by Mr. Cheng Siwei on behalf of the Central Committee of the China Democratic Construction Association in March 1998. In the same year, Mr. Cheng proposed the roadmap of taking "three steps" to promote the development of the GEM, that is, the first step was to set up a number of venture capital companies under the existing legal framework; the second step was to create venture capital funds; and the third step was to establish a venture capital system including the GEM.

In 1999, the CSRC put forward the motion of establishing a high-tech enterprise sector on the Shanghai and Shenzhen Stock Exchanges, and the Shenzhen Stock Exchange embarked on initiating the establishment of the Growth Enterprise Market (GEM), which was put on hold after the bursting of the galloping technology bubble in 2001.

In November 2002, the Shenzhen Stock Exchange proposed to the CSRC a move for progressively promoting the construction of the GEM market step by step. In 2004, the State Council decided to establish a multi-layer capital market system to meet the diversified financing needs of different types of enterprises, and to promote the building of the GEM market in a step-by-step manner. As a transition to the GEM, the Shenzhen Stock Exchange was approved to establish the SME Board market, with the aim of incubating sustainable high-tech enterprises and providing a financing platform for their entrepreneurial innovation.

The year 2009 saw a breakthrough made in the building of the GEM Board Market. In May 2009, the GEM Board Market was officially launched. On September 17, 2009, the first GEM Board IPO examination conference was convened, and seven companies attended the conference. On October 23, 2009, the inauguration ceremony of the China's GEM Board took place, with the first batch of 28 GEM companies being listed. On October 30, 2009, the GEM market was officially launched, marking that China's multi-layer capital market system has basically taken shape.

The GEM market was positioned to provide financing services for independently innovative enterprises and other growth-oriented start-ups, and to actively serve the national innovation-driven development strategy. As we all know, the bulk of companies listed on the GEM market were engaged in the high-tech business with huge growth potential, yet they were always newly established small-scale enterprises with a lackluster business performance. As compared to the Main Board market, the GEM market had relatively loose listing requirements and it was characterized by rigorous regulation yet low entry threshold and high risks. As an important complement to the Main Board, the GEM market offered an alternative channel to help SMEs with growth potential gain access to finance.

As of February 28, 2020, there were a total of 798 companies listed on the GEM Board Market, with the total volume of shares traded of 16,365 million, the total turnover of RMB 240,171 million, the total shares outstanding of 410,719 million and a free float market capitalization of RMB 314,041 million. The top 5 sectors had the turnover as follows: Manufacturing (RMB 143,464 million), information technology (RMB 63,607 million), finance (RMB10,344 million), research services (RMB 4,546 million), and cultural communication (RMB 4,314 million).

3.3.4 Opening of Special Third Board Markets

There is a distinction between the old and new third board markets. The old third board market stemmed mainly from the process of working towards the solutions on how to solve the issue related to the STAQs and NETs systems[16] applied in the market for legal person shares.

The STAQs, the abbreviation for the Securities Trading Automated Quotations System, refers to a comprehensive OTC market for trading negotiable securities through computer networks, with its centre in Beijing. On December 5, 1990, the STAQs was jointly established and operated for transferring legal person shares of joint-stock companies by the PBOC and the China Securities Market Research and Design Centre under the leadership of the Economic System Reform Commission of the State Council. On July 1, 1992, the STAQ system was put into trial operation for transferring legal person shares, creating a market for transferring legal person shares.

The NETs, the abbreviation of National Exchange and Trading System, was developed and designed by China Securities Trading System Corporation Ltd. (CSTS) and put into trial operation on April 28, 1993. With its center also in Beijing, it provided services such as centralized securities trading, quotation, clearing, settlement, registration, custody and inquiry by using its computer network system connected to satellite data communication networks which covered more than 100 cities across China. Likewise, The NETs, consisting of a trading system, a clearing and settlement system and a securities brokerage business system, was also launched for transferring legal person shares.

However, due to regulatory and other reasons, only 17 companies were listed for transferring via the STAQs and NETs. In contrast, 90% of the marketable shares in the market, which were originally intended for institutional investors, were actually held by natural persons. On September 9, 1999, the state forewent the operation of the STAQs and NETs systems during the overhaul of the OTC market, leaving a large amount of funds tied up in these two markets.

With a view to creating a market for addressing the historical legacy bequeathed by the shares of companies delisted from the Main Board Market, and the legal person

[16] STAQs stands for the Securities Trading Automated Quotations System, while NETs represents the National Exchange and Trading System.

shares of listed companies transferred on the former STAQs and NETs systems, the Agency Share Transfer System, also known as the Old Third Board Market, was officially launched for transferring the above-mentioned non-tradable shares, with a stock code starting with 4.

The development of the New Third Board market originated from the pilot transfer of shares of unlisted companies in Zhongguancun Science and Technology Park in 2006. On October 25, 2006, Sinosoft Co., Ltd. and Beijing Time Technologies Co., Ltd. both issued an official announcement of private placements, marking the official financing in the Third Board market. Thereafter, approximately one or two companied were allowed to make private placement offerings in the Third Board market each year. In 2009, unlisted companies settling in Zhongguancun Science and Technology Park were allowed to transfer shares via the Agency Share Transfer System on a pilot basis. As opposed to companies delisted from the Main Board Market and listed companies transferring legal person shares via the former STAQs and NETs system, the companies from Zhongguancun Science and Technology Park were all high-tech enterprises listed for transferring shares via the Agency Share Transfer System, marking the metamorphosis from old Third Board Market to New Third Board Market.

In September 2012, the National Equities Exchange and Quotations system (NEEQ, commonly known as the "New Third Board Market"), was legally approved to be registered for establishment according to the law and thereby the New Third Board Market was officially launched in the capital market. On January 16, 2013, it officially opened for business as the third national stock exchange following the Shanghai and Shenzhen stock exchanges. In compliance with the related requirements, companies allowed to transfer their shares on the NEEQ system were unlisted public companies which must have more than 200 shareholders and were subject to the unified regulation of the CSRC. On December 31, 2013, the NEEQ emerged as a national market when it commenced to accept the application for transferring shares from companies nationwide.

Since the New Third Board Market was created to mainly provide services in support of the development of innovative, start-up and emerging SMEs, all the qualified domestic joint stock companies were allowed to apply for conducting the business such as transfer of shares by transactions, equity and debt financing, and asset restructuring via securities brokerage companies. Nowadays, the NEEQ serves as a national equity trading platform which not only targets unlisted joint stock companies settling in the Zhongguancun Science and Technology Park, but also accommodates those from the pilot areas such as the New Binhai District in Tianjin city, the Donghu New Tech Development Park in Wuhan city and Zhangjiang High-Tech Park in Shanghai. In 2017, the NEEQ performed hierarchical management, and companies allowed to transfer shares on the NEEQ were categorized into companies in the "base" tier and those in the "innovation" tier.

As of December 31, 2019, there were a total of 8,953 companies allowed to transfer their shares in the New Third Board Market, with the total shares outstanding of 561,629 million and the total market capitalization of RMB2,939,960 million.

For the whole year, the NEEQ floated 637 stocks in total, with a total amount of outstanding shares of RMB26,463 million.

3.3.5 Incubation of Futures and Derivatives Markets

As early as the 1980s, China embarked on the exploration of how to develop a futures market. For example, the BOC was approved to conduct the spot and forward foreign exchange trading business on behalf of governmental organs, social groups, enterprises, public institutions, and other entities in China.

The 1990s saw a rapid emergence of the futures market. On October 12, 1990, the Zhengzhou Grain Wholesale Market was officially launched as China's futures industry in embryo. In 1992, Guangdong Wantong Futures Brokerage Co., Ltd. and China International Futures Co., Ltd. were established to deal in the foreign exchange futures business on a trial basis, and the Shanghai Stock Exchange commenced to conduct the treasury bond futures business. In October 1993, the public was allowed to deal in the treasury bond futures business. By the end of 1993, there had been a total of over 50 futures exchanges and over 300 futures brokerage companies in China. Meanwhile, some foreign financial companies affiliated to enterprise group had flocked to China to operate in the foreign exchange futures business in the form of cooperation, joint venture or sole proprietorship, etc.

The exponential development of the futures market has brought about a series of thorny issues, such as excessive number and unsound structure of futures market players, as well as mixed and uneven quality practitioners, which have seriously stunted the health development of the market. In 1994, financial regulators launched an overhaul campaign to restructure the futures market.

In June 1999, the Interim Regulations on the Administration of Futures Trading were promulgated, laying a foundation for regulating futures trading, tightening the regulation of futures trading, maintaining the order of the futures market, safeguarding the legitimate rights and interests of all parties involved in futures trading, and promoting the further development of the futures market. On December 28, 2000, the China Futures Association was founded. With its self-regulatory management function, the China Futures Association constituted a three-tier regulatory regime for the futures industry in tandem with the CSRC and the Shanghai and Shenzhen Stock Exchanges.

In 1999, the Shanghai Metal Exchange, the Shanghai Grain and Oils Exchange and the Shanghai Commodity Exchange merged to form the Shanghai Futures Exchange (SFE). On November 6, 2013, the SFE initiated the establishment of the Shanghai International Energy Exchange Co., Ltd. (INE), an international trading venue for futures market participants, which was approved to be registered for establishment in the China (Shanghai) Pilot Free Trade Zone according to the law. As of the end of 2019, the Shanghai Futures Exchange had 198 members, with 18 futures products approved for trading, as well as 3 options contracts on copper, natural rubber and gold.

Building on commodity futures business, financial futures and other derivatives markets have also sprung up nationwide. In December 2004, the Shanghai Stock Exchange issued the SSE 50 Exchange Traded Open-End Index Securities Investment Fund as the first ever domestic traded open-ended index securities investment fund product in China. In December 2005, the first batch of asset securitization products, namely the CDB Kaiyuan 05-1A credit ABS product and the CCB 2005-1 MBS product, was successfully issued in Beijing.

On September 8, 2006, the China Financial Futures Exchange was officially founded in Shanghai as a corporate exchange specializing in the trading and settlement of financial derivatives products (e.g. financial futures and options). Subsequently, the CSI 300 stock index futures product was officially listed for trading on April 16, 2010. Thereafter, other financial derivatives products such as stock index futures, stock futures, options and treasury bond futures were successively issued.

In March 2011, the Shanghai Futures Exchange was approved to list lead futures contracts for trading. On April 15, 2011, the world's ever first coke futures product was approved for trading on the Dalian Commodity Exchange. On April 21, 2011, China's first spot electronic non-ferrous metal exchange "Kunming Fanya Metal Exchange" was approved to open for operation, with silver and indium products being listed for trading. On October 13, 2011, Zhengzhou Commodity Exchange was approved to conduct the methanol futures trading business.

As of the end of 2016, there were 52 futures products traded in China's domestic futures market, including 46 commodity futures products, 5 financial futures products, and 1 financial options product. For the whole year, the volume of domestic futures traded stood at 4,138 million and the value of domestic futures traded amounted to RMB 195.63 trillion respectively. Specifically speaking, the cumulative volume of traded domestic commodity futures reached 4,119 million and the cumulative value of traded domestic commodity futures hit RMB177.42 trillion; financial futures 19 million and RMB18.21 trillion[17]respectively. It is worth mentioning that the aforesaid 52 listed futures and options products were issued by financial institutions in almost all the main sectors of the national economy, involving agriculture, metals, energy, chemicals, and finance. Most notably, China's futures turnover came top in the world for seven consecutive years.[18]

As of the end of 2019, the China Futures Association had 327 members, including 149 futures companies, 84 securities companies, 10 asset management companies, 80 risk management companies, and 4 private futures fund managers.

The Chinese futures market trading system consisted of five financial institutions, including the Shanghai Futures Exchange, the Shanghai International Energy Exchange, the Zhengzhou Commodity Exchange, the Dalian Commodity Exchange and the China Futures Exchange. Through enhancing its capability for serving the

---

[17] China Securities Regulatory Commission and China Futures Association (Eds), *China Futures Market Yearbook 2016*, China Financial and Economic Publishing House, 2017, p. 149.

[18] Liu Shiyu: To Effectively Make an Deployment of Reforming, Developing and Stabilizingthe Futures Market as National Strategy (Preface), the China Securities Regulatory Commission and the China Futures Association (Eds):*China Futures Market Yearbook 2016*, China Financial and Economic Publishing House, 2017, p. 1, p. 9.

real economy and boosting the efficiency of resource allocation, China's futures market has progressively won the recognition from the society in respect of price discovery, risk management and resource allocation optimization. Meanwhile, a regulatory regime and operational system for the futures market, as well as a mechanism for risk prevention and avoidance have basically taken shape.

3.4 Establishing a Bond Market System with Multiple Players

The Chinese government forewent the issuance of bonds in the 1960s and there was a resurgence and turnaround in China's bond market in the 1980s. From 2005 onwards, the bond market has been on the upturn, reaching the RMB10 trillion mark in 2010. From 2013 onwards, China's bond market's issuance registration system and interconnection have been further improved, ushering in a period of seizing strategic development opportunities. By 2016, the market had had the outstanding balance of bonds worth over RMB57trillion in aggregate, with RMB56.30 trillion of bonds held in custody and 15,300 institutional investors getting involved. In 2019, a bond market system characterized by a full range of products and a more reasonable product structure, as well as a reinforcing credit hierarchy basically took shape.

3.4.1 Market Participants and Bond Products

Bond market participants included: (1) Primary market participants and issuers (e.g. central and local governments, central bank, government-backed agencies, financial institutions, legal entities, international development agencies, underwriters and direct investors); (2) Secondary market participants (e.g. market makers,[19] money brokerage companies, settlement agents, and domestic and foreign investors); (3) Bond derivatives market participants, with the China Financial Futures Exchange (CFFEX) acting as trading front office in the exchange bond derivatives market and China Foreign Exchange Trading System (CFETS) serving as trading front office and central custodian in the OTC bond derivatives market.

Up to date, a monolithic and hierarchical bond market system has been established in China, which is composed of the interbank bond market, the exchange market, the commercial bank OTC market, and other niche markets such as regional trading centers (e.g. local financial exchanges), inter-agency product quotation systems and free trade zones (FTZ).

The interbank bond market made up the core of China's bond market. It was a block trading market characterized by bilateral enquiry and transaction, and a combination of trade-by-trade settlement and CCP settlement. The China Central Depository

[19] As of December 31, 2016, there were a total of thirty market makers in the bond market.

and Clearing Corporation Limited (CCDC) and the SHCH provided custody and settlement services for this market.

All the investors who met the relevant market access requirements of the PBoC were allowed to become a custodian and settlement member of the CCDC. The CCDC opened and centralized managed accounts in a classified manner depending on the nature of financial institutions and their business scope. Generally speaking, institutional investors opened a Tier-1 bond account directly with the CCDC, which was divided into proprietary account and escrow account. The proprietary account was opened to record bondholders' outstanding proprietary balances and their balance movements, and all of members such as settlement agent, direct trade settlement and entrusted settlement agent were required to open a proprietary account with the CCDC. The escrow account was used to record the outstanding balances and the balance movements of bonds held by secondary custodians and sub-custodians that were required to open an escrow account with the CCDC.

Participants in the bond exchange market included all kinds of social investors. The bond exchange market was a retail market for centralized match-trade, which employed a net settlement system operated by the CCDC. In addition, it employed a two-tier custody system, with the CCDC acting as primary custodian in charge of opening escrow accounts, and the CSDC serving as sub-custodian for recording sub-ledger for investors' transactions on exchanges. Therefore, there were no direct right and obligation relationships between the CCDC and investors operating in transactions on exchanges.

The commercial bank OTC market was a retail market that was complementary to the interbank bond market and operated a two-tier custody system. As compared to the exchange market, commercial banks operating in the OTC market business were required to transmit their balance change data to the CCDC by COB (close of business) each day. Meanwhile, the CCDC provided balance inquiry service for OTC market investors, which offered an important means to protect their rights and interests.

As another complement to the interbank bond market, the FTZ market defined its position as an "offshore market within the territory of China" in an attempt to open Chinese bond market to the outside world. The FTZ market was established to attract foreign investors to invest in the domestic bond market, broaden the channels for offshore RMB funds to flow back to China, and expedite the internationalization of the *renminbi*.

In the bond market, custodian institutions included the CCDC, the CSDC and the SHCH, and a multi-thronged regulation was exercised according to market segments and securities products. The NAFMII of the PBoC exercised the industry self-regulation of the issuance registration of debt financing instruments of non-financial enterprises; the MoF was responsible for regulating treasury bonds, local government bonds and panda bonds, and the National Development and Reform Commission took charge of regulating enterprise bonds, panda bonds, and rail bonds.

The CSRC was responsible for regulating the exchange market, the New Third Board Market, corporate bonds, commercial papers issued by securities companies, convertible bonds, exchangeable bonds, enterprise asset-backed securities and panda bonds, as well as financial bonds and credit asset-backed securities issued by banking financial institutions. The CBIRC was tasked with regulating the fixed-term subordinated bonds and financial bonds issued by insurance companies, and the State Administration of Foreign Exchange (SAFE) was in charge of regulating panda bonds.

In terms of interest payment methods, bonds are categorized into zero-coupon bonds, discount bonds, fixed coupon rate bonds, floating coupon rate bonds, and accrued bond. As regards currencies, bonds are divided into bonds denominated in RMB, foreign currencies and Special Drawing Rights (SDRs)[20] respectively. With respect to tradable or non-tradable nature, bonds are divided into tradable and non-tradable bonds. With regard to issuers, bonds are divided into government bonds (treasury bonds and local government bonds), central bank bills, government-backed agency bonds[21] (rail bonds and central Huijin bonds), corporate debentures, financial bonds, asset-backed securities, panda bonds,[22] interbank negotiable certificates of deposit, and special bonds (green bonds and social impact bonds), etc.

3.4.2 The Active Government Bond Market

As bonds with the highest credit ratings, treasury bonds were mainly issued by the central government via the MoF. From 1949 to 1958, People's Victory Bonds in Kind and National Economic Construction Bonds were major treasury bonds issued by the Chinese government and all of them were completely redeemed in 1965. Following the resumption of treasury bond issuance in 1981, a treasury bond market progressively took shape in China. From 1981 to 1990, treasury bonds were mainly issued through administrative allocation.

Fiscal policy bonds are a type of treasury bonds issued by the MoF. From 1988 to 1993, treasury bonds worth of RMB 36 billion were issued to four major state-owned specialized banks, as well as the BOCOM, the CITIC Industrial Bank, the PICC and urban credit cooperatives in five tranches to raise funds in support of national construction programs. The government allocated quotas to them as planned, and all of them made subscriptions and issuance to fulfill their respective quotas allocated to them by way of one-off issuance and repayment in installments. The bond coupon rate varied from year to year depending on the actual financial situation each year. The PBoC took charge of the issuance of government bonds and the repayment of principal and coupe rate on behalf of the MoF, and the MoF was responsible for

---

[20] In August 2016, the World Bank issued 500 million of RMB-denominated SDR bonds in China's interbank market.

[21] Government–backed agency bonds were issued through the CCDC, traded in the interbank bond market and mainly held in custody by the CCDC.

[22] Panda bonds are RMB-denominated bonds issued by foreign institutions in China. Currently, the issuers are mainly international development agencies and foreign banks.

setting an annual budget to ensure the repayment of principal and coupe rate at maturity.

In 1991, treasury bonds were traded and transferred in 400 prefectures and Tier-1 cities across China, bringing forth a relatively booming OTC market for treasury bonds. In 1992, a small number of certificated treasury bonds were issued. In 1993, a system of primary dealers for dealing in treasury bonds was introduced to change the original pattern of bond issuance through administrative allocation.

In 1994, the government reformed the treasury bond trading and regulation regime. On March 18, 1994, the first batch of treasury bonds was traded on the Shenzhen Stock Exchange. The traded products included the Treasury Bonds of 1991, the 3-Year and 5-Year Treasury Bonds of 1992, and the 3-year and 5-year Treasury Bonds of 1993. In the meantime, a series of reform measures including paperless issuance and tender issuance were adopted, and new bond products such as discount treasury bonds, zero-coupon treasury bonds and coupon treasury bonds were also launched as well, thereby progressively bringing forth a more healthy and sustainable treasury bond market. From 1997 onwards, treasury bonds were basically issued on a certificated, paperless and online basis.

Treasury bonds in China mainly consisted of book-entry treasury bonds, and savings treasury bonds. Among them, book-entry treasury bonds were issued through tender via the CCDC, traded in the interbank bond market and the bond exchange market, and held in custody by the CCDC. Additionally, savings treasury bonds were issued to individual investors via the OTC of commercial banks in the form of certificated savings treasury bonds and electronic savings treasury bonds, of which electronic savings treasury bonds were held in custody by the CCDC.

Tradable products in the treasury bond market included treasury bonds issued in 1981, discount treasury bonds and central bank bills in 1996, central bank bills in 2002, certificated treasury bonds (electronic book-entry) in 2004, savings treasury bonds in 2006, local government bonds in 2009, government-backed agency bonds in 2010, and local government private placement bonds in 2015.

As of the end of 2019, China's treasury bonds had an outstanding balance of RMB16,803,804 million, including a domestic outstanding bond balance of RMB16,603,213 million and a foreign outstanding bond balance of RMB200,591million, with both being controlled within the treasury bond balance cap of RMB17,520,835 million approved by the National People's Congress.[23]

Generally speaking, local Chinese governments had no power to issue bonds. However, huge local government bonds possibly running as high as trillions in RMB came into a spotlight during China's annual "Two Sessions" in 2010. One main reason for a rapid increase in local government bonds was that the Chinese government adopted a loose monetary policy in 2009 in an attempt to stimulate the economy.

---

[23] Liu Kun, *Report on the Central Final Accounting for Revenues and Expenditure* [EB/OL], the 19th Plenary of the Standing Committee of the 13th National People's Congress, June 20, 2020, http://www.npc.gov.cn/npc/c30834/202006/c6b4e1f6afa348dc8ea9e020dd1ebb80.shtml.Accessed on June 30, 2020.

Out of the RMB10 trillion loans newly issued during the whole year, 40–50% were issued through financing platforms which had a local government background.

In reality, financing platforms refer to local investment companies set up by local governments using land or public facilities as capital funds. As the local governments were not allowed to directly apply for loans, they attempted to address such an issue by setting up investment companies for borrowing money from banks or issuing enterprise bonds to finance their infrastructure programs. Altogether, there were at least more than 8,000 companies of this sort in China in history.

As of the end of 2010, local government debts in China had an outstanding balance of RMB10,717,491 million, of which RMB6,710,951 million or 62.62% were debts for which local governments were liable to clear and settle; RMB2,336,974 million or 21.80% were contingent debts for which the local governments were liable to guarantee; and RMB1,669,566 million, or 15.58% were other related debts for which the local government might assume certain bailout liability.

In 2011, heavy local government debts were publicly exposed as a result of the reinforcement of comprehensive audits and the exercise of comprehensive regulation of local government debts. According to a survey report released by the National Audit Office on June 27, 2011, local government debts passed the RMB 10 trillion mark. Additionally, related audit data revealed that local government debts totaled RMB 17.9 trillion at the end of 2013. In 2016, the MoF claimed that the central government would not underwrite local government debts.

Local government bonds were mainly issued by the local governments and they were divided into general obligation bonds and special bonds. Generally speaking, they were issued by the CCDC through tender or private placement, traded in the inter-bank bond market and the bond exchange market, and held in custody by the CCDC.

In March 2019, the MoF allowed local government bonds to be issued through the commercial bank OTC market. Subsequently, local government bonds were issued through the commercial bank OTC market in twelve provinces and prefectures (cities), including Ningbo city and Zhejiang province, with actual subscriptions totaling RMB10,984 million.

According to the statistics data released by the MoF, China's local government debts had an outstanding balance of RMB 22,092.3 billion as of the end of January 2020, including RMB11, 939.7 billion of general obligation debts and RMB10,152.6 billion of special debts; or RMB 21,903.4 billion of government bonds and RMB188.9 billion of government debts in the form of non-government bonds. The average remaining term to maturity of the local government bonds was 5.2 years, of which 4.9 years were for general obligation bonds and 5.6 years were for special bonds. In addition, the average coupe rate was 3.54%.[24]

---

[24] The Budget Department of the Ministry of Finance of the People's Republic of China, On the Issuance and Outstanding balance of Local Government Bonds as of January 2020 [EB / OL], http://yss.mof.gov.cn/zhuantilanmu/dfzgl/sjtj/202002/t20200221_3472494.htm. Accessed on February 29, 2020.

3.4.3 *The Enterprise Bond Market with Diversified Products*

In China's enterprise bond market, bond products in trading were roughly divided into enterprise bonds, corporate bonds, debt financing instruments of non-financial enterprises, convertible corporate bonds, SME private placement bonds, among others.

With the approval of the National Development and Reform Commission, **enterprise bonds** are issued by enterprises to the interbank bond market and the exchange market via the CCDC's issuance system on a unified basis, and traded in the interbank and bond exchange markets, as well as registered with and held in custody by the CCDC. Generally speaking, enterprise bonds included SME joint bonds, project revenue note (PRN), and perpetual bonds.

Enterprise bonds were debuted in China in 1984. Prior to 2007, the enterprise bond market was basically in a fledging stage. In September 2007, China Yangtze Power Co., Ltd. successfully issued its enterprise bond for the first time in the country as a real enterprise bond traded in the bond market.

As of the end of December 2009, 165 enterprise bonds totaling RMB421,433 million were issued in China. In March 2010, the outstanding balance of enterprise bonds reached RMB1,100,088 million, passing the RMB1 trillion mark for the first time.

With the approval of the CSRC and the National Development and Reform Commission, **corporate bonds** are issued by listed companies or unlisted public companies via the CCDC's issuance system for trading in the interbank and bond exchange markets, or transferred through the National Equities Exchange and Quotations system, and held in custody by the CCDC. In March 2016, "entrepreneurship and innovation" corporate bonds were issued on a pilot basis, and the funds raised were mainly channeled to support the technological innovation, product R&D and market expansion of innovative start-ups.

In February 2020, the National Development and Reform Commission made a decision on the adoption of a registration system for the issuance of enterprise bonds in accordance with the newly amended Securities Law, and the CCDC served as enterprise bond registration agency in charge of bond registration for issuance.

Debt financing instruments of non-financial enterprises are registered with the NAFMII for issuance and issued by non-financial enterprises with a legal person status to the interbank bond market for trading, and registered with and held in custody by the SHCH. Non-financial corporate debt-financing instruments mainly included six products, namely commercial paper maturing in less than one year and super and short-term commercial papers at maturity within a period of less than 270 days; medium-term notes with a maturity of more than one year; SME collective notes (SMECN) issued by small and medium-sized non-financial enterprises; private placement notes (PPN); asset-backed notes (ABN) backed by the cash flows generated from the underlying assets of enterprises; and project revenue note (PRN) issued by non-financial enterprises.

Convertible corporate bonds are mainly issued by domestic listed companies for trading in the exchange market, as well as registered with and held in custody by the CSDC, which can be converted into shares as per the agreed terms to maturity within a prescribed time limit ranging from three to five years. Bond with attached warrant, also known as equity warrant bonds (EWBs), are a type of convertible corporate bonds with a minimum maturity of one year, that incorporate warrants which are detachable and may be traded separately from bonds. In 1997, the first batch of RMB 4 billion convertible bonds was issued in the Chinese bond market, and 500 unlisted key state-owned enterprises were selected for the pilot scheme.

SME private placement bonds are privately placed by domestic SMEs to qualified investors for inter-qualified investor transfer in the bond exchange market, and held in custody by the CSDC through registration.

Asset-backed securities are divided into credit asset-backed securities, and corporate asset-backed securities. The former are mainly issued and traded by specialised trust financial institutions (e.g. trust companies) to the interbank bond market or cross-market issued for trading, and are registered and held in custody by the CSDC. In addition, the latter are mainly issued and traded on the exchange market by securities companies, as well as registered and held in custody by the CSDC in the form of collective asset management schemes, where the underlying assets are other assets other than credit assets, and fee-charging rights, etc.

Additionally, there are also **other special enterprise bonds** such as financial enterprise bonds, green bonds, and social impact bonds. Financial bonds are enterprise bonds issued by financial enterprises via the CCDC for trading in the interbank bond market, and held in custody by the CCDC, including policy financial bonds, commercial bank bonds,[25] and non-banking financial bonds.[26] As of 1985, financial bonds were issued to raise funds in support of the relevant national reform policies and the development of infrastructure, pillar industries and primary industries. In 1995, the ICBC and the ABC took the initiative to issue financial bonds in China for the first time.

Green bonds are issued to raise special funds in support of green industry programs, which is divided into labeled green bonds, and unlabeled green bonds. In 2016, Chinese issuers issued RMB238 billion of green bonds at home and abroad, including RMB201,785 million of labeled green bonds issued in the domestic market.

Social impact bonds refer to bonds issued to raise funds for the social public service sector, with a focus on using market-oriented means to address social issues. For example, the Shandong Yinan County Poverty Alleviation Social Impact Bond was registered with the NAFMII in 2006 as China's first social impact bond and it was issued to raise RMB 500 million for local poverty alleviation.

---

[25] Issuers are domestic commercial banks with a legal status. These bonds are divided into general obligation financial bonds, special SME loans bonds, special financial bonds for agriculture, rural areas and rural residents, subordinated bonds, Tier-2 capital instruments and other products.

[26] Issuers are domestic commercial banks with a legal status. These bonds are divided into general obligation financial bonds, special SME loans bonds, special financial bonds for agriculture, rural areas and rural residents, subordinated bonds, Tier-2 capital instruments and other products.

3.5 Price Reform in the Financial Market: Market-Oriented Interest Rate

From 1949 onwards, a primitive dual-track system in which official and market-based interest rates co-existed was in place for a long period. In those days, market-oriented interest rates were relatively higher while official bank interest rates were relatively lower and remained unchanged for ages. From the 1980s onwards, the Chinese government embarked on the reform in the interest rate regime which oriented towards market-based interest rates.

3.5.1 Applying Differentiated Interest Rates on Loans with Differential Loan Terms to Maturity and Floating Interest Rate

China's market-oriented interest rate reform was instituted in the 1980s. In October 1980, the Jinxiang Credit Cooperative of Cangnan County in Wenzhou city of Zhejiang province took the initiative to pilot in floating up the interest rate at 1% per month on large-sum (no less than RMB500) 1-year individual savings deposits, and hiking that at 1.5% on loans to individual businesses or township enterprises and cooperatives with outstanding business performance. In May 1986, the Wenzhou Branch of the Agricultural Bank of China undertook the interest rate pilot reform, which was upscaled across Wenzhou city in September 1987.

China's interest rate reform was rolled out nationwide in 1983, with differential lending rates on loans to different sectors, regions and products with differential repayment periods.

In January 1986, state-owned specialized banks commenced to impose the floating interest rate regime and their head offices were empowered to float their interest rates within the range determined by the PBoC's head office; credit cooperatives were allowed to float up or down deposit and loan interest rates as per the provisions and empowerment of the PBoC. In July 1986, the CCB was mandated to apply differentiated interest rates to the infrastructure construction loans in the sectors of coal, electric power, crude oil exploitation, railway, transportation, posts and telecommunications, civil aviation, iron and steel, nonferrous metals, chemicals, building materials and logging. In January 1987, the PBoC allowed commercial banks to float up the interest rate by up to 20% based on loan prime rate as prescribed by the state.

Generally speaking, the first step in the market-oriented interest rate reform in the 1980s was to adjust deposit and loan interest rates in a progressive and proper manner by applying differentiated interest rates on loan with differential loan terms to maturity and floating interest rate. Nevertheless, bank interest rates were put under stringent control again in the early 1990s. In February 1990, the PBoC stipulated that banks, urban and rural credit cooperatives or other non-banking financial institutions were no longer allowed to float up their deposit and loan interest rates, and the adjustment range of the floating interest rate on loans was narrowed from 30 to 20%. Additionally, the power to float loan interest rate still remained in the hands of the PBoC's head office. The PBoC prescribed that a 50% loan interest rate ceiling was imposed on urban and rural credit cooperatives, and loan projects for floating up loan interest rates were subject to the approval from the branches of the PBoC at or above the county level.

3.5.2 Setting Benchmark Interest Rate and Adjusting Loan Interest Rate

After the 14th National Congress of the Communist Party of China was convened in 1993, the market-oriented interest rate reform was put on the agenda again, aiming to install a market-oriented interest rate regime dictated by money supply and demand in the money market, with the benchmark interest rate set by central bank at the core.

First, the interbank benchmark lending interest rate was determined. In January 1996, the PBoC applied the Chibor interbank lending rate as benchmark interest rate. On June 1, 1996, the interbank lending rates were liberalized to allow lenders and borrowers to determine their lending rates at their discretion in view of money supply and demand in the interbank lending market. This is an important step taken in the reform of market-oriented interest rates.

Second, the interest rate reform of the bond market was initiated. In June 1997, interest rate reform was instituted in the inter-bank bond market to liberalize bond repurchase and spot trading interest rates. In September 1998, the market-oriented interest rates on financial bonds issued by policy banks such as the CDB, EIBC and ADBC were liberalized. In September 1999, tender issuance was successfully applied to the treasury bond interest rate in the interbank bond market.

Third, the rediscount and discount interest rate formation regime was reformed. In March 1998, the PBoC allowed commercial banks to determine their discount rate and transfer discount rate at their discretion provided that their discount rate and transfer discount rate were no more than current loan interest rate. In other words, commercial banks were allowed to determine their discount rate and transfer discount rate by adding basis points to rediscount rate. By liberalizing discount rate and transfer discount rate, rediscount rate was used as an important monetary policy instrument for the PBoC.

Fourth, the floating range of the loan interest rate of financial institutions was increased. In 1998, the PBoC expanded the floating range of the interest rate on the loans granted by financial institutions to small enterprises from 10 to 20%, and it also raised the floating loan interest rate ceiling of rural credit cooperatives from 40 to 50%. In September 1999, financial institutions below the county level were allowed to float up their loan interest rates by up to 30%. The policy of imposing the ceiling of floating up the interest rates on loans to small businesses by 30% was also applied to all medium-sized businesses, while for large enterprises, the ceiling still remained at 10% and the floor was determined at 10%. In April 2003, the methods of interest accrual and settlement in relation to loans denominated in RMB were liberalized to be determined by lenders and borrowers through consultation at their discretion.

In January 2004, the PBoC expanded the floating range of the loan interest rates of financial institutions again. Specifically speaking, the floating loan interest rate floor for commercial banks and urban credit cooperatives remained unchanged at 10%, while the ceiling increased to 70 and 100% respectively. The floating loan interest rate ceiling of rural credit cooperatives grew to twofold and the floor dropped to 0.9-fold. In the meantime, the restrictions on the ownership and size of enterprises imposed on floating loan interest rates since 1999 were lifted. In March 2004, a floating interest rate regime for the PBoC to grant loans to financial institutions was also imposed by adding basis points to its benchmark lending interest rate in a proper manner. In October 2004, the floating interest rate ceiling on loans denominated in RMB granted by financial institutions (excluding urban and rural credit cooperatives) was raised to 2.3 times as much as loan prime rate while the floor remained 0.9 times as much as loan prime rate.

By determining benchmark interest rate and reforming loan interest rate, the market-oriented interest rate reform has made quick headways, thereby installing an interest rate regime dictated by market supply and demand.

3.5.3 Liberalizing Local and Foreign Currency Interest Rates and Applying Benchmark Interest Rate

The second step of the market-oriented interest rate reform was to liberalize foreign currency deposit and loan interest rates by allowing domestic financial institutions to float up and down their deposit interest rates, as well as determining and applying a new benchmark interest rate.

First, the interest rates on foreign currency loans and deposits were liberalized. In September 2000, the PBoC reformed the foreign exchange interest rate regulatory regime and liberalized foreign exchange interest rates, stipulating that financial institutions were allowed to negotiate with their customers to determine the interest rates on large-sum foreign exchange deposits in excess of US$3 million. In March 2002, it reformed the policy of differential foreign exchange interest rate control over Chinese and foreign financial institutions, bringing Chinese residents' small-sum foreign exchange deposits made at domestic and foreign financial institutions under the PBoC's interest rate control on small-sum foreign exchange deposits. As such, Chinese and foreign financial institutions could be treated equally in terms of foreign exchange rate policy.

In June 2003, the PBoC commenced to liberalize the interest rates on small-sum deposits denominated in pound sterling, Swiss Franc and Canadian dollar in China, while imposing interest rate ceiling on small-sum deposits denominated in US dollar, Japanese yen, euro, and Hong Kong dollar. In November 2003, commercial banks were allowed to determine their own interest rates on small-sum foreign currency deposits denominated in US dollar, euro, Japanese yen, and Hong Kong dollar provided that such interest rates did not exceed the interest rate ceiling published by the PBoC. In November 2004, the PBoC liberalized both the interest rate on the aforesaid small-sum foreign currency deposits with a term of more than one year and the interest rate on two-year small-sum foreign currency deposits, and commercial banks were allowed to determine and publish them at their discretion.

Second, deposit and loan interest rates for financial institutions were no longer determined in a uniform manner. The PBoC used policy instruments to directly control the interest rates in the money market, thereby indirectly affecting the deposit and loan interest rates of financial institutions. In March 2005, it decided to completely liberalize the interbank deposit interest rate for financial institutions, substantially lower the interest rate on excess deposit reserves, and allow financial institutions to determine their own methods for accruing and settling the interest rates on deposits other than demand deposits and time deposits of small savings for lump-sum withdrawal. In September 2005, the PBoC conferred commercial banks the power to determine the interest rates on six types of deposits other than time deposits and demand deposits.

By the end of 2005, only a few interest rate products such as the deposit rate ceiling, the loan interest rate floor and the statutory deposit reserve requirement ratio had not undergone the market-oriented interest rate reform process. The market-based interest rate reform has largely achieved the milestone of "controlling loan interest rate floor and deposit interest rate ceiling".

Third, a new benchmark interest rate was launched and applied. In January 2007, the Shanghai Interbank Offered Rate (Shibor) was officially launched as a new benchmark interest rate for the Chinese financial market. As a simple, unsecured and wholesale rate, the Shibor is an arithmetic average rate calculated based on the RMB interbank lending rates independently quoted by a quotation syndicate of banks with high credit ratings. The move is intended to comprehensively launch a new benchmark rate for the Chinese money market and progressively determine the Shibor as the benchmark rate in the money market interest rate system.

In 2007, the market-oriented interest rate reform made breakthrough headways. Through a series of reforms, the power to determine interest rates was progressively handed over to financial institutions, allowing them to adjust the level of interest rates based on their capital adequacy ratio and judgments on the dynamics of the financial market at their discrete. As a result, a market-oriented deposit and loan interest rate formation regime for financial institutions has taken shape, which is dictated by market demand and supply, affected by the money market interest rates, and built on the benchmark interest rates of the PBoC such as Shibor and LPR (Loan Prime Rate).

3.5.4 *Abolishing Interest Rate Control and Applying Market-Oriented Interest Rate*

The ultimate objective of the market-oriented interest rate reform is to lift interest rate control and apply market-oriented interest rates. To that end, the PBoC has adopted the following reform policies.

First, the floating range of loan interest rate was further increased. On June 8, 2012, the PBoC adjusted the floating deposit interest rate ceiling for financial institutions to 1.1 times as much as benchmark interest rate, and the floating loan interest rate floor to a 0.8-folddecrease in loan prime rate. On July 6, 2012, it adjusted the floating loan interest rate floor for financial institutions to a 0.7-fold decrease in loan prime rate, and allowed commercial banks to float down loan interest rate by up to 30% from loan prime rate.

Second, loan interest rate floor were abolished and interest rate control were removed. The PBoC decided to forego lending interest rate floor 0.7 times as much as loan prime rate (LPR) from July 20, 2013 onwards, allowing financial institutions to determine their own lending rates at their discretion; to remove the control on commercial paper discount rates; and to officially operate the centralized quotation and publication mechanism for commercial banks' loan prime rate (LPR), marking that the market-oriented interest rate reform has made great headways.

Third, the deposit interest rate ceiling was abolished. On March 1, 2014, the interest rate ceiling for small-sum foreign currency-demoninated deposits was liberalized in the Shanghai FTZ, and thereby the market-oriented interest rates for foreign currency-demoninated deposits were applied for the first time.

The PBoC adjusted the floating deposit interest rate ceiling for financial institutions from 1.2 times to 1.3 times as much as benchmark interest rate on March 1, 2015, and then to 1.5 times on May 11, 2015. On August 26, 2015, it liberalized the floating interest rate ceiling for time deposits with a term of more than one year (exclusive). From October 24, 2015 onwards, it lowered the benchmark interest rate of deposits and loans denominated in RMB and the statutory deposit reserve requirement ratio of financial institutions, and no longer imposed the floating deposit interest rate ceiling on commercial banks and rural cooperative financial institutions.

As of 2019, the PBoC only imposed the interest rate ceiling on demand deposits and up-to-1-year time deposits (inclusive) equaling to 1.5 times as much as benchmark interest rate. Merely one step from comprehensive interest rate liberalization, it has basically completed its 20-year reform in market-oriented interest rates.

The roadmap for China's market-oriented interest rate reform is to liberalize RMB interest rates following foreign currency interest rate; deposit interest rates following loan interest rate; the *renminbi* following foreign currencies; deposits following loans; short-term and small-sum deposits and loans following long-term and large-sum ones; progressively expand the floating range of interest rate and eventually lift the control over interest rates, thereby establishing a market-oriented interest rate regime based on the Shibor and the LPR. Even after the control over interest rate is lifted, the market-oriented interest rate reform is still underway and it still has a long way to go.

Chapter 4
The Evolution Trajectory of the Central Bank System and Monetary Policies

In the past 70 years from 1949 to 2019, China's central banking system went through distinct stages in the evolutionary trajectory of the financial sector. As the central bank of the country, the PBoC has completed its institutional restructuring into a modern central bank, and it has also established a macro-financial and economic regulatory regime with itself at the core and modern monetary policy as its instrument.

4.1 Evolutionary Trajectory of the Composite Central Bank System

From the 1950s to the 1980s, the Chinese government operated a composite central banking system in which the PBoC was China's largest commercial bank and the state agency for allocating financial resources. Following the national strategy of reform and opening up, the PBoC has undertaken institutional reforms for several times, shifting its role from the sole state bank to a modern central bank that independently performed central bank functions.

4.1.1 The PBoC Founded in Times of China's War of Liberation

On December 1, 1948, while China's War of Liberation still raged on, the People's Government of North China merged the North China Bank with the Peihai Bank and the Northwest Peasant Bank to form the PBoC in Shijiazhuang city, which issued the

Y. Wu, *A Financial History of China (1949–2019)*, Research Series on the Chinese Dream and China's Development Path,
https://doi.org/10.1007/978-981-99-6571-7_4

renminbi for the first time as standard money[1] in circulation across North China, East China and Northwest China. Nan Hanchen was appointed general manager of the PBoC and subsequently he was named the governor of the PBoC in October 1949.

In February 1949, the PBoC, which was founded in times of China's War of Liberation, moved from Shijiazhuang city to Beiping city (today's Beijing city) to take over bureaucratic capital banks and to conduct the banking business. According to the Organic Law of the Central People's Government of the People's Republic of China adopted by the Chinese People's Political Consultative Conference on September 27, 1949, the PBoC functioned as state bank and it was tasked with issuing currencies, managing treasuries on behalf of the MoF, administering financial affairs, stabilizing the financial market order, propping up the economy, and supporting national rehabilitation. In terms of its organizational structure, the PBoC was placed under the administration of the Government Administration Council and the guidance of the Financial and Economic Affairs Committee of the National People's Congress, and it maintained a close working relationship with the MoF. In those days, the PBoC functioned as state bank and the *renminbi* served as legal tender after the founding of the People's Republic of China.

In the early 1950s, the PBoC played a leading role in promoting the recovery of the national economy, and making effort to improve the country's financial and economic situation.

First, it stabilized the financial situation in the country. The PBoC assisted the Chinese government in maintaining financial market stability, involving reining in inflation, overhauling the private financial sector, administering financial activities in a unified manner, and regulating the flow of hot money; as well as cracking down on the black market for trading gold, silver and foreign currencies, revoking the privileges of foreign banks in China, prohibiting the circulation of foreign currencies, and exercising unified foreign exchange control. Additionally, it also actively conducted the deposit and loan, remittance, and foreign exchange business to facilitate the interflow of raw materials and commodities between urban and rural areas, and thereby propped up the economy.

Secondly, it strengthened cash management. In accordance with the Decision on the Performance of Cash Management by State Agencies adopted by the Government Administration Council on April 7, 1950, the PBoC was designated as a state agency for making cash allocation and managing state treasures on the behalf the MoF, and it was mandatory that all the cash of military and government agencies and public enterprises must be deposited with the PBoC. Meanwhile, the PBoC was also mandated to adjust foreign exchange rate and make foreign currency allocation. Through the channels for "pooling deposits, building treasuries and making flexible allocation", the PBoC shall assist the industry and commercial authorities in

---

[1] For information on the development of the People's Bank of China prior to the reform and opening up, please refer to Wu Xiaoling, editor-in-chief, *A Chronology of Major Events in China's Financial Reform and Opening up*, China Financial Publishing House, 2008, pp. 1–15; and the official website of the PBoC for relevant data on the historical development trajectory and chronology of events of the PBoC.

propping up the state-run economy by jointly reforming policies, flexibly allocating funds, and strengthening cash management.

Third, it overhauled the money supply sector. On August 1, 1950, the PBoC held a joint meeting for the Chinese Finance Association to enact unified administrative measures for China's money supply sector. According to the Provisional Regulations of the People's Republic of China on the Control of Gold and Silver promulgated by the Government Administration Council on February 4, 1952, the PBoC served as the competent authority for controlling gold and silver, and the gold and silver trading business shall be conducted by the PBoC or its authorized agencies. Besides, conducts such as the smuggling, trafficking, unlicensed trading of gold and silver, using gold and silver as currency or collateral, and unauthorized gold and silver smelteries were all strictly prohibited.

Fourth, it set out business revenue and expenditure plans and credit fund management measures. In January 1951, the PBoC formulated and promulgated corresponding business revenue and expenditure plan compilation measures and statistics report procedures, and specified the targets, purposes, type, method, and tenure of loans. In April 1951, the PBoC and the Ministry of Internal Trade jointly issued the Joint Instructions on Banning Commercial Credit, stipulating that all internal and external transfers of funds from agencies under the Ministry of Trade must be handled through the PBoC and that the agencies under the Ministry of Trade were not allowed to have debt relationships with any entity.[2]

As of the end of 1952, the PBoC installed a nationwide vertical leadership and organizational structure regime, issued the *renminbi* in a unified manner, banned and exchanged all the old currency issued by the Kuomintang government within a prescribed time limit, and used the *renminbi* as unified legal tender nationwide. Meanwhile, it exercised the unified regulation of financial institutions and their financial business, and resorted to practicable means (e.g. People's Victory Parity Savings based on the price index of certain commodities and the deposit and lending interest rates) to balance money supply and demand. As a result, it has reversed the chaotic situation in the financial market in the early years of the People's Republic of China, and laid the foundation for establishing a national banking system in a planned economy period.

4.1.2 Establishing a Monolithic National Banking System

During the first five-year plan period from 1953 to 1957, the PBoC both served as a currency-issuing and financial-managing agency and a full-fledged commercial banking institution, progressively developing into a state financial hub for lending,

[2] In March 1955, the Block worked together with the MoF as well as the relevant departments to jointly conduct related researches, and they unanimously agreed to abolish commercial credit under the instructions of the State Council.

cash management, transfer and settlement. As such, a monolithic national banking system has taken shape.

First, it developed into the sole state bank which both specialized in monetary management and the banking business such as credit loans, clearing and settlement, wage fund oversight, and cash management. In 1953, the PBoC established a loan plan management regime characterized by unified lending and unified deposit, developed eight settlement methods, controlled foreign exchange, and designated the BOC to operate in the foreign exchange business. In 1955, it issued a new edition of the *renminbi* as well as banned and exchanged for the old edition of the *renminbi* still in circulation. In 1956, the PBoC laid down relevant rules and regulations on national cash management, and worked with the BOC to conduct the foreign currency deposit business in Beijing city, Tianjin city, Shanghai, Guangzhou city, Fuzhou city, Xiamen city, Shantou city and other regions.

Second, it served as state bank in charge of fund management. In the early 1950s, 70% of the working capital quotas for the central industrial authorities were allocated by the MoF and the remaining 30% were borrowed by loans from the PBoC. In 1958, all such working capital was centrally managed by the PBoC. In other words, all working capital originally allocated to enterprises by the MoF were borrowed from the PBoC in the form of loans, with the relevant interest rates being calculated uniformly. The system of the unified management of working capital by the PBoC was designed to balance state financial revenues, credit loans, and raw material and goods supplies, and to manage them in a unified manner. In other words, infrastructure investments and working capital must be managed separately, and working capital must be leveraged for purposes such as the production and distribution of commodities, among other things. It is recommended that funds be allocated and used in a rational and economical manner.

Third, it accumulated working experience in the fiscal and banking reform and oriented towards safeguarding national interests. At the national finance and banking conference held on November 21, 1964, Vice-premier and Finance Minister Xiannian Li proposed ten guidelines on the reform of the financial and banking system, which were referred as state bank's general guidelines in fiscal and financial management.

These ten guidelines included: Separately managing financial revenues and credit funds, prohibiting the use of bank money to finance fiscal expenditures; drawing a clear line between liquid and fixed funds, central and local fiscal revenues, and ownership by the whole people and collective ownership; prohibiting the use of working capital for infrastructure; prohibiting the withholding of profits, illegal apportionment of charges to enterprises, and arbitrary tax cuts, etc., or prohibiting any act that is detrimental to the interests of farmers or to supply and marketing cooperatives and handicraft industry cooperatives; doing year-end stock-taking, and prohibiting the false reporting of inventories and income; perpetuating the system for managing the funds, goods and supplies as prescribed by the state, and prohibiting the misappropriation of funds and materials from enterprises; repaying loans in a planned, guaranteed and timely manner, and prohibiting defaults, arbitrary credit sales, down payments and deposits; establishing a cash management model; adopting a system of recording, calculation and accounting, properly setting up the accounting department, prohibiting accounting without proper book-keeping, and the dissolution of the accounting department; applying a system of prices set by the state, and prohibiting unauthorized price hiking, reduction or skimming; and pressing ahead with the national employment and remuneration plan; prohibiting the arbitrary increase in the number of permanent employees, the exceeding of the state wage limit, and the raising of state minimum remuneration, and other standards and limits on expenditure without authorization.

Fourth, it explored the reform on the national banking system and gave better play the role of the PBoC. In March 1966, the PBoC reformed the procedures for loans and settlement in urban and rural areas, which stipulated that where goods and commodities were directly cross-county, cross-prefecture and cross-province distributed to neighboring regions between urban and rural areas, banks in two neighboring regions between urban and rural areas were required to directly handle the settlement; where loans were granted in regions between urban and rural areas, such urban–rural loans must be repaid to banks located in regions where loans were borrowed; where grass-roots supply and marketing cooperatives supplied agricultural and sideline products to state-owned companies, it was recommended to adopt remittance payment method by sticking to the principles of "delivery and acceptance, making a payment within a prescribed time limit, and banks in charge of oversight".

In July 1970, the MoF held the National Finance and Banking Work Conference to press for the reform on finance and banking. At the conference, a propose was put forward to call for delegating financial revenue and credit loan administrative power and imposing financial revenue and expenditure quotas, infrastructure investment quotas and rural credit loan quotas each year. In September 1972, the MoF convened the National Banking Work Conference to deliberate on the PBoC's independent organizational structure, business operation models and funds.

On November 28, 1977, the State Council decided to officially re-separate the PBoC from the MOF by re-designating the PBoC as a ministerial-level agency directly under the State Council, and restoring its original organizational structure. In this way, the PBoC was conferred the sole power to issue money, and its fundamental polices on issuing money and managing credit loans, wage fund, gold, silver and foreign currencies were carried out. The separation work was completed in December 1977, and the PBoC and the MOF officially commenced to work as separate agencies on January 1, 1978.

The PBoC imposed a national banking regime which was attuned to the business transaction and regulation needs in a planned economy era. In those days, it was a compound central bank which both functioned as state central bank and the largest commercial bank in China. Meanwhile, it made full use of effective instruments such as currency issuance and credit and loan schemes for cash management, and performed the functions of regulating the circulation of currency and exercising financial supervision.

4.1.3 Transforming the National Bank into the Central Bank

In the late 1970s, the PBoC embarked on an exploratory reform of the national banking system, which was progressively transitioned into a central banking system in the 1980s.

First, the PBoC reformed the centralized credit fund management regime. In October 1976, the PBoC commenced to explore the reform of the credit loan management regime. In this regard, it proposed that the power to issue money should rest with central bank which was mandated to comprehensively plan and coordinate the money issuance and credit loan work in a unified manner. Nevertheless, financial revenue funds and credit loan funds must be separately managed.

In view of domestic reform and opening-up situation and economic work requirements at that time, the PBoC reformed the centralized credit loan fund management regime. Xiaoping Deng pointed out that "Economic work is a political task of prime importance, and economic issue is an overriding political issue. Only when banks operate as real banks can we prop up the economy".[3]Through power delegation, the PBoC actually granted banks and enterprises at all level a certain degree of autonomy in their leveraging funds.

Second, the PBoC imposed the regime for carrying out hierarchical and centralized fund management by the competent authorities. The roles of the PBoC and the MoF in managing funds were clearly defined respectively. Specifically speaking, long-term funds, grants, and funds on quota fell within the purview of the MoF while short-term funds, loans and over-quota funds were under the management of the PBoC. For instance, the PBoC granted over-quota working capital loans and seasonal loans to state-owned enterprises, certain loans for working capital in manufacturing granted to collective enterprises, the self-employed, and private enterprises in urban and rural areas, as well as production loans, grain ration loans and other subsistence loans to poor peasants in rural areas. The regime for carrying out hierarchical and centralized fund management by the competent authorities was imposed from the 1970s to the 1980s and it retained framework pattern regardless of piecemeal reforms therein.

Third, the PBoC was mandated to maintain the stability of the financial market order and grant policy loans. In January 1980, the PBoC was mandated to safeguard the monolithic *renminbi* market and preserve financial market order.[4] Meanwhile, it granted policy loans to enterprises in line with the government's economic development policies in different historical periods. In response to the State's calling for developing the light industry and the textile industry in January 1980, the PBoC worked with the BOC to jointly grant short and medium-term special loans to the light industry and the textile industry, and foreign exchange loans to purchasers, which were mainly earmarked for fixed asset investments

[3] Xiaoping Deng: *Selected Works of Xiaoping Deng*, Vol. 2, People's Publishing House, 1994, pp. 194, 199–200.

[4] The People's Bank of China and the CCCPC Party Literature Research Office (eds): *Selected Literature on the Financial Work (1978–2005)*, China Finance Publishing House, 2007, pp. 10–14.

such as adaptive-reusing, refurbishing, and renovating old factories, as well as the rehabilitation and extension work related to old factories.

Fourth, the PBoC separated its commercial banking business and performed central banking functions. In July 1982, the State Council endorsed and forwarded the Request for Instructions on the Central Bank Functions of the People's Bank of China and its Relationships with Specialized Banks, effecting its transition from a national bank to a central bank. In January 1983, the CCB and the ABC were designated as financial institutions directly under the State Council while they conducted the financial business under the leadership of the PBoC.

On September 17, 1983, the State Council issued the Decision on the Performance of Central Banking Functions by the People's Bank of China, which conferred central bank status on the PBoC, and mandated it to separate its commercial banking business while establishing a financial system with specialized banks as the mainstay.[5]

In January 1984, the newly established ICBC took over the industrial and commercial credit loan and savings business previously handled by the PBoC, and thereafter the PBoC ceased to handle the credit loan business for enterprises and individuals. As a result, a national bank system has transitioned to a central banking system and the PBoC has developed into a modern central bank in a new era. As a state agency directly under the State Council in charge of administering state financial affairs, the PBoC specialized in properly studying and making macroeconomic decisions, strengthening the management of credit loan funds, and maintaining monetary stability. Meanwhile, it also established the Board of Governors as its decision-making body.

4.2 Reform and Optimization of the Central Bank System

From 1984 to 1993, the PBoC commenced to perform the functions of central bank by persistently reforming and optimizing its central banking system and management regime, so as to better perform its central bank functions.

4.2.1 Establishing the Basic Framework of the Central Bank System

First, the Chinese government defined the pivotal roles of the PBoC, involving issuing money, managing state treasuries on behalf of the MoF, and regulating the circulation of RMB; laying down the strategic plans for the reform and development of the financial sector, related laws and regulations, and monetary policies; formulating and implementing RMB exchange rate policies, managing and operating

[5] The People's Bank of China and the CCCPC Party Literature Research Office (eds): *Selected Literature on Financial Work (1978–2005)*, China Finance Publishing House, 2007, pp. 30–32.

state foreign currency and gold reserves; serving as lender of last resort, regulating the national financial market; and attending and supporting relevant international financial events on behalf of the Chinese government.

Second, the Chinese government reformed the credit fund management regime and established a national macro-regulation regime. In July 1979, the PBoC decided to switch from a credit fund management regime of "unified collection and allocation" to a regime of "unified planning, hierarchical management, deposit-pegged lending and deposit- loan gap control".[6] The regime was imposed on a trial basis by the PBoC's branches in regions such as Shanghai, Jiangsu province, Fujian province, Hubei province, Tianjin city and Shaanxi province at first, and then nationwide in February 1980.

In February 1981, the PBoC imposed the quota on deposit-loan gap to exercise deposit-loan gap control, and it required its branches to implement the year-end deposit-loan gap (excess of deposits over loans) plan and the mid-year minimum deposit plan; and strictly stick to the year-end loan-deposit gap (excess of loans over deposits) plan, the mid-year maximum loan-deposit gap plan, or the general short- and medium-term loan plan. Excess funds within the head office's approved deposit-loan gap quota plan may be borrowed or lent between provincial branches.

In January 1985, the PBoC further reformed the credit loan deposit-loan gap control regime, and imposed the regime of "unified planning, allocation of funds, borrowing and lending, and mutual financing".[7] Under the newly installed regulatory regime, the deposits and loans of specialized banks were all incorporated in the national comprehensive credit loan plan, and specialized banks were required to formulate their annual credit loan plans which were then balanced and compiled by the PBoC into the national comprehensive credit loan plan. With the approval from the central government, the PBoC was mandated to ratify the credit loan plans of specialized banks based on the national comprehensive credit loan plan and then forward them to specialized banks for allocation and implementation.

In 1987, the PBoC imposed a four-tier management regime for credit loan plans, including the credit loan plan of the PBoC, the credit loan plans of state-owned specialized banks, the credit loan plans of non-banking institutions (e.g. non-banking institutions with ownership by the whole people and urban and rural credit cooperatives), and the national comprehensive credit loan plan consolidating the three above plans.[8]

In March 1988, the PBoC established a financial macro-regulation regime for controlling credit loan quotas by deepening the reform of the credit loan fund management regime. Specifically speaking, credit loan quotas, structure of credit funds and amount of money issued were set out in the national comprehensive credit loan plan.

[6] Wu Xiaoling (ed): *A Chronicle of Major Events in China's Financial Reform and Opening up*, China Finance Publishing House, 2008, p. 19.

[7] Wu Xiaoling (ed): *A Chronicle of Major Events in China's Financial Reform and Opening up*, China Finance Publishing House, 2008, pp. 85–86.

[8] Wu Xiaoling (ed): *A Chronicle of Major Events in China's Financial Reform and Opening up*, China Finance Publishing House, 2008, pp. 123–124.

It is noted that the credit loan plan of the PBoC were crucial to achieving macro-regulation targets, while the credit loans plans of specialized banks and non-banking financial institutions played an important role in macro-regulation and micro-funding operations.

In June 1988, the PBoC laid down the general guidelines for managing credit funds, that is controlling the amount of credit loan funds, adjusting the structure of credit loan funds, and regulating credit loan quotas; implementing a policy of "deposit-pegged lending" (other than CCB's working capital loans); properly regulating base currency and central bank loans; the total amount of financial bonds issued nationwide was determined by the PBoC in line with the national comprehensive credit loan plan, and all the funds raised must be channelled to grant special loans.

Under the centralized credit fund management regime of the PBoC, specialized banks and financial institutions were required to turn over the following proportion of deposits to the PBoC: 20% for deposits from enterprises, 40% for savings deposits, and 25% for deposits in rural areas (including transfer deposits of rural credit cooperatives). Additionally, deposits turned over by specialized banks were adjusted on a ten-day basis and that of the sub-county branches of the ABC on a monthly basis.

Third, the PBoC and the MoF coordinated to perform financial regulatory functions. Specially speaking, the PBoC was in charge of administering the establishment, disbanding or mergering of financial institutions, managing the funds, foreign debts, foreign currencies, money, commercial papers and other financial products of enterprises, as well as overseeing the credit standing of enterprises. Additionally, the MoF was mandated to administer its registered specialized banks, insurance companies and other financial institutions. In July 1988, the MoF ordered specialized banks to establish a bad debt reserve system. Meanwhile, the PBoC was mandated to oversee and inspect specialized banks, cooperatives and other non-banking financial institutions, as well as manage their assets and liabilities, and urge them to establish a bad debt reserve system for ensuring the solvency of financial institutions.

Fourth, the Chineset government explored and optimized macro-regulation models. In addition to regulating the amount of credit loan funds, the PBoC also used other means such as interest rates, the deposit reserve requirement ratio, central bank lending and rediscount to control credit loans and money supply, thereby increasing its economic macro-regulation capability. Nevertheless, since its roadmap remained to allocate funds by way of credit loan quota control and implement monetary policy, the PBoC was far from being a central bank which was discharged with legal mandates for exercising financial regulation. In reality, it was merely in charge of general administration and inspection, e.g., approving and administering the establishment and business scope of financial institutions, conducting special on-site inspection, and meting out administrative punishments.

In March 1991, the PBoC decided to establish a prospect survey system for 5,000 industrial enterprises to keep abreast of the relevant data on industrial production, operation, and demand and supply of funds, as well as the dynamics of microeconomic entities. In the end, it was capable of providing accurate and timely data available for formulating effective monetary and credit loan policies, and regulating economic operations.

4.2.2 *Establishing a Regulated Central Bank System*

From 1993 onwards, the central banking system of the PBoC has been constantly reinforced and regulated through financial system reforms.

First, the roles and powers of the PBoC were further defined. Following the reform of the financial system in 1993, the PBoC became a central bank for exercising the macro-economic regulation of credit loan quotas and money supply, and administering all types of financial institutions (e.g. financial regulation, supervision and services) in a unified manner, and thereafter it no longer carried on the policy and commercial business.[9] The power to adjust loan quota was concentrated in the hands of the head office of the PBoC, and the power of the PBoC's provincial branches to adjust 7% of loan quota was revoked. By formulating and implementing unified national monetary policy, the PBoC could control money supply, ensure the security of the financial system, maintain monetary stability, and promote a healthy economic growth.

According to the Law on the Peoples Bank of China adopted for implementation in 1995, the PBoC was accorded the status of China's central bank under the new legislation for the first time, marking the establishment of a law-based and regulated central bank system in the country.

Second, macro-economic regulation was imposed through indirect means. In compliance with the policy requirements associated with the reform of the financial system imposed in 1995, the PBoC set up the Monetary Policy Committee in 1997, which was mandated to formulate and implement the monetary policy independently under a separate operation system. Meanwhile, the Monetary Policy Committee also used major policy instruments such as statutory deposit reserves, central bank loan prime rate, open market operations and exchange rate policy to indirectly regulate money supply, thereby maintaining monetary stability.

In terms of exchange rate policies, the PBoC intervened in the foreign exchange market through open market operations in foreign exchange following the reform of China's unification of exchange rates in January 1994. Due to controls on capital account transactions and interest rates, and autonomy in monetary policy operations, there was a lack of correlation between China's RMB policy and exchange rate policy. Therefore, the PBoC was only allowed to purchase large amounts of foreign currencies to maintain exchange rate stability in the event of a persistent oversupply of foreign currencies in the foreign exchange market. Meanwhile, it was mandated to hedge base currency injected as a result of foreign currency purchase by way of recovering its loans granted to financial institutions, controlling the amount of loans

---

[9] The People's Bank of China and the CCCPC Party Literature Research Office (eds): *Selected Literature on Financial Work (1978–2005)*, China Finance Publishing House, 2007, pp. 196–203.

granted by financial institutions, and increasing the limits on the liquidity position of designated foreign exchange banks.

Third, the reform for the deposit reserve system was carried out. In 1998, the PBoC comprehensively carried out the reform of the deposit reserve system. Specifically speaking, the PBoC consolidated "deposit account" and "reserve account" of financial institutions into "reserve deposit account"; it lowered the statutory reserve requirement ratio from 13 to 8% (excess deposit reserves were determined by financial institutions at their discretion); and it assessed the statutory deposit reserves of financial institution by legal entity on a ten-day basis. Where the statutory deposit reserves of financial institutions deposited with the PBoC by legal entity on a unified basis were less than 8% of the outstanding deposit balance at the end of the last one third of month, the shortfall was liable to damages of 0.06%, and penalties were imposed for overdraft on "reserve deposit account" and failure to submit relevant financial statements as required; the interest rate on reserve deposits of financial institutions was lowered to 5.22 from 7.56% for paid-in general deposits and 7.02% for reserve deposits (weighted average of 7.35%) in a unified manner; categories of deposit of financial institutions were redefined, and financial institutions were required to deposit a prescribed portion of their general deposits with the PBoC as statutory deposit reserves, etc.

Fourth, the roles of the PBoC in exercising macro-regulation as well as preventing and controlling systemic financial risks were consolidated. The Law on the People's Bank of China (Amendment) was adopted in December 2003 and it re-defined the roles of the PBoC in formulating and implementing monetary policy, shifting from its direct regulatory role (e.g. approving the establishment and business scope of financial institutions, assessing the qualifications of senior management and supervising and guiding them in their performance of duties and functions) to risk assessment of the financial sector, financial holding companies and hybrid financial instruments, with a view to preventing and mitigating systemic financial risks and maintaining national economic and financial security.

4.2.3 Reforming the Management Regime of the PBoC

In 1998, the PBoC commenced to reform its internal management regime by upholding the spirit of the National Working Conference on Finance held in 1997.

First, the PBoC's provincial branches were dissolved and newly established and their roles were redefined. From October to December 1998, the PBoC disbanded 31 provincial branches, and it newly established 9 branches in cities such as Tianjin, Shenyang, Shanghai, Nanjing, Jinan, Wuhan, Guangzhou, Chengdu and Xi'an as dispatched offices to perform central banking functions in different regions.

Additionally, it also set up two business departments in the cities of Beijing and Chongqing to conduct corresponding business.[10]

Second, the Party Committee of the PBoC was set up. In December 1998, the PBoC decided to exercise the vertical leadership of the Party Committee and the vertical management of cadres in the financial sector according to the Circular of the Central Committee of the Communist Party of China on Issues Relating to Improving the Leadership System of the Party in the Financial System and Strengthening and Improving the Work of the Party in the Financial System.[11] As the central bank of the country, the PBoC must establish and improve the Party leadership system to better leverage the institutional advantages of central bank, perform its central banking functions and duties according to the law, and devote itself to safeguarding China's economic and financial security, and propping up the economy.

Third, the organizational structure and the regulatory roles of the Monetary Policy Committee were reformed and redefined respectively. In March 2000, the State Council reformed the organizational structure of the Monetary Policy Committee of the PBoC by appointing chairman, vice-chairman and 10 commissioners and then 14 commissioners afterwards, and the Monetary Policy Committee was mandated to hold a meeting four times each year. During the institutional reform of the State Council in 2003, the CBRC was newly established to take over the PBoC's regulatory functions and duties towards banking financial institutions. In August 2005, the PBoC's Shanghai Head Office was approved for establishment and the Monetary Policy Bureau II was set up to perform the functions of preventing anti-money laundering and regulating the credit reference industry, and to promote the building of a social credit system.

4.3 Main Instruments and Target System of Monetary Policies

When performing central bank functions, central bank leveraged policy instruments to achieve the ultimate goal of successfully exercising macro-regulation and maintaining financial stability.[12] In practice, the PBoC had both conventional and innovative instruments available at its disposal.

[10] Wu Xiaoling (ed): *A Chronicle of Major Events in China's Financial Reform and Opening up*, China Finance Publishing House, 2008, p. 471 and p. 475.

[11] The constituents of the financial system hereby mentioned refers to the PBoC, the CSRC, the CIRC, policy banks, state-owned commercial banks, state-owned commercial insurance companies, BOCOM, etc.

[12] This section mainly makes reference to the official PBoC website for relevant monetary policy literature and documents.

4.3.1 The Monetary Policy System and Targets

Monetary policy is a generic term referring to various instruments that state central bank has available to achieve its specific economic objectives by controlling and regulating money supply or credit loan quota. Monetary policy is a broad concept that includes a range of elements and components such as ultimate goal, monetary policy instruments, monetary policy intermediate targets, and monetary policy effectiveness. As an important part of the country's macroeconomic policies, it is central to central bank's fulfillment of its major functions.

As necessitated by macroeconomic development, monetary policy mainly aims to achieve price stability (monetary stability), economic growth, full employment, and international balance of payments (financial market stability, interest rate stability and foreign exchange market stability). Internationally prevailing monetary policy instruments included open market operations, discount window policies, and adjustments to the statutory reserve requirement ratio. Nevertheless, each country leverages instruments in a different manner, with some focusing on quantity-oriented targets while others concentrating on price-oriented targets.

In 1995, the ultimate goal of monetary policy was established by the PBoC to maintain monetary stability and thereby promote economic growth. Meanwhile, money supply, aggregate financing to the real economy (total social financing), China interbank offered rate and the deposit reserve requirement ratio were used as intermediary and operational targets for monetary policy.

The instruments leveraged by the PBoC to carry out monetary policy included open market operations, the statutory reserve requirement ratio, the rediscount rate, central bank lending, central bank foreign exchange operations, credit loan quotas, central bank deposit and loan benchmark interest rates, etc. By taking stock of the macroeconomic situation, the PBoC would flexibly choose and apply the above policy instruments to regulate money supply. Meanwhile, it may adopt innovative monetary policy instruments to effectively exercise macroeconomic regulation in the light of the changing dynamics of the economic and financial system in a new era.

In the midst ongoing economic downturn and the transition from old to new growth incentives, challenges to its macro-regulation capabilities faced the PBoC. How to stimulate demand and promote economic growth? How to allocate limited financial resources in a rational and appropriate manner? And how to control money supply, maintain monetary stability and rectify the financial market order? In particular, a major task for which there is no standard answer is how to maximize financial efficiency while preventing financial risks.

4.3.2 Conventional Monetary Policy Instruments

As compared to its foreign counterparts, the PBoC also had conventional monetary instruments available for use (e.g. statutory deposit reserve ratio policy, rediscount policy, and open market operations). Additionally, some special monetary policy instruments were also available for the PBoC to perform its functions as central bank. These special instruments included interest rates, consumer credit ratings, margin level control and other indirect methods, as well as bank credit loan quota control and central bank lending, among others.

First, the statutory deposit reserve system was established. This prime conventional monetary instrument allowed the PBoC to regulate the credit fund supply capacity of financial institutions by adjusting the statutory reserve requirement ratio and thereby indirectly control money supply.

As early as 1984, the PBoC fixed the statutory reserve requirement ratios by type of deposit as follows: 20% for corporate deposits, 25% for rural deposits, and 40% for savings deposits. All these ratios were uniformly adjusted to 10% in 1985 and then 12% and 13% in 1987 and 1988 respectively which remained at the same levels for 10 years.

During the PBoC's reform of the deposit reserve system in March 1998, the statutory reserve requirement ratio was lowered from 13 to 8%. In 1999, it was reduced to 6%. In September 2003, the statutory reserve requirement ratio was unified at 7%. On April 25, 2004, domestic financial institutions commenced to operate a differential deposit reserve requirement ratio system, which stipulated that where financial institutions had the capital adequacy ratio of less than 4%, their reserve requirement ratio was increased by 0.5–7.5%; where the capital adequacy ratio was not less than 4%, their reserve requirement ratio remained at 7% while that of urban and rural credit cooperatives remained at 6%. On January 15, 2005, the foreign exchange reserve requirement ratio for financial institutions was adjusted to 3% in a unified manner.

In June 2006, the PBoC commenced to progressively increase the statutory reserve requirement ratio by a range of 0.5 and 1%, hitting 17.5% in June 2008. From September 2008 to December 2008, the statutory deposit reserve requirement ratio was lowered for several times by 4% in aggregate, down to 13.5%. From 2010 to June 2011, it was raised as many as 12 times, up to 21.5%. From November 30, 2011 onwards, the statutory reserve requirement ratio was lowered for seven consecutive years, with a minimum ratio of 9.5% for large financial institutions and 9% for small and medium-sized financial institutions. As of June 2018, it was increased to 15.5% for large financial institutions and 13.5% for small and medium-sized financial institutions.

By analyzing the above data for adjusting the statutory reserve requirement ratio, we can learn that the PBoC used to apply the statutory reserve requirement ratio as a monetary policy instrument.

Second, the rediscount policy was implemented. Discount is the act of central bank discounting outstanding discounted commercial drafts held by financial institutions. By pursuing the rediscount policy, the PBoC could regulate the total amount of rediscounting commercial drafts and related interest rates in a timely manner to control base money and exercise financial macro-regulation.

To address the serious default problem among enterprises in their business operations, the PBoC decided to conduct the rediscount business for specialized banks in ten cities including Beijing and Shanghai on a trial basis in 1986. It is the first time that the PBoC has resorted to rediscount since it independently performed its central banking functions.

With a view to coping with the issues of payment defaults and cash shortage of enterprises in some key industries, as well as the hampered distribution and sales of some agricultural and sideline products, the PBoC allocated rediscount quotas totaling RMB10 billion for the coal, electric power, metallurgy, chemical, railway, cotton, pig, sugar and tobacco sectors to promote the commercial paper business in the above sectors in the second half of 1994. As an alternative monetary policy instrument, rediscount played a positive role in supporting key industrial and agricultural production sectors.

As of the end of 1995, the PBoC regulated the rediscount business, incorporated the rediscount business into the monetary policy instrument system, attached importance to monetary policy signals transmitted for the rediscount business, and initially established a rediscounting business system. To be attuned to the needs of financial macro-regulation and structural adjustment, it also published prioritized industries, enterprises and product catalogues for the rediscounting business from time to time.

From 1998 onwards, the PBoC introduced a series of policies to enhance the management of commercial drafts and rediscount operations, and reform the rediscount and discount rate formation mechanism, making rediscount rate an independent benchmark interest rate of central bank and bringing into play effective rediscount monetary policy. Thereafter, it continued to expand rediscount business operations and services by leveraging rediscount as a policy instrument to alleviate the short-term financial crunch of some small and medium-sized financial institutions. Actually, it allowed enterprises with good credit standing to rediscount their issued commercial acceptance bills. It is worth mentioning that it also extended maturity from four months to six months.

In the aftermath of the financial crisis in 2008, the PBoC further reformed rediscount policies. Firstly, it reasonably increased the number of sub-licensed rediscount windows to facilitate the application for conducting the rediscount business filed by financial institutions, especially local small and medium-sized financial institutions. Secondly, it rationally expanded rediscount business operations and provided rediscount services for more financial institutions. Specifically speaking, urban and rural credit cooperatives, foreign depository institutions with a legal person status, newly established rural depository financial institutions, and financial companies affiliated to enterprise groups were all eligible for applying for conducting the rediscount business. Thirdly, it encouraged the use of commercial acceptance bills and commercial credit notes. By prioritizing rediscount bills and targeted financial institutions, priority was given to rediscounting agricultural-related bills, and bills issued, accepted and held by county-level enterprises and financial institutions as well as small and medium-sized financial institutions. Finally, it allowed to conduct the rediscount business in the form of pledged repo and outright repo to improve efficiency..

Third, central bank lending instrument was leveraged. Central bank lending means that central bank grants loans to financial institutions to regulate base currency.

By properly regulating the amount of its loans granted to financial institutions and related interest rates, central bank could regulate base currency, manage to achieve the targets of controlling money supply and credit loans, and properly regulate the flow of funds and credit loans.

From 1984 onwards, central bank lending was used by the PBoC as an important monetary policy instrument. In recent years, the amount of loans of the PBoC granted to financial institutions has diminished as a proportion of base currency while there has been a marked shift in its structure and targeted financial institutions. It is learned that loans have been newly granted to facilitate the adjustment of credit loan structure and guide an increase in credit loan supplies for counties as well as for agriculture, rural areas and rural peasants.

Fourth, open market operation transactions were conducted. The PBoC conducted opened market operation transactions in both RMB and foreign exchange. Open market operations in foreign exchange were launched in March 1994, while open market operations in RMB commenced in 1996 yet were discontinued in 1997 due to too low trading volume, and they resumed in May 1998. Meanwhile, it established a primary dealer system for open market operations by selecting a group of commercial banks capable of handling large-sum bond transactions to act as its trading counterparties for open market operations, and designating the CCDC to provide business and technical support for open market operations. Therefore, transaction volume has progressively increased therefrom.

From 1999 onwards, open market operation was used as an important instrument for the routine operation of the PBoC's monetary policy, and it played a positive role in regulating money supply, the liquidity position of commercial banks, and the interest rates of the money supply market.

In terms of transaction types, bond transactions in PBoC's open market operations mainly involved repo transactions, spot transactions and issuance of central bank bills.

In recent years, the primary dealer system for open market operations has been continuously reformed and optimized by successively establishing related management systems (e.g. the primary dealer assessment and regulation system and information reporting system), and extending the choice of primary dealers from commercial banks to other financial institutions (e.g. securities companies). As of the end of 2018, there were a total of 48 financial institutions selected as primary dealers in open market operations.

Fifth, the interest rate policy was implemented. The PBoC has been optimizing the market-oriented interest rate formation mechanism through the reform in market-oriented interest rate. Additionally, it regulated money supply by adjusting the benchmark deposit and loan interest rates for financial institutions, implementing a flexible interest rate policy, and controlling the costs of the lending market. In March 1998, the PBoC was approved to lower the deposit and loan interest rates for financial institution, with the annual deposit interest rate going down by 0.16%, and the annual loan interest rate dropping by 0.6% on average.

In October 2004, the PBoC decided to raise the deposit and loan benchmark interest rates for financial institutions, abolish the ceiling of loan interest rates for financial institutions, raise the ceiling of floating loan interest rates for urban and rural credit cooperatives to 2.3 times as much as loan prime rate, and establish a system for floating down RMB deposit interest rates. From November 18, 2004 onwards, it raised the interest rate ceiling on small-sum foreign currency deposits denominated in USD. In the meantime, the PBoC would no longer publish the interest rates for 2-year small-sum foreign currency deposits denominated in US dollars, Euro, Japanese yen and Hong Kong dollar. Instead, commercial banks were granted the autonomy in determining the rates of this sort.

In the aftermath of the financial crisis in 2008, the PBoC adjusted the interest rate floor on individual commercial housing loans to 0.7 times as much as loan prime rate; and lowered the benchmark interest rate for the 1-year RMB-denominated deposits of financial institutions from 3.87 to 3.60%, and the loan prime rate for 1-year loans from 6.93 to 6.66%, while it also adjusted the loan prime rate for other kinds of loans accordingly. Meanwhile, it also lowered the benchmark interest rate for the deposits of financial institutions by reducing the benchmark interest rate for demand deposits from 0.72 to 0.36%, and adjusting the interest rates for other kinds of deposits accordingly. On June 28, 2015, the PBoC re-lowered the benchmark interest rates for RMB loans and deposits of financial institutions. Specifically speaking, it reduced the loan prime rate for 1-year loans to financial institutions by 0.25–4.85%, and the benchmark interest rates for 1-year deposits by 0.25–2%. Meanwhile, it also adjusted the benchmark interest rates for other kinds of loans and deposits, and the interest rates for individual housing provident **fund** deposits and loans accordingly.

4.3.3 Innovative Monetary Policy Instruments

With a view to catering for the actual needs of money supply regulation, the PBoC has been innovating monetary policy instruments in recent years.

First, it innovated short-term liquidity operation instrument. In January 2013, the PBOC innovated short term liquidity operations (SLO) as a necessary supplement to open market operations by building on the existing monetary policy operating framework and drawing on international experience. Generally speaking, it may use SLO at its discretion when temporary fluctuations in liquidity occur. This instrument helped the PBoC to properly regulate short-term money supply in the market, control the rapid fluctuations in money supply and demand arising from emergencies, contingencies or other unexpected swings, promote the smooth operation of the financial market, keep financial market expectations well anchored, and effectively prevent financial risks.

Second, it innovated standing lending facility. By drawing on international experience, the PBoC innovated standing lending facility (SLF) in early 2013, with a maturity of 1 month to 3 months. SLF is mainly used to meet the long-term demand for high liquidity of financial institutions such as policy banks and state-owned commercial banks. The interest rate of SLF is determined to be attuned to the needs of monetary policy regulation and market-oriented interest rate regulation.

SLF is issued on a collateral basis, with eligible collaterals including highly credit-rated bond assets and high-quality credit assets, etc. Besides, it means "one-to-one" transactions between central bank and counterparties referring to a wide array of financial institutions including depository financial institutions.

In order to cater to the temporary liquidity needs of financial institutions, the PBOC launched a total of RMB 61.03 billion in SLF for financial institutions in June 2018, of which RMB 28.88 billion was for SLF with a maturity of 7 days and RMB 32.15 billion was for SLF with a maturity of one month. In terms of policy effectiveness, the interest rate of SLF functions as the upper limit of China's interest rate corridor, which is conducive to maintaining the stability of interest rates in the money market.

Third, it innovated medium-term lending facility. In September 2014, the PBoC innovated medium term lending facility (MLF), a monetary policy instrument for central bank to lend medium-term base currency to commercial banks and policy banks that meet prudential macroeconomic regulation requirements on a tender basis.

MLF is issued on a collateral basis. In other words, financial institutions pledge high-quality bonds such as treasury bonds, central bank bills, policy financial bonds and highly-rated credit bonds as eligible collaterals, and the PBoC gives full play to the medium-term policy interest rate. By controlling the medium-term financing costs of financial institutions to prop up their balance sheets and influence market expectations, the PBoC motivates financial institutions to lend low-cost funds to the real economy pursuing state policies, and thereby reduces the costs for total social financing. In order to maintain the overall smooth and moderate liquidity of the banking system and to increase the money supply and credit loan quotas reasonably, the PBoC must continuously innovate and optimize its product portfolio in view of market liquidity and enhance targeted regulation in a more flexible and effective manner.

Fourth, it innovated credit asset-pledged relending instrument. From October 2015 onwards, the PBoC continued to pilot the credit asset-pledged central bank lending program in 11 provinces (cities) including Shanghai and Jiangsu province. Specifically speaking, the PBoC assigned its internal rating of 3,022 eligible local financial institutions with a legal person status in the pilot regions, and included their eligible credit assets in the scope of eligible collateral acceptable for the PBoC to grant central bank loans. In this way, the PBoC helped to address the relative lack of high-grade bond collaterals from local financial institutions with a legal person status and facilitated the provision of liquidity support by central bank to local financial institutions with a legal person status.

As of the end of 2015, the PBoC's branches in the pilot regions granted credit policy support loans of RMB 4,973 million to 31 local financial institutions with a legal person status by way of credit asset pledge, and guided them to grant loans to the key state economic sectors and underdeveloped sectors (e.g. agriculture, rural areas, rural peasants, and micro and small enterprises). In this way, it has diminished social financing costs, and propped up the real economy. From 2016 onwards, the PBoC continued to implement a sound prudential money supply regulation policy, and steadily push forward with the credit asset-pledged central bank lending pilot program.

Fifth, it innovated pledged supplementary lending instrument. In April 2014, the PBoC innovated pledged supplementary lending instrument (PSL) to finance the rehabilitation of urban slums. As a long-term stable source of funds with reasonable costs, PSL offers large-sum financing with relatively longer maturities to financial institutions mainly in support of the development of the key sectors, underdeveloped sectors and social undertakings. PSL is issued in a collateral manner, and eligible collaterals for PSL include high-grade bond assets and high-quality credit assets.

As of July 2018, the PBoC granted PSL loans of RMB 30.3 billion to three banks, namely the CDB, the Export–Import Bank and the ADBC, with the outstanding balance of PSL hitting RMB 3,215.5 billion in late July.

4.4 Theory and Practice on the PBoC's Independence

It was not until 1983 that the PBoC was far from a central bank in a real sense and therefore it is nonsense to explore the PBoC's independence. From 1984 to 1994, the PBoC functioned as central bank and differed from state-owned specialized banks in organizational structure. With the promulgation of the People's Bank of China Law in 1995 and its revision in 2003, as well as initiation of a series of financial system reforms, the issue of PBoC's independence gradually came to the fore, prompting many scholars to analyze and explore this issue from the perspectives of jurisprudence and institutional economics.

In this regard, we need to address the following thorny issues such as How to examine the independence of the central bank in theory? How does the PBoC practice its central bank independence? And what legal and institutional safeguards are in place?

4.4.1 Independence of the Central Bank and Its Characteristics

The issue of central bank independence was explored as early as the 19th century. In 1824, the economist David Ricardo argued: "It is said that Government could not be safely entrusted with the power of issuing paper money; that it would most certainly abuse it…There would, I confess, be great danger of this, if Government-that is to say, the ministers–were themselves to be entrusted with the power of issuing paper money. In 1913, Keynes assumed that the goals of policy should be set by the government, not by the central bank itself; and the central bank must regularly demonstrate that it is appropriately pursuing its mandated goals. Additionally, the independence accorded to central banks for the making of monetary policy should not be presumed to extend without qualification to its non-monetary functions. Nevertheless, both David Ricardo and Keynes did not expound on how to regulate the degree of central bank's dependence from the government.

The independence of central banks was in the spotlights in the 1920s and then interrupted by the war, yet the issue of central bank independence re-gained attention in the 1970s. In the face of the financial crisis arising in 2008, central banks delivered different financial performances and whereupon the effectiveness and independence of central bank monetary policy were extensively and thoroughly explored among the financial sector and academia.

Independence of central banks refers to the relative independence of central banks from the government in its operations, i.e. the central banks is placed alongside the legislature, administrations, and the judiciary as an independent agency of the government and its activities are subject to the interpretations of the judiciary.

American scholar Frank Southard (1969) believes that central bank independence refers to "that the central bank must be allowed to be a full-fledged partner at the stage when major economic policy decisions are made affecting the price level, the balance of payments, and monetary and credit conditions; and must be enabled to help to carry out these policies with vigor and courage." and "that the government should avoid creating situations of fait accompli where its commitment can only be honored through endorsements of public deficits by the central bank."[13] Eijffinger et al. (1996) of Tilburg University argued that central bank independence actually involves matters related personnel independence (degree of government influence on the central bank's appointment process), deficit financing independence (i.e. direct or indirect financing for the government), and policy independence (independence of monetary policy targets and instruments).[14]

When the economy runs smoothly, there is no independence of central bank from the government. Nevertheless, this is not the case when the economy is in a downturn or runs into trouble. Generally speaking, the government is more concerned about employment and social security, while central bank attaches importance to price stability and how to properly exercise macroeconomic regulation.

Through the study of the evolutionary trajectory of national central banks and theoretical exploration, central bank independence refers to the degree of autonomy granted to or actually enjoys by central bank in its performing functions and duties, making decisions and taking actions. Generally, central bank independence is more centrally embodied in the relationship between central bank and the government (state administration), in which it enjoys a certain degree of independence, yet merely has relative independence.

How to measure the degree of central bank's independence? ① The functions and duties assigned to the central bank by law and its initiative in carrying out its functions and duties; ②The affiliation of the central bank, whether it affiliates to

[13] Frank A. Southard Jr., *Central Bank Independence* [J], The American Journal of Economics and Sociology, Vol. 28, No. 4 (Oct., 1969), p. 404.

[14] Sylvester Eijffinger, Maarten Van Rooij and Eric Schaling, *Central Bank Independence: A Paneldata Approach* [J], Public Choice, Vol. 89, No. 1/2 (Oct., 1996), pp. 163–182.

the legislature (Congress or Parliament) or to the government or its departments; ③ The procedures for the appointment, office tenure and powers of the governor of central bank; ④The funding and financing relationship between central bank and the MoF; and ⑤The composition of the highest decision-making body of central bank and whether government personnel get involved in decision-making. In this regard, the degree of independence of central bank is classified as stronger, weaker and intermediate accordingly.

Central bank independence falls into three categories by capital structure:① State-owned central banks with state-owned capitals, which are low-degree independent central banks yet fairly commonplace, and the PBoC belongs to this category; ②Central banks where the state and the private sector jointly own capitals, which are relatively higher-degree independent central banks, such as the Bank of Japan, the Bank of France and the Bank of England; and ③Central banks owned by the private sectors, which are the highest-degree independent banks, such as the Federal Reserve System (FRS).

In terms of affiliation, central banks are the most independent central banks when they are placed under the administration of the Parliament or Congress yet the least independent central banks when they affiliate to the MoF or other government departments. Regardless of the degree of central bank independence, there are some certain links between central banks and government departments all the time. Generally speaking, central banks enjoying higher degree of independence may bear a loose relationship with government departments, while central banks enjoying a lower degree of independence may have close ties with government departments. In general, central banks tend to have the closest relationships with the MoF alongside other departments in charge of economic operations, trade administration and statistics.

Without taking account of tax hikes, the government may make up fiscal deficits by way of monetary financing, debt financing, government asset sales and other means of financing. The more independent a central bank is, the less likely it is forced to issue more money or financing deficit. Therefore, a highly independent central bank is capable of curbing inflation and stimulating economic growth.

4.4.2 Practicing the Independence of the Central Bank

It has been almost 40 years since the PBoC commenced to practice central bank independence in September 1983, when it officially assumed central bank functions.

First, the PBoC enjoyed a relatively independent legal status. In 1986, the Provisional Regulations on the Administration of Banks were promulgated by the State Council, which explicitly stipulated that the PBoC was the central bank of the country and a state agency for leading and administering the national financial sector under the administration of the State Council. Additionally, it also explicitly stipulated 12 functions and duties of the PBoC as central bank and a financial regulatory authority, as well as the business philosophies and business scope of commercial banks and non-banking institutions.

Under the financial system reform scheme in 1993, the PBoC performed three functions of imposing financial regulation, exercising financial macro-regulation, and providing financial services, and it also had four powers including power to issue money, power to regulate funds, power to adjust interest rates, and power to allow financial institutions to gain access to the market.

According to the Law on the Peoples Bank of China adopted in March 1995, the PBOC was accorded the status of China's central bank under the new legislation for the first time. Under the leadership of the State Council, the PBoC was mandated to formulate and implement monetary policy, prevent and control financial risks, and preserve financial stability, with its monetary policy targets of maintaining monetary stability and thereby promoting economic growth.[15] Additionally, the PBoC was discharged with legal mandates by law for performing 12 functions and duties, including issuing relevant orders and regulations, formulating and implementing monetary policy, issuing the *renminbi* and managing its circulation, regulating financial and foreign exchange markets, carring out and managing the operation of China's foreign currencies and gold reserves, managing state treasuries on behalf of the MoF, and maintaining the normal operation of the payment and clearing system.

From 1995 onwards, there were provisions governing the relationships between the PBoC and the government, the ultimate goals, the choice of policy instruments, the relationships between the head office and branches, and the financial budget system. Under the legislation, the PBoC enjoyed relative independence.

The PBoC enjoyed a relatively independent legal status, and it was mandated to serve for the central government, yet it was not allowed to become completely independent of the government, let alone overrode government agencies. Meanwhile, the PBoC must take China's economic development objectives as its fundamental goals, follow the laws of economic development, and independently formulate monetary policy and measures necessitated for economic development. As an agency directly under the leadership of the State Council, the PBoC was neither allowed to become completely independent of the government, nor did it cater to all the political needs of the government or completely obey its orders.[16]

The relative independence of the PBoC refers primarily to its relatively independent powers to issue money, to formulate and implement monetary policy, and to perform management of, exercise controls of and impose sanctions on the financial system and the financial market.

Second, the PBoC enjoyed relatively greater independence in the formulation and implementation of monetary policy. The PBoC was allowed to independently implement monetary policy using monetary policy instruments, including the statutory reserve requirement ratio, the central bank benchmark interest rate, conducting

[15] The People's Bank of China and CCCPC Party Literature Research Office (eds): *Selected Literature on Financial Work (1978–2005)*, China Finance Publishing House, 2007, pp. 555–562.

[16] Bai Weihua: On the Relative Independence of the People's Bank of China, Journal of Beijing University of Technology (Social Sciences), Issue 4, 2002, pp. 36–39.

the rediscount business for banking institutions, granting loans to commercial banks, and conducting open market operation transactions in treasury bonds, other government bonds, financial bonds and foreign exchange. Nevertheless, it must submit monetary policy targets such as money supply, interest rates and exchange rates to the Standing Committee of the National People's Congress in tandem with working reports on monetary policy and the operational performance of the financial sector.

Third, the PBoC enjoyed substantive independence in financial regulation. The PBoC may have the sole regulatory authority over the financial sector according to the law. From 1983 to 1993, the PBoC adopted a compliance regulation system. In other words, it was mainly tasked to supervise and inspect whether financial institutions complied with laws and regulations as well as policies.

The PBoC-centered regulatory system has been established for the administration purposes. Specifically, a centralized and unified financial management system was in place, in which the PBoC administered all types of financial institutions. The PBoC acted primarily as the competent authority for administering financial institutions or the financial industry, rather than a regulator of all types of financial institutions and their business operations, with a focus on the approval of the establishment of financial institutions, their business scope and related re-registration instead of prudential regulation. In the absence of sound legal basis, norms and transparency, the PBoC tended to arbitrarily intervene in the approval for the establishment and business scope of financial institutions. Conversely, compliance regulation refers to carrying out an audit of the business operated by the financial sector through specific audit methods in compliance with national policies, related policies and banking regulations, systems and provisional regulations, with the aim of imposing regulations and reinforcing internal control regime.

The PBoC was tasked with overseeing the operation of the financial market, exercising macroeconomic regulation of the financial market, and promoting its coordinated development according to the law. Additionally, it had the power to inspect and supervise the deposit reserves of financial institutions as well as other entities and individuals, the interbank lending market, the bond market, foreign exchange, gold, clearing and settlement, and anti-money laundering.

With the exception of state-owned commercial banks, many local financial institutions were controlled by provincial governments, making it difficult for for the PBoC to carry out independent and impartial judicial enforcement when regulating the closures and debt repayments by financial institutions, debt evasion and defaults by enterprises, and illegal charges by financial institutions.

The PBoC enjoyed greater economic independence (e.g. financing the government's fiscal deficit and choice of financial instruments) than political independence. Needless to say, there were certain limitations on political independence (e.g. capital and personnel). Specifically, the PBoC's entire capital was funded and owned by the state, and its governor was determined by the National People's Congress upon nomination by the Premier of the State Council. During the adjournment of the National People's Congress, the Governor of the PBoC was determined by the Standing Committee of the National People's Congress and appointed and removed by the President of the People's Republic of China, and the Deputy Governor was appointed and removed by the Premier of the State Council.

At the legal and institutional level, the independence of the PBOC primarily refers to its autonomy and legal status in formulating and implementing monetary policy, which is divided into legal and practical independence. The PBoC enjoyed greater practical independence than legal independence. In practice, the PBoC had the advantage of gaining access to information for monetary policy decisions. In other words, the decision options it submits tended to be the sole options or one of few alternatives available for the central government to make decisions. In general, the PBoC's decision options were technically difficult to be vetoed because they truly reflected the central government's intentions. The technical monopoly of the PBOC therefore made up its deficiencies in terms of legal independence.[17]

4.4.3 Institutional Safeguards for an Independent Central Bank

A general consensus that a central bank must have independence has emerged in the financial sector and the theoretical circles. Nevertheless, there is still a controversy surrounding how to ensure central bank independence. Specifically speaking, we still need to address the following issues: Must central banks be independent of the government in organizational structure? Or only by subordinating itself to the legislature can central bank ensure its independence? For the PBoC, What principles should be adhered to maintain relative independence?

First, it was imperative to foster an awareness of law-based finance and ensure the enactment of the PBoC-related legislation in a stable and continuous manner. As compared to its counterparts in the UK and the US, the PBoC had a relatively short history of actually performing central banking functions. However, it has been attaching importance to the rule of law right from the outset. In 1986, the Provisional Regulations on the Administration of Banks were promulgated, in which the PBoC's dependence was not set forth, but nevertheless its status and functions were explicitly conferred and defined. In the Law on the the People's Bank of China promulgated in 1995 and amended in 2003, the PBoC's status and specific functions were detailed and reformed. In the past 20-odd years of enforcing PBoC-related laws and statutes, enacting PBoC-related laws in a proper and continuous manner was a prerequisite for central bank independence.

Second, the PBoC enjoyed monetary policy independence on the basis of national macroeconomic objectives. According to Article 3 of the Law on the PBoC, the PBoC implemented monetary policy to maintain monetary stability and promote economic growth. In other words, the PBoC pursued two-faceted instead

[17] Yang Song and Yan Hai: The Independence of the People's Bank of China: Clause Analysis and Norms Reshaping, *Present day Law Science*, Issue 3, 2008, pp. 18–26.

of monolithic money policy targets. In terms of the choice of monetary policy intermediate targets, there was a gradual shift from quantity-oriented to price-oriented intermediate targets. Specifically speaking, M2 supply and total social financing were chosen as quantity-oriented monetary policy intermediate targets while central bank's benchmark deposit and lending rate curve and foreign currency prices were used as price-oriented intermediate targets; and operational targets included reserves and base currency, etc.

Third, relevant central bank independence systems were built in conformity with the laws of financial activities to keep pace with the times. As of the financial crisis in 2018, the PBoC continuously reformed its central bank functions and repeatedly used direct or indirect regulatory means to regulate the operation of the domestic economy and the financial sector. In the end, it has achieved the desired effect.

According to the report of the 19th National Congress of the Communist Party of China (CPC) held in September 2017, it explicitly set forth that sound monetary policy and macro-prudential regulation policy constituted a two-pillar regulatory framework.[18] As an important deployment made after reflecting on the lessons of the global financial crisis and taking into account China's actual situation, it helped the PBoC to promote financial stability while maintaining monetary stability at the same time, improve the effectiveness of financial regulation, prevent systemic financial risks, and thus effectively safeguard macroeconomic stability and national financial security.

Under the two-pillar regulatory framework, policy makers placed premium on CPI-based monetary policy, while also incorporating two prime targets for the financial cycle (total credit and real estate prices) into the regulatory framework. The former refers to the terms and conditions for financing, while the latter reflects investor's perceptions and attitudes towards risks. As real estate is used as important collateral for credit lending, the two amplify each other, exacerbating the swing in the economic cycle (pro-cyclicality). In turn, total credit and asset prices further linked finance to the real economy through channels such as balance sheets.

Only when the macro-prudential regulation policy framework and central bank's monetary policy complement each other can we better preserve and safeguard both monetary stability and financial stability at the same time.®

Monetary policy is a set of tools that a nation's central bank has available to promote a sustainable economic and employment growth by controlling money supply and maintaining price stability. Conversely, macro-prudential regulation policy is designed to reform and overhaul the financial system for the sake of safeguarding financial stability and preventing systemic risks, which is complementary to monetary policy. By comprehensively and properly pursuing two complementary policies can we better create a sound monetary and financial environment for carrying out supply-side structural reforms and promoting a high-quality economic development.

---

[18] 第61-62页。Monetary Policy Analysis Group of the People's Bank of China: Report on the Implementation of China's Monetary Policy (2017Q3), November 17, 2007, pp. 61–62.

Finally, it was imperative to constantly reform the financial regime and properly deal with five relationships. Tracing back to the PBoC's evolutionary history, the separation of government and enterprises was a watershed in the reform of the financial system, whereby the PBoC was separated from governments at all levels and became a truly independent central bank, with its local branches also being independent of local governments at all levels, as well as accountable only to the National People's Congress and subject to the supervision of the Standing Committee of the National People's Congress. Meanwhile, the PBoC was also separated from the MoF, and fiscal deficits could only be financed through the issuance of government bonds. Neither was the PBoC forced to make overdrafts to finance fiscal deficits, nor were government bonds allowed to be sold to the PBoC.

At the legal and practical work levels, the PBoC was mandated to properly handle its relationships with the State Council, the National People's Congress, the MoF, local governments and other financial institutions, and to continually improve the modern central banking system, thereby establishing a comprehensive monetary policy system and a regulatory framework.

Chapter 5
Evolutionary Trajectory of China's Financial Regulatory Regime

From 1949 to 2019, the Chinese government established a PBoC-centered financial regulatory regime. In the 1990s, there formed a regime of separate operation and separate regulation. From the twenty-first century onwards, the Chinese government has been exploring the establishment of an effective regulatory regime for promoting financial globalization and mixed operation to ensure a secure, sound and efficient operation of China's financial system, with a focus on exercising prudential regulation, preventing systemic financial risks, and strengthening modern financial governance.

5.1 Historical Evolution of the Financial Regulatory Regime

During the seventy years from 1949 to 2019, China's financial regulatory system evolved through five major stages.

5.1.1 Integrated Regulatory Regime with the PBoC at the Core

When a planned economy reined in the financial market from the 1950s to the late 1970s, an integrated regulatory model with the PBoC at the core was in place.

In accordance with the Interim Regulations on the Organizational Structure of the People's Bank of China and the Interim Regulations on the Organizational Structure of the Regulatory Authorities adopted in November 1950, the PBoC was officially established as China's financial regulatory authority, in which the CPC Committee

Y. Wu, *A Financial History of China (1949–2019)*, Research Series on the Chinese Dream and China's Development Path,
https://doi.org/10.1007/978-981-99-6571-7_5

of the PBoC Head Office (Office of Inspections) was set up to oversee the financial industry on behalf of the State. Meanwhile, the Internal Auditing Division was created as an affiliate to the PBoC's Accounting and Treasury Department in charge of financial auditing. Under the direct leadership of the Government Administration Council, the PBoC also maintained a close working relationship with the MoF in accordance with relevant rules and regulations.

There were no overhauls in the integrated regulatory regime, nor were other financial regulatory authorities established prior to the outbreak of the Cultural Revolution which had brought the national economy to the brink of collapse. Under an integrated regulatory regime, the PBoC concurrently operated in the business of central bank and commercial banks as well as oversaw China's financial sector as well. Nevertheless, it was not discharged with legal mandates for regulating the market entry, operation and exit of financial institutions.

During the Cultural Revolution, the PBoC's integrated regulatory regime underwent massive overhauls. First, the Internal Auditing Division under the PBoC's Accounting and Treasury Department was disbanded, and officials in charge of internal audit were transferred elsewhere, both of which have severely hampered the audit work.[1] Second, the PBoC was consolidated into the MoF and it only retained its official title. Meanwhile, some of its branches at various levels were merged with the MoF to create the Bureau of Finance as the administrative body. Third, financial business was slack and there was no way of exercising financial regulation at all in those days.

5.1.2 The Centralized Financial Regulatory Regime Consisting of the PBoC and the SAFE

In 1979, the SAFE was established directly under the leadership of the State Council to administer foreign exchange and related business, resulting in the formation of a centralized financial regulatory regime consisting of the PBoC and SAFE. It is worth mentioning that the PBoC-led regime was not abolished until 1992.

Under the centralized financial regulatory regime consisting of the PBoC and the SAFE, the PBOC was tasked with formulating monetary policy, with money supply control as the main intermediate target of monetary policy. Meanwhile, it also resorted to administrative means to exercise financial regulation by shifting its original "cashier" role of the State during the planned economy period. Additionally, it also made efforts to explore ways to better perform its financial regulation functions.

First, the PBoC reformed its organizational structure to strengthen specialized and law-based regulation. In 1982, the PBoC set up the Financial Institution

[1] The BoC's overseas brancheshave been implementing an internal audit system and their audit work has been ongoing all along as well.

Administration Department to conduct researches on the reform of financial institutions, enact measures for administering financial institutions, and approve the establishment, dissolution and merger of financial institutions. Subsequently, the Laws and Regulations Department, the Non-banking Financial Institutions Department, and the Insurance Department were separated from the Financial Institution Administration Department which was renamed the Banking Department thereafter. Additionally, the Foreign Financial Institution Administration Department was also established. In 1985, the PBoC separated the Internal Audit Department from the CPC Committee of the PBC Head Office (Office of Inspections), and then installed the Internal Audit Department in the PBoC's head office and all the branches, which was conducive to progressively optimizing the organizational structure for financial regulation. In January 1987, the PBoC set up the Money Management Department and the State Treasury Department. Meanwhile, it also reorganized the Planning Department as the Comprehensive Planning Department, the Survey and Research Department as the Survey and Statistics Department, and the Inspection and Audit Department as the Audit Department respectively.

After the PBoC officially served as China's central bank in September 1983, specialized banks were no longer under its administration. Instead, the PBoC could only resort to economic means to lead and oversee the business operations of specialized banks, supplemented by necessary administrative means.

According to the Interim Regulations of the People's Republic of China on the Administration of Banks adopted in 1986, the PBoC was a state organ under the leadership of the State Council and it was mandated to administer China's financial affairs, issuance and circulation of currency, cash, credit loans, all types of financial institutions, insurance companies and financial markets in accordance with national laws and regulations. This marks an important step on the way to law-based financial regulation.[2]

Second, the PBoC highlighted its role in regulating financial institutions in China. In October 1984, the PBOC was established by law as the competent authority for regulating financial organizations across China. Specifically, financial affairs such as operations in financial business or establishment, merger and dissolution of financial institutions by any government departments and entities must be subject to the approval from the PBoC or its authorized agencies. In 1988, the PBoC was conferred the power to approve the establishment of securities companies or similar financial institutions.

In practice, the PBoC or its authorized agencies had the power to take necessary economic and administrative measures to order unlicensed financial institutions to suspend their financial business. In 1989, the PBoC disbanded its illegal affiliated financing companies according to law, and recovered all its loans that had been irregularly used as capital for financing companies. Meanwhile, it also dissolved all of its established non-conforming securities companies and credit rating agencies. In 1990, all the financing companies, securities companies, leasing companies and

---

[2] The State Council: *Interim Regulations of the People's Republic of China on the Administration of Banks*, January 7, 1986.

financial companies affiliated to enterprise group that had been established without the approval of the PBoC and failed to meet the acceptance inspection criteria were disbanded. Moreover, all of unlicensed finance companies and financial companies affiliated to enterprise group, and financial companies or other internal financial institutions set up by non-enterprise groups were also dissolved.

Third, the PBoC compiled four-tier credit loan plans for the whole society to control credit loan quotas. With the reform of the credit loan regulation regime from 1984 to 1985, the Chinese government imposed the borrowing and lending regime for credit loan quota control. In this context, the PBoC took credit loan quota as an important metric for implementing monetary policies and exercising macro-regulation. The PBoC commenced to install a four-tier regulation regime for compiling credit loan plans to impose quotas on loans and grant loans based on deposits in central bank, including the credit loan plan of the PBoC, the credit loan plans of state-owned specialized banks, the credit loan plans of non-banking institutions, and the national comprehensive credit loan plan consolidating the three above plans.

In 1990, the PBoC officially formulated and pressed ahead with four-tier credit plans for the whole society, which included: (1) Credit quota plans for banks, urban and rural credit cooperatives and various trust companies, as well as for bonds, stocks, fund-raising and other credit activities; (2) Credit loan plans for state-owned banks including the PBoC, specialized banks, the BOCOM and the CITIC Industrial Bank; (3) Credit loan plans for other financial institutions such as trust and investment companies and urban and rural credit cooperatives; and (4) Credit loan plans for bonds, stocks, fund-raising and various other forms of credit loan activities. Meanwhile, it also imposed targeted regulation according to different levels of credit loan plans.

Fourth, the PBoC investigated and imposed penalties on illegal trust institutions and business to rectify financial market order. In April 1986, the PBoC stipulated that financial trust and investment companies shall be only approved for establishment in medium-sized and large cities at national, provincial and prefectural levels (excluding counties or sub-county regions), and individuals shall be prohibited from operating in the trust business. Trust and investment companies at the three levels shall be required to have an equity capital of RMB50 million, RMB10 million and RMB5 million, plus a minimum paid-in equity capital denominated in foreign currencies of US$5 million, US$2 million and US$1 million respectively.

In October 1988, the PBoC took decisive measures to call for all the trust and investment companies to effectuate "three cessations" nationwide (i.e. cease to grant trust loans, cease to borrow and lend funds, and cease to make investments), and to promptly overhaul the trust industry. In September 1989, it further overhauled trust and investment companies, investment companies and other financial institutions established by the administrative authorities.

5.1.3 The Financial Regulatory Regime Consisting of the PBoC, the SAFE, the CSRC and the CIRC

From 1992 to 2002, the PBoC-centered financial regulatory regime consisting of the PBoC and the SAFE progressively switched to one which was comprised of the PBoC, the SAFE, the CSRC and the CIRC as a result of the establishment of both CSRC and CIRC and the introduction of a separate regulation model.

First, the CSC and the CSRC were set up to separate securities regulation from the PBoC. On October 26, 1992, the CSC and the CSRC were established respectively. Specifically, the former served as the competent authority for regulating the securities market in a unified manner on behalf of the State, while the latter acted as the executive body of the CSC for regulating the securities market in accordance with laws and regulations. The CSC and CSRC were established to separate certain functions of securities regulation from the PBoC and they worked together with the PBoC to jointly oversee the securities industry, successfully reforming the original monolithic regulatory model with the PBoC at the core.

Second, the CSRC was reorganized as an agency specializing in securities market regulation. From April to August 1998, the State Council decided to merge the CSC with the CSRC to form its newly affiliated CSRC which was elevated to the ministerial level, and the PBoC delegated all its securities regulatory powers to the newly established CSRC.

Third, a separate operation and separate regulation model was established. In 1994, the State Council set out the requirements for the banking, insurance, securities and trust industries to carry out separate operations. Meanwhile, it formulated and revised different management rules and regulations as well as regulatory norms and requirements for administering various types of financial institutions. In March and May 1995, the Law of the People's Republic of China on the People's Bank of China, the Law of the People's Republic of China on Commercial Banks and the Insurance Law were respectively promulgated for implementation, which stipulated the requirements for separate operation and separate regulation in the banking and insurance industries.

Fourth, the CIRC was established. In November 1998, the State Council approved the establishment of the CIRC to officially separate insurance regulation from the PBoC. As a ministerial-level agency directly under the State Council, the CIRC was in charge of administering national commercial insurance and ensuring the sound operation of the insurance industry. In 2002, the Insurance Law was revised and adopted, defining the role of the CIRC as the insurance regulatory authority directly under the State Council for overseeing the insurance industry according to the law.

Following the reform of the aforementioned financial regulatory regime, a financial regulatory regime consisting of the PBoC, the SAFE, the CSRC and the CIRC was officially installed as of the end of 1998. The PBoC was responsible for regulating commercial banks, trust and investment companies, credit cooperatives, financial companies affiliated to enterprise group and other banking financial institutions, the SAFE specialized in administering foreign exchange business and activities, the CSRC was in charge of regulating securities companies (including investment banks), and the CIRC was mandated to oversee the insurance industry.

As a regulation race model, the financial regulatory regime consisting of the PBoC, the SAFE, the CSRC and the CIRC was conducive to defining regulatory roles and duties as well as improving regulatory efficiency, whereas it also posed an obstacle for business innovations and brought forth overlapped business among financial institutions at the same time. In particular, the aforementioned three regulatory authorities lacked communication with each other and this resulted in their poor coordination and cooperation in financial regulation.

In September 2000, the PBoC, the CSRC and the CIRC decided to establish a joint tripartite regulatory meeting system to give full play to their respective roles and promptly solve policy coordination problems arising in the separate regulation process. A joint meeting might be convened from time to time at the proposal of any of the aforesaid regulators, with members of the tripartite joint meeting acting as meeting conveners in rotation. Following each joint meeting, the three regulators would coordinate relevant regulatory policies under the relevant resolutions adopted at the joint meeting.

5.1.4 The Financial Regulatory Regime Consisting of the PBoC, the SAFE, the CSRC, the CIRC and the CBRC

From 2003 to 2017, China imposed the financial regulatory regime consisting of the PBoC, the SAFE, the CSRC, the CIRC and the CBRC, which differed from its predecessor in the newly establishment of the CBRC.

On April 28, 2003, the CBRC was officially established to mainly perform banking regulatory functions separated from the PBoC, involving the regulation of commercial banks, asset management companies, trust companies and other depository financial institutions. On October 19, 2003, 36 provincial-level dispatched offices of the CBRC were officially set up to carry out their respective functions. As such, a new banking regulatory regime has taken shape.

Therefore, an integrated separate financial regulation regime consisting of the PBoC, the SAFE, the CSRC, the CIRC and the CBRC has been since created and this put an end to a long-standing era of the PBoC administering the banking, insurance, securities and futures industries.

Under the financial regulatory regime consisting of the PBoC, the SAFE, the CSRC, the CIRC and the CBRC, the PBoC was empowered to formulate monetary policies, maintain financial stability, and enact financial laws and regulations, shifting the focus from compliance management to compliance and risk management. Under the leadership of the State Council, the PBoC was tasked with exercising macro-prudential regulation and coordinating micro financial regulation. The SAFE was responsible for regulating the foreign exchange market directly under the administration of the PBoC, while the CSRC, CIRC and CBRC were discharged with legally mandates for exercising micro-regulation respectively within their purview in the financial sector. Overall, there was both a division of functions and coordination between the aforementioned three regulatory authorities. Despite their explicitly defined roles and functions, the CSRC, CIRC and CBRC were all subordinate to and under the leadership of the State Council.

As financial globalization and mixed operation emerged as a prevailing trend in the wake of the 2008 financial crisis, it was imperative to explore new effective regulatory models to fill in gaps in authorities and remedy regulation lags underlying the separate regulation model. In terms of building a counter-cyclical financial macro-prudential regulation regime and reforming the separate regulation model, certain basic consensus has been progressively arrived at among domestic practitioners and theoretical circles.

5.1.5 The Financial Regulatory Regime Consisting of the PBoC, the FSDC, the SAFE, the CBIRC and CSRC

At the National Conference on Financial Work held in Beijing from July 14 to 15, 2017, it was announced that the Financial Stability and Development Committee (FSDC) would be set up under the State Council to assist in consolidating the PBoC's role for carrying out macro-prudential regulation and preventing systematic risks. On November 8, 2017, the FSDC was officially established and it held its first plenary meeting. As an executive body of the State Council for coordinating to tackle major issues pertaining to financial stability, reform and development, the FSDC was tasked with overseeing the shadow banking system, the asset management industry, Internet finance and financial holding companies.

On April 8, 2018, the China Banking and Insurance Regulatory Commission (CBIRC) was officially inaugurated to primarily oversee the banking and insurance industries, safeguard the legal and sound operation of the banking and insurance industries, prevent and resolve financial risks, protect the legitimate rights and interests of financial consumers, and maintain financial stability according to the law.

From April 20, 2018 onwards, the CBIRC took over the responsibilities for regulating the business operations and formulating regulatory rules and regulations in relation to financial leasing companies, factoring companies, and pawn shops, which were previously regulated and formulated by the Ministry of Commerce.

With the establishment of the FSDC and the merger of CBRS and CIRC into the CBIRC, the financial regulatory regime consisting of the PBoC, the FSDC, the SAFE, the CBIRC and CSRC was officially installed to rise to the challenge of the separate regulation model in the financial sector, and follow the mainstream trend towards the internationalization of financial regulation on the threshold of a new era of asset management.

Under a new financial regulatory system, the CBIRC and CSRC were empowered to collect information and data from financial institutions under their supervision respectively, and to consolidate, compile and publish data and financial statements of different financial institutions in accordance with relevant national rules and regulations. Meanwhile, a "Joint Regulatory Meeting Mechanism" and a "Regular Liaison Mechanism" have been established to enhance a close cooperation between the MoF and the PBoC in jointly maintaining the stability of the financial system and bolstering the confidence of the financial market.

The year 2008 is the first year for China to comprehensively implement the communiqué adopted at the 19th National Congress of the Communist Party of China. Additionally, it is a key year for implementing the 13th Five-Year Plan and the year of reforming the financial regulatory regime consisting of the PBoC, the FSDC, the SAFE, the CSRC and the CBIRC.

From 1949 to 2019, there was a transition from comprehensive regulation to separate regulation in China's financial regulatory regime which was eventually reverted to comprehensive regulation to address the changing domestic and international situations in a new era. To be attuned to the needs of financial globalization and domestic mixed financial operations, the financial regulatory regime consisting of the PBoC, the FSDC, the SAFE, the CBIRC and CSRC was officially installed in line with policy and institutional requirements. This newly installed financial regulatory regime were imposed to remedy the previous over-expansion of the financial sector at the expense of quality improvement and risk prevention, and to redefine the objectives of building socialism with Chinese characteristics in a new era.

5.2 Securities Institutions and the Market Regulatory Regime

The regulation of the securities industry is usually predicated on a combination of factors such as financial institutions, markets and various operational mechanisms. Although regulatory regimes vary from country to country, there are essentially three regulatory regimes in different countries: centralized regulation regime, self-regulation regime, and regulatory regime that falls somewhere in between. The variation between these different regulatory regimes lies in whether there exist national securities regulatory laws and authorities. China's securities regulatory regime falls into the category of a centralized regulation regime, in which corresponding laws and regulations are in place, national administrative regulatory authorities have been established, and various industry self-regulatory organizations have been created.

5.2.1 *Legal Regulation at the Judicial Level*

From 1949 to 1990, there was neither real capital market and securities industry nor competent regulatory authorities in China, and the PBoC assumed the responsibility for overseeing related business.

With the establishment of the Shanghai and Shenzhen stock exchanges and the emergence of the securities industry, specialized regulation was put on the agenda from the 1990s onwards. In terms of law-based financial regulation, laws and regulations pertaining to the regulation of the securities market were enacted and promulgated, including national laws, administrative rules and regulations, judicial interpretations, departmental rules and regulations as well as normative documents.

First, five laws and one decision were successively promulgated, including the Law of the People's Republic of China on the People's Bank of China, the Law of the People's Republic of China on Commercial Banks, the Insurance Law, the Bill Law and the Guarantee Law, as well as the Decision of the Standing Committee of the National People's Congress on Punishing Those Who Disrupted Financial Market Order adopted in 1995. According to the aforementioned laws and regulations, the PBoC was designated as central bank for overseeing the financial sector in China, and it was not until the establishment of the CSRC in 1992 that the securities market and securities companies were directly regulated by the PBoC. Additionally, the basic business philosophies behind the market-oriented and regulated development of securities institutions were also set forth in the above documents.

Second, a number of national laws applicable to the regulation of the securities industry were promulgated and revised, including the Company Law (1993, 2004 and 2005), the Securities Law (1998, 2004, 2005 and 2013), the Trust Law (2001), the Securities Investment Fund Law (2003), the Bankruptcy Law (2006), the Law on the Promotion of Small and Medium-sized Enterprises (2002 and 2017), the General Provisions of Civil Law (2017), the Anti-Unfair Competition Law (1993 and 2017) and the Enterprise Income Tax Law (2017), among others.

The Securities Law was adopted in December 1998 as a fundamental law governing the regulation of the securities market in China. After its coming into force on July 1, 1999, this law was amended for three times in 2004, 2013 and 2014 respectively and it was revised in 2005 for the first time. The second revised edition of this law was officially adopted on December 28, 2019, effective on March 1, 2020.

The Securities Law covers almost all aspects of securities issuance, securities trading and investor protection etc. In particular, the newly revised Securities Law set out new provisions for comprehensively operating the registration system for securities issuance, increasing the costs of illegality, optimizing the investor protection system, strengthening information disclosure, and expanding the scope of application of the Securities Law. This marked a solid step towards law-based securities market regulation, and laid a legal foundation for comprehensively deepening the reform of China's capital market.

As an important law on securities investment funds, the Securities Investment Fund Law was adopted on October 28, 2003 and it was revised in 2012 and amended in 2015 to clarify the status and role of the fund industry in the securities market. It is learned that the Securities Investment Fund Law has significance for regulating the activities of securities investment funds, protecting the legitimate rights and interests of investors and the parties involved, and promoting the healthy development of securities investment funds and the securities market. There is no doubt that the Securities Investment Fund Law is another important law for regulating the securities market following the Securities Law.

Third, relevant administrative regulations were promulgated by the State Council. In 1993, the Interim Regulations on the Administration of Stock Issuance and Trading were promulgated to set out detailed provisions on stock issuance, trading and related activities within the territory of China. In March 2007, the Regulations on the Administration of Futures Trading was promulgated to set forth provisions on futures, futures exchanges, futures companies and futures trading rules, as well as futures trading regulation. In February 2014, the Circular on Issuing the Scheme for Reforming the Registered Capital Registration System was promulgated to reform the registered capital and other registration items of companies, further relax the control on the market access of market participants, lower entry threshold, improve a business environment, and promote the rapid development of market participants.

Fourth, judicial interpretations of the Supreme People's Court and other departmental rules and regulations were laid down and promulgated. The former refers to judicial interpretations on the application scope of some financial and economic laws and regulations; the latter means rules and regulations formulated and issued by the CSRC, including general provisions, issuance in the securities market, listed companies, market trading, securities companies, securities service agencies, funds and futures. In October 1990, the Interim Measures for the Administration of Securities Companies were formulated for promulgation by the PBoCto stipulate that the PBoC shall serve as state securities administrative authority, and securities companies must be subject to its leadership, management, audit, supervision and coordination. On December 26, 1997, the Rules Governing the Listing of Securities on the Shanghai Stock Exchange and the Rules Governing the Listing of Securities on the Shenzhen Stock Exchange were issued by the Shanghai and Shenzhen Stock Exchanges with the approval of the CSRC. In addition, the Guidelines on Financial Regulation were issued by the PBoC in June 2001, and the Measures for the Administration of Securities Companies were promulgated by the CSRC in December 2001.

5.2.2 Heteronomy Regulation of Executive Administration

The securities market falls into the category of regulation in the form of executive administration. Before the CSRC was established, the PBoC had regulated the market. From 1992 onwards, the CSC and CSRC were created as securities regulators. The former was responsible for the overall oversight of the securities market, while the latter was the executive body.

In October 1992, the CSC was established with the former Executive Meeting on Securities of the State Council as its predecessor, and its General Office was set up to attend to the routine work under the direct leadership of the General Office of the State Council. Vice Premier Rongji Zhu of the State Council was the first chairman of the CSC, whose members consisted of the heads of 13 ministries and commissions, including the PBoC, State Commission for Structural Reform, State Planning Commission, MoF, Economic and Trade Office, Ministry of Supervision, Supreme People's Court, Supreme People's Procurator ate, Ministry of Economy and Trade, State Executive Administration, State Administration of Taxation, State-Owned Assets Supervision and Administration Commission, and SAFE.

Apart from the CSC and CSRC, the relevant departments of the State Council and local governments also performed the following securities regulatory functions and duties:

The State Planning Commission was tasked to balance supply and demands, and compile securities plans based on the CSC's plans and proposals; the PBoC was responsible for approving and administering securities institutions and filing them with the CSC; the MoF administered certified public accountants and accounting firms, whose qualification review fell within the remit of the CSRC; the State Commission for Structural Reform was in charge of drafting the regulations on pilot joint-stock schemes and coordinating the related pilot work. With the supervision of the CSRC, the Shanghai and Shenzhen stock exchanges were under the centralized administration of their respective local governments. Additionally, the establishment of new stock exchanges was subject to the review of the CSC and the approval of the State Council. The pilot joint-stock system programs of existing local enterprises were examined and endorsed by the competent departments authorized by provincial governments or the governments of cities specifically designated in the state plan in conjunction with the competent departments of the enterprises, while those of existent central enterprises were subject to approval by the State Commission for Structural Reform in tandem with the competent departments of the enterprises.

In 1992, the CSRC was established as a ministerial agency directly under the State Council, which consisted of a Public Offering Supervision Committee, an Administrative Sanction Committee, four directly affiliated public institutions and twenty functional departments. In addition, thirty-eight regional bureaus were set up in different provinces, autonomous regions, municipalities directly under the central government, and cities specifically designated in the state plan. Meanwhile, the CSRC established commissioner's offices in Shanghai and Shenzhen to respectively administer nineteen branches. In this way, a unified and orderly national securities and futures regulatory system has progressively taken shape to regulate and maintain the order of the national securities and futures market and to safeguard its lawful and healthy operation.

From 2013 onwards, the CSRC has been further pressing ahead with regulatory reform in line with the market-oriented and law-based guidelines, shifting its regulatory focus from pre-event approval to in-event and post-event regulation. Additionally, it has also curtailed or cancelled some items subject to administrative approval, enhanced institutional building and market overhaul, and reinforced the enforcement of institutional rules and regulations.

Apart from the above government administrative bodies, China Securities Investor Protection Fund Corporation Limited (SIPF), which was approved for establishment with capital contributions from the State Council on August 30, 2005, is also worth mentioning. As a wholly state-owned enterprise, it served as a securities industry regulatory body under the centralized administration of the CSRC. In the past fifteen years since its establishment, the SIPF pulled off a brilliant feat in preventing and resolving financial risks, supporting and assisting with service regulation, and protecting the legitimate rights and interests of investors.

5.2.3 Self-regulation of Industry Associations

Self-regulatory organizations in the securities market refer to organizations that self-regulate their market activities in compliance with institutional conventions, articles of association, norms and by-laws. These organizations generally operate on a membership basis, and financial institutions such as eligible securities operators may apply for joining them as members (e.g. the Securities Industry Association, the Stock Exchange, etc.).

Self-regulatory organizations in China's securities market mainly included the Securities Association of China, China Futures Association, China Association for Public Companies, the Asset Management Association of China, Shanghai and Shenzhen stock exchanges, as well as other securities service intermediaries (e.g. accounting, auditing, law and appraisal firms), among others.

Established in accordance with the relevant provisions of the Securities Law and the Administrative Provisions on the Registration of Social Organizations in August 1991, the China Securities Association was a non-profit self-regulatory securities organization subject to the operational guidance and supervision of the CSRC and the Ministry of Civil Affairs. On July 6, 1998, the Association deliberated and adopted the China Securities Association Membership Convention (for Trial Implementation) and Conduct Code for Securities Practitioners, requiring securities operators to strengthen self-regulation and regulate their operations in business according to the law. As of the end of February 2020, there were 133 statutory members (securities companies), 249 general members, 78 special members and nearly 1,000 observer members in the China Securities Association.[3]

[3] Securities Association of China: *Association Members: Member Organizations*[EB/OL], https://jg.sac.net.cn/pages/publicity/hydw-list.html.

Founded on December 29, 2000, the China Futures Association was a non-profit social organization and a national futures self-regulatory body subject to the operational guidance and regulation of the CSRC (securities regulatory body) and the Ministry of Civil Affairs (the register office of social organizations in China).

As of the end of February 2020, the China Futures Association had a total of 401 members, including 331 general members (149 futures companies, 84 securities companies, 10 asset management companies, 84 risk management companies and 4 private futures funds), 5 special members (futures exchanges), and 75 affiliate members (4 futures service agencies, 12 margin custodian banks, 36 local associations and 23 members in relation to Zhengzhou Commodity Exchange, Dalian Commodity Exchange and Shanghai Futures Exchange).[4]

Established on February 15, 2012, the China Association for Public Companies was a national self-regulatory organization which was composed of listed companies and related financial institutions. As a non-profit social corporation, it adopted a membership system, and the CSRC was the competent authority for overseeing its business operations.

The China Association for Public Companies had 228 sponsor members, 249 board members, 119 executive board members (including 24 non-member managing directors), and 34 supervisory board members (including 1 non-member supervisor), playing a self-regulatory role in imposing the requirements for self-regulation and self-regulating the maturity and integrity of the capital markets.

As of the end of February 2020, the China Association for Public Companies had a total of 2,912 general members and 18 affiliate members (related institutions providing services for public companies).

Approved for establishment as a social legal entity registered with the Ministry of Civil Affairs on June 6, 2012, the China Asset Management Association was a self-regulatory organization for the securities investment fund industry, subject to the operational guidance and regulation of the CSRC and the Ministry of Civil Affairs. Despite its late establishment, the Association differed from general industry associations in that it acted as an industry association with administrative functions and assisted the CSRC in performing its regulatory duties.

According to the Securities Investment Fund Law, fund managers and fund custodians shall join the Association, and fund service providers were also allowed to join it. As of the end of February 2020, the Association had 4,416 members, including 629 general members, 308 affiliate members, 3,352 observer members and 127 special members.[5]

In addition, there were also three other industry self-regulatory organizations in China, namely Shanghai Stock Exchange, Shenzhen Stock Exchange and China Financial Futures Exchange.

---

[4] China Futures Association: *Profiles of Association Members*[EB/OL], http://www.cfachina.org/XHJS/XHHY/.

[5] Asset Management Association of China: *Research & Statistics: Membership Data*[EB/OL], http://www.amac.org.cn/researchstatistics/datastatistics/membershipdata/. Accessed on March 15, 2020.

The Shanghai and Shenzhen stock exchanges were both non-profit legal entities under the direct administration of the CSRC. Their securities regulatory functions included: Providing securities trading venues and facilities; formulating rules and regulations on stock exchange business operations; accepting applications from companies for listing, and arranging for the listing of stocks; organizing and supervising securities trading; regulating members and listed companies; and managing and releasing market information.

The securities regulatory functions of the China Financial Futures Exchange included organizing and arranging for the listing for trade, clearing and settlement of financial derivatives (e.g. financial futures), formulating business management rules and regulations, exercising self-regulation, releasing market trading information, providing technologies, venues, facilities and services, and performing other functions as permitted by the CSRC, among others.

5.3 Oversight and Administration of Financial Intermediaries

The regulation of financial intermediaries involved institutional management (including market entry, establishment of branches, requirements for personnel appointment and dismissal, etc.); business operation management (including financial product market reforms in product price and product governance mechanisms), operational process monitoring (including all types of target-based off-site and on-site regulation based on compliance and risk prevention), exit mechanisms for financial institutions, and so on.

5.3.1 Regulation and Self-regulation of Commercial Banks

In terms of regulation, several regulatory laws have been enacted, including the Law of the People's Republic of China on Commercial Banks (1995, 2003, 2015), the Banking Regulation Law of the People's Republic of China (2003) and the Anti-Money Laundering Law of the People's Republic of China (2006), among others.

With the introduction of the core guidelines for banking regulation formulated by the Basel Committee on Banking Supervision, the Law of the People's Republic of China on Commercial Banks was deliberated and adopted in 1995 and revised twice in 2003 and 2015 respectively to provide for tightening up the regulation of commercial banks. Meanwhile, the relevant provisions were also amended accordingly.

The provisions as to the establishment and organizational structure of commercial banks, protection of depositors, fundamental rules and regulations for lending and other business, financial accounting, regulation, takeover and dissolution, and legal liabilities were all set forth in the Law of the People's Republic of China on Commercial Banks. By espousing the business philosophy of ensuring security, liquidity and profitability, commercial banks were required to operate in their business independently in a risk-bearing, self-financing and self-regulating manner. Additionally, they shall conduct business according to the law without the interference from any entity or individual while assuming civil liability independently with their entire corporate property.

In 2003, the Banking Regulation Law of the People's Republic of China was adopted to empower the CBRC to regulate banking financial institutions and their business activities nationwide. The regulatory work involved regulating and administering the activities of the banking industry, preventing and resolving banking risks, protecting the legitimate rights and interests of depositors and other customers, promoting the healthy development of the banking sector and its lawful and sound operation, and bolstering public confidence in the banking industry.

In terms of regulation, relevant administrative regulations were formulated by government administrative departments in respect of financial industry administration, business operations, corporate governance, risk prevention and information disclosure. These regulations included the Interim Regulations on Banking Administration (1986) issued by the State Council; the Circular on Carrying out Asset Liability Ratio Management of Commercial Banks (1994) released by the PBoC; and the Core Risk Management Metrics for Commercial Banks (for Trial Implementation, 2005), Measures for the Capital Management of Commercial Banks (for Trial Implementation, 2012) and Interim Measures for the Equity Management of Commercial Banks (2018) issued by the CBRC, among others.

In 2003, the CBRC was approved for establishment as a national competent regulatory authority. Under the reformed financial regulatory regime, national laws and the mandates of the State Council, the CBRC was reorganized as the CBIRC in 2008 to impose unified regulation on commercial banks, financial asset management companies, trust and investment companies and other depository financial institutions nationwide.

By upholding the principles of legality, openness, fairness and efficiency, the CBRC has jointly established a regulatory information sharing mechanism in tandem with the PBoC, the State Council and other financial regulatory authorities. Meanwhile, it has also jointly installed a regulatory cooperation mechanism in conjunction with the banking regulatory authorities in other countries or regions to facilitate cross-border regulation.

The indirect financing system with commercial banks at its core has formed the backbone of China's financial sector, placing the regulation of commercial banks on top agenda for the regulation of the financial sector.

The regulation of commercial banks covered all depository banks and financial institutions. The ultimate goals were to protect the interests of depositors and consumers of financial products, promote fair competition, and safeguard the security and stability of the entire financial system.

The comprehensive regulation of commercial banks involved institutional and business regulation, e.g. market access such as establishment and re-registration of financial institutions, license transfer, merger and acquisition, etc.; as well as requirements for prudential regulation of business operations, and prevention of various risks such as credit risks, market risks, interest rate risks and liquidity risks. The prudential regulation was primarily imposed in respect of risk management, internal control, capital adequacy ratio, asset quality, loss reserves, affiliate transactions, asset liquidity, and so on.

According to the Law of the People's Republic of China on Commercial Banks adopted in 1995, the loan-deposit ratio shall not exceed 75%, which was regarded as a red line for regulating the loan-deposit ratio to curb the rampant lending growth of commercial banks. In other words, commercial banks were required to retain at least 25% of their deposits in a bid to protect the safety of depositors and prevent the liquidity risks of banks.

In May 1998, the PBoC was allowed to officially implement a five-tier classified loan management system for commercial banks. Additionally, it also liberalized loan quotas for state-owned commercial banks and gradually adopted asset liability ratio management and risk management.

It has been more than 20 years since the loan-deposit ratio regulation was imposed on commercial banks. From 1995 to 2003, the loan-deposit ratio in China's banking industry actually exceeded 75%, indicating that this regulatory metric ended in failure. From 2004 to 2010, the over all loan-deposit ratio fell below 75%, while it came close to 75% for some small and medium-sized banks.

With a view to addressing the above issues, the CBRC reformed the metrics and norms for regulating the business operations of commercial banks by applying new metrics such as capital adequacy ratio, leverage ratio, liquidity and loan loss reserve ratio in May 2011. Additionally, it refined the basic principles, calculation methods and regulatory models of leverage ratio regulation, and made differentiated transitional arrangements in the light of the actual situation of different financial institutions. As a result, a preliminary policy framework for applying new regulatory metrics and norms in China's banking industry has taken shape.

In 2005, the 75% loan-to-deposit ratio requirement, which had been enforced for more than 20 years, was abolished in the newly adopted the Law of the People's Republic of China on Commercial Banks, shifting the loan-deposit ratio from a statutory regulatory metric to a liquidity monitoring metric.

Established in May 2000, China Banking Association was primarily empowered to oversee the self-regulation of banking financial institutions, and the first batch of 22 member banks included policy banks, wholly state-owned commercial banks, joint-stock commercial banks and urban commercial banks, etc. On October 25, 2005, forty member banks jointly signed on documents such as the China Banking Industry Self-Regulation Convention and China Banking Industry Rights Protection Convention. In this way, they have reached a consensus on industry-wide self-regulation.

As of May 2020, the China Banking Association had a total of 736 member organizations and 32 specialized committees. Specifically, its member organizations included all depository banking institutions, foreign-funded financial institutions, new rural financial institutions, China Union Pay, other financial institutions, as well as banking industry associations of all provinces (autonomous regions, municipalities directly under the central government and cities specifically designated in the state plan), etc.

5.3.2 The Regulatory Regime for Overseeing Insurance Institutions

As far as the legal system is concerned, the Insurance Law adopted in 1995 is the first fundamental insurance law enacted after the founding of the PRC. The Insurance Law is modeled on the international style of legislation prevalent in some countries and regions that integrates the Insurance Act and the Insurance Contract Act into a complete and systematic insurance law, and it was revised four times in 2002, 2009, 2014 and 2015 respectively.

Through its legislative provisions set forth on insurance contracts, insurance companies, insurance business models, regulation of the insurance industry, insurance agents and brokers, as well as legal liabilities, the Insurance Law played an important role in regulating insurance activities, protecting the legitimate rights and interests of the parties involved in insurance activities, tighten up the regulation of the insurance industry, and promoting the healthy development of the insurance industry.

Specific provisions on compulsory motor vehicle insurance, etc. were set forth in administrative regulations on insurance supervision, including the Regulations on the Compulsory Insurance for Motor Vehicle Traffic Accidents Liability (2006), and the Decision on Amending the Provisions on the Compulsory Insurance for Motor Vehicle Traffic Accidents Liability (2013).

Normative documents on the regulation of the insurance industry in China were mainly issued by the CIRC, including various types of regulations in respect of general regulations, institutional management, property insurance, life insurance, capital utilization, accounting, statistics and information technology application, intermediaries and audit, among others.

In the meantime, the PBoC also issued insurance regulatory regulations, including the Insurance Industry Regulatory Targets promulgated in September 1998. The regulatory targets fall into four categories, namely non-life insurance business, life insurance business, capital utilization and financial standing, or they were categorized into obligatory targets and focused targets by nature. Such a target system applied to Chinese insurance companies and Sino-foreign joint venture insurance companies, while branches of foreign insurance companies and reinsurance companies were allowed to apply the target system by reference.

Upon its establishment on November 18, 1998, the CIRC took over the administration of the insurance industry from the PBoC. In 2003, the CIRC was reorganized as a ministerial-level body directly under the administration of the State Council, and it then commenced to set up functional departments and dispatched agencies, as well as employ staff. Specifically, it had 15 functional departments, 2 public institutions, 36 CIRC bureaus in provinces, autonomous regions, municipalities directly under the central government and cities specifically designated in the state plan, and 5 CIRC branch bureaus in the cities of Suzhou, Yantai, Shantou, Wenzhou and Tangshan respectively.

In March 2003, the CIRC issued the Regulations on the Management of Solvency Margin and Regulatory Targets of Insurance Companies, which led to the preliminary establishment of the first generation of China's business operation scale-oriented solvency margin regulatory system for the insurance industry. In other words, insurance companies were required to have capital commensurate with their scale of business operations.

As the insurance industry galloped ahead, this system has been proven to be too simple to measure the level of risks faced by insurance companies. In January 2016, the CIRC officially implemented the second generation of the risk-oriented solvency margin regulatory system. Meanwhile, it also established a framework supported by "three pillars", namely quantitative and qualitative regulation requirements, a market constraint mechanism, and a metric system.

Following its establishment in April 2018, the CBIRC took over the regulation of the insurance industry from the CIRC. Under the Financial Regulatory Regime consisting of the PBoC, FSDC, SAFE, CBIRC and CSRC, the CBIRC was tasked with exercising the unified regulation of the national insurance market and maintaining the lawful and healthy operation of the insurance industry in accordance with national laws and the mandates of the State Council.

In terms of self-regulation, 13 Chinese insurance companies signed on China's first National Insurance Industry Convention on September 9, 1997, which was an important move aiming at self-restraint and self-regulation of the insurance industry. Additionally, the Insurance Association of China was established on February 23, 2001 as the first national insurance industry self-regulatory organization which was discharged with legal mandates for self-regulation, rights protection, service provision, mutual exchanges, and publicity.

The Insurance Association of China assisted the insurance regulatory authorities in urging members to exercise self-regulation, and lawfully carry out business operations. Additionally, it also organized its members to sign on self-regulation conventions, formulate self-regulatory rules and regulations, restrain unfair competition, safeguard a fair and orderly market environment, and organize the establishment of industry standards.

As of September 2019, the Insurance Association of China had 326 members altogether, including 12 group (holding) companies, 86 property insurance companies, 89 life insurance companies, 10 reinsurance companies, 14 asset management companies, 33 specialized insurance brokerage companies, 5 specialized insurance surveyors and loss adjusters companies, 16 specialized insurance agencies, 42 local insurance associations (including intermediaries associations) and 17 insurance agencies.

5.3.3 Supervision of Non-banking Financial Institutions

Apart from banking and insurance financial institutions, there were a large number of non-banking financial institutions that had been established with the approval of the regulatory authorities. Prior to 2018, the Other Non-banking Financial Institution Supervision Department of the former CBRC and the relevant competent departments of the former CSRC and CIRC were tasked with regulating non-banking financial institutions.

In addition to the general financial regulatory laws and regulations mentioned above, regulations and basic principles governing the regulation of non-banking financial institutions were mainly issued by the CBRC, including the Measures for the Administration of Financial Companies Affiliated to Enterprise Group (2000) and the Guiding Opinions on Strengthening the Application and Management of Information Technology of Non-Banking Financial Institutions (2016), among others.

On November 30, 2017, the CBRC issued the Service Guidelines Concerning Matters Related to the Approval of the Establishment, Re-registration, Dissolution and Business Scope of Non-Banking Financial Institutions (Branches), which set forth specific and detailed provisions on trust companies, financial companies affiliated to enterprise group, asset management companies, financial leasing companies, auto finance companies, and money brokerage companies, etc.

Trust companies were regulated primarily in accordance with the Trust Law (2001), the Banking Regulation Law of the People's Republic of China, and the Measures on the Administration of Trust Companies (2006).

The regulation of finance companies were mainly governed by the Company Law, the Law of the People's Republic of China on Commercial Banks, the Measures for the Administration of Financial Companies Affiliated to Enterprise Group formulated by the PBoC (revised in 2000, 2004 and 2006), and the Interim Measures for the Assessment of Risk Management Indicators of Financial companies Affiliated to Enterprise Group (2006) issued by the CBRC. The CBRC was responsible for regulating financial companies affiliated to enterprise group.

Financial leasing companies adopted multi-pronged regulation by multiple regulators in accordance with the Measures for Regulating Financial Leasing Companies (2000) issued by the CBRC, while regulation imposition varied from regulator to regulator. Financial leasing companies filed with the Ministry of Commerce were not allowed to engage in interbank lending and other financial business that had not been approved by the CBRC. Financial leasing companies under the supervision of the CBRC could obtain financing through their own funds, absorption of shareholders' deposits, interbank lending, issuance of financial bonds, and special loans for leasing projects. From 2017 onwards, the financial leasing business was brought under the unified supervision of the CBRC in the light of actual business operations.

FAMCs were imposed regulation in accordance with the Guidelines for the Supervision of Financial Asset Management Companies on a Consolidated Financial Statement Basis (for Trial Implementation, 2011) formulated and promulgated by the

CBRC, which set out the capital regulation rules and requirements for FAMCs for the first time.

In 2014, the CBRC worked with five ministries and commissions including the MoF, PBoC, CSRC and CIRC to jointly formulate and issue the Measures for Regulating Asset Management Companies (effective in January 2015), which are a holistic regulation governing the asset management industry in China. In this Measures, the capital regulation rules and requirements for FAMCs were further revised, including the reiteration that the parent company and affiliated legal entities of a financial asset group must comply with the uniform capital regulation rules and requirements imposed by their respective regulators on a consolidated financial statement basis.

In addition, the CBRC issued the Measures for the Capital Management of Financial Asset Management Companies (for Trial Implementation) in December 2017, which set out specific requirements and provisions for the capital regulation of asset management companies (e.g. developing proper capital management metrics for capital adequacy ratio and differentiated risk weights for assets).

By espousing the principles of separation of business and regulation, financial holding companies were brought under the supervision of competent regulatory authorities depending on the nature of their business. In addition, the internal departments and business operations of financial holding companies were also subject to separate regulation according to the nature of their business. Specifically, for FHCs operating abroad, the competent regulatory authorities were tasked with establishing external liaison and working together with the local regulatory authorities. Meanwhile, specific and targeted countermeasures such as regulatory policies, metrics and models have been studied and developed to regulate financially controlled groups that originated from industrial capital investments.

In the absence of legislation in some areas, regulatory legislation lagged behind the development progress of the Internet finance and fintech industries in old days. It was not until June 21, 2010 that the PBoC issued the Measures for the Administration of Payments by Non-financial Institutions. On September 21, 2010, it also issued the Detailed Rules for the Implementation of the Measures for the Administration of Payment Services Provided by Non-financial Institutions (Draft for Public Comments). Thereafter, third party payments were brought under the regulatory regime.

In May 2011, the PBoC announced the list of the first batch of 27 enterprises to be granted third-party payment licenses and business permits. Nevertheless, it was only on June 21, 2011 that the PBoC issued the Provisions on the Administration of the Testing and Certification of Non-financial Institution Payment Service Business Systems. In the following three years, it also issued business licenses to 269 third-party payment enterprises in five batches. However, these regulatory provisions were mainly concerned with regulation of market access rather than protection of financial consumers' rights and interests.

As a major statutes for regulating Internet finance, the Guiding Opinions on Promoting the Healthy Development of Internet Finance were jointly issued by ten ministries and commissions including the PBoC, CBRC, CSRC and CIRC in July 2015 to assign regulatory duties, exercise regulation and clarify main business such as online payments, online lending, equity crowd-funding, online fund sales, online insurance, online trust, and online consumer finance. Among them, major financial business such as online lending, online trust and online consumer finance were all subject to the regulation by the CBRC.

Non-banking financial institutions constituted a large part of financial institutional system and each industry had a corresponding industry association as a self-regulatory organization (e.g. the China Trustee Association and China National Association of Financial companies affiliated to enterprise group). For instance, the specialized committees of the China Banking Association were in charge of overseeing the self-regulation of financial leasing companies, auto finance companies and money brokerage companies respectively. On March 25, 2016, the National Internet Finance Association of China was established in Shanghai as a national self-regulatory organization for the entire Internet finance industry, which played a proactive role in tightening up industrial self-regulation, promoting industrial regulated development, protecting the rights and interests of consumers, and engendering the innovative enthusiasm of market players.

The China Society for Finance and Banking was responsible for overseeing the self-regulation of financial institutions and organizations, including local banks, funds, fund management companies, small loan companies, guarantee companies, investment companies, investment management companies, financial leasing companies, factoring companies and insurance companies.

5.4 Financial Risk Management and National Financial Security

As far as national financial security is concerned, financial risk regulation refers not only to the static regulation of financial markets and financial institutions, but also to the dynamic regulation of financial risk control and financial security network construction. Finance is the core competitiveness of the country, and financial security makes up the core of national security. Therefore, preventing and resolving financial risks, especially preventing the occurrence of systemic financial risks, is a fundamental task of our financial work. It is imperative to "effectively regulate financial practitioners, bring funds under control, and build a powerful institutional firewall".[6]

[6] Jinping Xi: Speech at the 13th Collective Study Session of the Political Bureau of the CPC Central Committee, February 22, 2019, http://www.gov.cn/xinwen/2019-02/23/content_5367953.htm.

5.4.1 Preventing and Defusing Systemic Financial Risks

Financial risk refers to the likelihood that an economic entity would suffer losses when engaging in financial activities, usually in terms of economic downturn risks, i.e. potential financial losses and the degree of uncertainty, including all types of risks associated with financing, which are characterized by uncertainty, pervasiveness, diffusion, hazard and contingency. In general, financial risks tend to severely undermine economy.

Financial risk includes micro financial risk and macro systemic risk. Micro financial risk is associated with the uncertainty of returns on specific assets, which can be measured by standard deviation or volatility. In theory, systemic risk refers to aggregate micro market risk that cannot be eradicated through diversification and it tends to provoke financial crises. In the related reports issued by the International Monetary Fund, the Bank for International Settlements and the Financial Stability Board in 2011, systemic risk was defined as the risk of widespread failure of financial services due to partial or total impairment of the financial system, with serious implications for the real economy. Systematic risk was measured and identified through an early warning indicator system and risk contagion measurement methods.

From the reform and opening up onwards, the economic philosophy of reform, development and openness underlay in China's financial sector. However, financial disruptions and turmoil have been bubbling away in the financial markets and the financial risks have been exposing in the development trajectory of the financial sector. In the 1980s and 1990s, recurrent inflation episodes and multiple campaigns for overhauling the financial industry and market brought about financial risks. How to prevent and mitigate these risks has posed a major challenge to the construction of China's financial regulatory system.

Internally, risks on the part of financial institutions were mainly incurred due to a combination factors: (1) The irregular and non-market-oriented business activities and practices of traditional state-owned commercial banks and other financial institutions, such as rural credit cooperatives and trust and investment companies (e.g. "irregular borrowing", "irregular fundraising" and "irregular approval for establishing financial institutions"); (2) The failures to address non-performing assets and bad or doubtful debts over the years in the reform of state-owned enterprises.

Risks in the financial market primarily stemmed from irregularities and illegality occurring in the process of the joint-stock reform and booming securities market as a result of "stock fever" since 1992, or arose from inflation caused by a rapid economic development. The speculation frenzy in real estate and land swept over China in the 1990s, particularly in Hainan province, Zhuhai city and Huizhou city of Guangdong province, and Beihai city of Guangxi province, setting off the first wave of China's property bubble since the reform and opening up. The bubble peaked in 1993, and the hyperinflation triggered by the property bubble continued until 1997.

During the eight-year overhaul of the financial market order in the 1990s, the government resorted to various political and economic instruments to eventually resolve various financial risks and successfully defuse the Asian financial crisis in

1997. Through institutional building, it strengthened the macro management of the securities market, and regulated all the financial activities according to the law.

In 1998, China's securities market achieved a steady and balanced development. Throughout the whole year, 120 enterprises issued shares at home and abroad, raising a total of RMB84,014 million from the market; and there were 851 domestic listed companies with a gross market capitalization of RMB1,950.5 billion, as well as 39 million investor accounts.[7] From 1998 to 2001, Chinese enterprises raised RMB503 billion from domestic and foreign securities markets, and national insurance premium income increased from RMB124.7 billion in 1998 to RMB210.9 billion in 2001.[8]

By the end of 2000, the Chinese government had basically established a financial risk management early warning system and a regulatory accountability system, and had progressively learned to defuse and manage financial risks in response to major domestic and international emergencies. Specifically, it had significantly reduced the non-performing loan ratio of four major reformed state-owned commercial banks, defused the payment risks of small and medium-sized financial institutions, rectified financial market order and maintained national financial security; cracked down on irregular and illegal fund-raising, establishment of financial institutions and financial business operations, defused systemic financial risks, and ensured national financial security and stability. Meanwhile, efforts had been made to support the implementation of the national strategy to expand domestic demand and develop the western regions, push through with the reform of state-owned enterprises and fulfill the three-year task of extricating them from difficulties; strengthen credit loan support for agriculture, science and technology and education so as to achieve a high economic growth and lay a solid foundation for accession to the World Trade Organization in December 2001.

Nevertheless, the so-called financial risks could not be eventually managed and controlled unless the structural problems of the economy were eradicated. In the long run, it was difficult to bail commercial banks out of financial risks and preserve their viability merely by injecting capital.

From the late 1990s to the early twenty-first century, the Chinese government instituted two major economic reforms that acted against the interests of tens of millions of people. The first reform aimed to restructure state-owned enterprises (SOEs) by introducing a policy of privatizing or closing down small state-owned enterprises while merging large state-owned companies into large industrial groups. With the exception of some SOEs that might affect the welfare of the state and the livelihood of the people, smaller SOEs were required to remove financial burdens and recover funds to pay off their debts through market-oriented reforms. The second reform was to re-launch the commercial housing market, whereby the welfare policy

[7] Wu Xiaoling (ed): *A Chronicle of Major Events in China's Financial Reform and Opening up*, China Finance Publishing House, 2008, p. 487.

[8] The People's Bank of China and *the Party Literature Research Center of the CPC Central Committee (ed): Selected Documents on Financial Work (1978–2005)*, Rongji Zhu: Herald a New Era of Financial Reform and Development in China, February 5, 2002, China Financial Publishing House, 2007, p. 464.

of allocating public housing to state-owned organizations has been progressively abolished.

Following these two economic reforms, the root causes of most perennial problems in China's economic reform and development were addressed, which has effectively alleviated the operating pressure on state-owned commercial banks. Those seemingly financial problems such as inflation, real estate bubbles and financial risk control and resolution went far beyond the financial realm. Actually, they were genuine political and economic issues.

In February 2002, the central government decided to take two major measures to prevent and control risks in the state-owned commercial banking system. First, central bank commenced to inject money into state-owned commercial banks by deploying foreign exchange reserves. Second, it encouraged state-owned commercial banks to go public abroad (mainly in Hong Kong) and bring in strategic investors while strengthening internal corporate governance in hope that the reform would bring down their bad debt ratio in excess of 15%.

In addition to these two economic reforms, China's booming economy was another key contributor to diffusing this round of financial risks. As a result of China's accession to the World Trade Organization, China's industrial and economic development coincided with a new wave of globalization, and global industrial chain restructuring. Meanwhile, the domestic private economy, with private enterprises at the core, was flourishing, and the real economy entered a golden development period at home. With the ongoing development and restructuring of the economy, the risk problems of the financial system have been partially mitigated and resolved.

Financial and economic globalization is a double-edged sword. By virtue of globalization, risks existing in China's economy and financial system have been mitigated to a certain extent. In the wake of the financial crisis of 2008, global systemic financial risks spread across China's financial sector, and therefore China's banking system and the real economy both have been affected to varying degrees. In response, the Chinese government has launched a $4 trillion crisis bailout programme, while lifting restrictions on local government borrowing.

From 2009 to 2019, the above bailout policy brought about a number of problems such as over-prosperity of the financial industry, volatility of the stock and housing markets, overcapacity in the real economy, and serious mismatch between supply and demand. It is worth mentioning that local government debt ballooned from zero to RMB22.53 trillion at the end of February 2020, posing a potential crisis risk to China's current and future economic development.

Since the launch of China's supply-side structural reform in 2016, a de-stocking campaign has been launched in the real estate industry to alleviate the problem of financial risks arising from enterprise and government debts. Although it failed to achieve the desired effect, this macro-regulation policy has highlighted the problem of debt risks across society.

In terms of the financial system as a whole, internal financial risks arise from the mismanagement of individual institutions, and stem from problems and hidden dangers occurring in the development trajectory of internal financial markets, which eventually leads to local or overall problems in the entire financial system; external financial risks are incurred as a result of the transmission of risks in relevant markets. By tracing the history of 40 years of reform and opening up, we have learned that the root causes of China's financial risks still lay in internal problems such as economic structure and business operating system, with risks mainly cropping up in the real estate market, stock market and debt market. Undoubtedly, policy and irrationality factors also contributed to financial risks.

From an endogenous and exogenous perspective, systemic financial risks in China were not only incurred in the financial sector, but also in non-financial sectors, which included over-financialization, high leverage ratio and ballooning asset bubbles of real estate; bond market risks such as high leverage ratios prevalent in the whole society, especially state-owned enterprises; spiking hidden local government debts, and serious asymmetry of relevant information; existing bad debt risks in economic downturns; frequent occurrence of financial disruptions and irregularities due to a lack of oversight over shadow banking; ramifications of fast-developing fintech on the traditional financial industry and financial regulation; greater risks and difficulties arising from uncertainties in the international economic and political environments.

By surfing the wave of fintech, unlicensed finance in the form of third-party payment companies, P2P companies and consumer finance companies has cropped up for the purposes of illegally raising massive private money in the name of Internet finance and financial inclusion. In other words, unlicensed finance has amplified credit and liquidity risks and made it more difficult for government departments to exercise regulation, thus inviting fintech risks. Another example is the capital operation crises of private enterprises such as such as Tomorrow's Empire in 2017, which exposed extremely complex financial risks, e.g. regulatory arbitrage, capital flight, insider trading, affiliate transactions and financial corruption incurred in the capital operations of private enterprises in the financial sector, as well as their intricate relationships with state-owned financial institutions. It was evident that the aforesaid financial risks and contributing factors were prone to spark off systematic risks.

It is well known that cumulative systemic financial risks would undermine and endanger the economic and financial security of a country. The work report at the 19th Party Congress highlighted the aforementioned issues and stressed that during the decisive period of building a moderately prosperous society, the Chinese government must resolutely fight in the three major battles of preventing and resolving major risks, eradicating poverty with precision and preventing and controlling pollution, and place the prevention and resolution of financial risks at the top agenda of the "three major battles".

In 2017, the Chinese government and the regulatory authorities launched the campaign for the "Toughest Financial Regulation Year" to impose proactive countermeasures to prevent and avoid illegal financial activities and risky incidents by relying on existing administrative and judicial systems. In the end, this campaign has prevented and resolved financial risks to a certain extent. By promptly cracking down on initial coin offering and crypto asset trading platforms, seven ministries and commissions including the PBoC commenced to overhaul Internet finance to prevent the financing risks of initial coin offering and preliminarily curb the financial risks in crypto asset-related areas.

However, these policies and measures have only scratched the surface of financial risks. Only by combining toughest regulation with proper guidance can we ultimately prevent and resolve financial risks. As finance and financial risks are closely bound up with the real economy, it is vital to avoid financial disruptions and irregularities, tighten institutional loopholes, and guide the flow of funds from the financial sector to the real economy. Needless to say, the synergy between finance and the real economy is the cornerstone of a country's financial stability and security.

Systemic financial risks refer to financial risks that may undermine and endanger the entire financial system and the real economy system, including potential and real systemic financial risks. Potential systemic financial risks can be prevented and resolved whereas real systemic financial risks (financial crises) are difficult to defuse. In the past 40 years of reform and opening up, the Chinese government held the bottom line of non-occurrence of systemic financial risks, i.e. non-occurrence of financial crisis. The underlying cause laid in a high long-term growth of the real economy, which has made the economic system more resilient to risks. Generally, the incomplete internationalization and non-convertibility of the *renminbi*, and the incomplete liberalization of capital accounts were the three main contributory factors for China to guard against systemic financial risks.

In a new era of socialism with Chinese characteristics, the Chinese government is slate to build an opener economy and therefore the three factors mentioned above are not prerequisites for the prevention and resolution of systemic financial risks. Therefore, the prevention and resolution of systemic financial risks is not only placed at the forefront of financial regulation, but also emerges as an eternal theme running throughout China's economic development trajectory. In the work report at the 19th Party Congress, both the decisive role of the market in the allocation of resources and systemic financial risks existing in the market were highlighted and reiterated, and the guidelines of holding the bottom line of non-occurrence of systematic financial risks were laid down as a prerequisite to ensure a country's financial security.

5.4.2 Micro and Macro Prudential Regulation

There is a need to establish a prudential regulation system to prevent systemic financial risks. With a focus on regulating the risks of individual institutions to reduce the likelihood of failure of individual institutions arising from imprudent operations, serious irregularities and excessive risk-taking, micro-prudential regulation embodies the conventional business philosophy of the financial stability policy model which assumes that by safeguarding individual institutions, the financial system will be safe and stable as a whole. In other words, a financial system consisting of all financial institutions will function properly if the operations of individual financial institutions run smoothly. Therefore, financial regulation merely needs to focus on how to ensure the smooth operation of individual financial institutions.

The existing core international standards for micro-prudential regulation included the Core Principles for Effective Banking Supervision and the Basel III Accord issued by the Basel Committee on Banking Supervision (BCBS), and the Insurance Core Principles promulgated by the International Association of Insurance Supervisors.

With the primary objective of mitigating systemic risk and lowering the macroeconomic costs of financial instability, macro-prudential regulation is viewed as a necessary factor for filling the gap between macroeconomic policies and conventional policies focusing on micro-prudential regulation of financial institutions, examining the interconnectivity of individual financial institutions and markets with the rest of the financial system, and mitigating the overall quantum of risk in the financial system (systemic significance), including correlated risk exposures to economic risk factors which jointly undermine the stability of the financial system. The macro-prudential regulators exerted top-down regulation against negative externalities.

In the aftermath of the financial crisis in 2008, the PBoC established the Financial Stability Bureau with a number of affiliated departments to comprehensively analyze and assess systemic financial risks as well as put forward proposals for preventing and mitigating systemic financial risks, etc. In 2011, the dynamic adjustment mechanism for differential reserves and the macro-prudential assessment system were officially introduced, shifting from exercising the prudential regulation of individual financial institutions to establishing a macro prudential assessment system. In 2012, an institutional framework for counter-cyclical macro-prudential regulation was continuously improved as an important move for improving the financial macro-regulatory regime.

On August 15, 2013, the State Council took an important step to prevent systemic financial risks by approving the establishment of a financial regulation coordination inter-ministerial joint meeting system (the "Joint Meeting") which was initiated by the PBoC with the participation of the CBRC, CSFC, CIRC and SAFE. Under this regulatory framework, financial issues such as cross-sector and cross-financial market innovations or regulatory arbitrage were supposed to be addressed to a certain extent.

The existing international macro-prudential financial regulation regime is primarily based on the relevant provisions set forth by the Financial Stability Board and the Basel Committee on Banking Supervision, such as Global Systemically Important Banks (G-SIBs). It is worth noting that the ICBC, ABC, BOC, CCB, and Ping An Insurance (Group) Company of China, Ltd. were all on the list of Global Systemically Important Financial Institutions (G-SIFIs), or Global Systemically Important Banks (G-SIBs) released by the Financial Stability Board in previous years. In compliance with the requirements imposed the Financial Stability Board, they have set up a crisis management group respectively to develop and update their recovery and resolution plans on an annual basis. In 2016, the Ping An Insurance (Group) Company of China, Ltd. completed its first round of resolvability assessments, the BOC and ICBC completed their second round of resolvability assessments, while the ABC and CCB completed their first round of resolvability assessments.

In 2016, the PBoC integrated the differential reserves dynamic adjustment mechanism with consensus loan management mechanism to officially upgrade the original regulatory regime to the macro-prudential assessment system (MPA), which guided banking financial institutions to strengthen self-restraint and self-regulation in terms of capital adequacy ratio, leverage ratio, assets and liabilities, liquidity, pricing, asset quality, cross-border business risks, and credit loan policy implementation. The assessment results were applied to the approval for differential deposit interest rates and differential insurance premiums, MPA, monetary policy tools, window guidance and counter-cyclical minimum capital requirements, thereby imposing "hard constraint" on the prudential regulation of financial institutions.

With a view to implementing the requirements of the Third Plenary Session of the 18th CPC Central Committee regarding the establishment of a sound management system for foreign debts and capital flows under a macro-prudential regulation framework, the PBOC has preliminarily established a macro-prudential policy framework for foreign exchange and cross-border capital movement. From the first quarter of 2017 onwards, the CBRC took the off-balance-sheet wealth management business of commercial banks as a broad credit loan target for macro-prudential assessment in an attempt to guide financial institutions to strengthen the management of their off-balance-sheet business risks and to better play the counter-cyclical market regulation and structural guidance role of the macro-prudential framework. Meanwhile, it also strengthened the prudential regulation of the asset management business and the shadow banking system, and continuously enhanced targeted and effective regulation.

As an important initiative to strengthen prudential regulation, the Financial Stability and Development Commission of the State Council was established in July 2017 to deploy financial reform, development and regulation, coordinate among monetary policy, fiscal policy and industrial policy, and strengthen authoritative and effective regulatory coordination.

In compliance with macro-prudential regulation requirements, all financial institutions were subject to regulation, including commercial banking institutions and their business operations, cooperative finance and other depository financial institutions, as well as non-banking financial institutions. In the future, an increasing number of financial activities that may have a significant ramification for the financial system (e.g. fintech, Internet finance and cross-border capital movement) will be brought under macro-prudential regulation.

In order to exercise macro-prudential regulation and prevent systemic risks, the PBoC launched the campaign for assigning ratings to central banking financial institutions. In the first quarter of 2018, it assigned ratings to 4,327 central banking financial institutions. On April 27, 2018, it also formulated and issued the Guiding Opinions on Regulating the Asset Management Business of Financial Institutions (the "Guiding Opinions"), which is the first fundamental instrument for prudential regulation. At its core, the Guiding Opinions aimed to overcome regulatory weaknesses, combat financial market disruptions and prevent systemic financial risks, and it was of great significance to the regulated development of the asset management industry.

5.4.3 The Deposit Insurance System and Security Network

As an important initiative to protect depositors against the loss of their insured deposits caused by depository financial institutions in the event of their failures, the deposit insurance system constitutes an integral part of financial security network. The world's first deposit insurance system originated in the United States in 1933 and it has played an important role in protecting the interests of depositors and maintaining the security and stability of the financial system.

In December 1993, the Chinese government proposed to establish a deposit insurance system, and the work to establish such a system covering all of depository financial institutions has gathered pace from 2006 onwards. On March 31, 2015, the State Council issued the Regulations on Deposit Insurance and the deposit insurance system was officially operated on May 1, 2015, eventually perpetuating the deposit insurance system that had been in the pipeline for 22 years.

The deposit insurance system was established according to the law to provide institutional protection for the legitimate rights and interests of depositors. Under such a system, the market-oriented exit mechanism for financial institutions has been further reformed and optimized, a long-term mechanism for the resolution of financial risks has been established, and a conventional implicit government guarantees model for financial institutions has been shifted.

In a new era, the launch of the deposit insurance system is attuned to an inevitable reform and development need for of China's financial sector. In reality, the deposit insurance system is conducive to protecting the interests of depositors, bolstering public confidence and maintaining financial stability; encouraging fair competition and promoting a balanced development in the banking sector; tightening up risk control and creating a healthy industrial environment; and building up a security network to ensure the smooth operation of the financial system under new circumstances.

As an important part of the financial security network, a deposit insurance system was introduced to address some important financial risk issues. Nevertheless, it has also posed certain system paradoxes. For example, the moral hazards of the deposit insurance system are of great concern. Under such an explicit deposit insurance system, depositors no longer need to choose their deposit banks in view of their qualifications because the safety of their deposits is guaranteed. Instead, the level of interest rates on deposits becomes the sole criterion for depositors to choose a bank. Undoubtedly, this reveals that banks are virtually immune from market oversight by depositors and that there is a potential for magnifying risks due to speculative incentive to achieve higher returns. Therefore, how to avoid the moral hazard of a deposit insurance system is a perennial thorny issue we need to tackle and it has posed a long-term challenge to us.

There are also issues arising from the "regulatory competition" between the deposit insurance system and existing regulators. On the one hand, deposit insurance agencies are assigned multiple regulatory responsibilities under this system.

Nevertheless, it is difficult to establish its regulatory boundaries with other regulators in relation to similar regulatory functions, which may undermine the authority of the regulator. On the other hand, multiple regulators may lead to increased regulatory costs. Therefore, it is also worth noting and addressing how to avoid gaps in the scope of regulation or gaps in authority arising from overlapping regulators and regulatory functions.

Apart from avoiding institutional paradoxes, a deposit insurance-based financial security network system also needs to fit in with other systems. This is the only way to establish an effective mechanism for the exit of financial institutions. To ensure the orderly and reasonable exit of "problematic financial institutions" from the market, a risk compensation system, a legal system for the insolvency of financial institutions, as well as a legal framework, judicial systems, regulatory rules and handling procedures applicable to the closure, merger, acquisition and reorganization and insolvency liquidation of financial institutions are all required.

5.4.4 Protection of Financial Consumers' Rights and Interests

In terms of both financial closed-loop regulation and financial security network construction, the Chinese government placed a premium on the protection of the rights and interests of financial consumers. In October 1993, the Law of the People's Republic of China on the Protection of Consumer Rights and Interests was deliberated and adopted by the National People's Congress. However, it is the earliest domestic legislation that protects the rights and interests of general customers instead of financial consumers, making it difficult to safeguard the rights and interests of financial consumers.

In the aftermath of the financial crisis in 2008, strengthening the protection of the rights and interests of financial consumers has become an international consensus and development trend, and protection of the rights and interests of financial consumers was regarded as an important initiative to maintain the stability of financial markets. In 2009, the Chinese government piloted a reform of protecting financial consumer rights and interests. Nevertheless, there was no legislation on the protection of the rights and interests of financial consumers in China. Under the legal system of financial regulation, which was centered on the aforementioned laws and administrative regulations, the concept of financial consumers has not been introduced, nor has the protection of the rights and interests of financial consumers been explicitly defined as an important target of financial regulation. Instead, only unworkable provisions such as "protecting the legitimate rights and interests of depositors and other customers", "protecting the legitimate rights and interests of investors" and "protecting the legitimate rights and interests of the parties involved in insurance activities" were generally set forth.

In 2012, the PBoC, CBRC, CSRC and CIRC set up the Financial Consumer Protection Bureau, the Banking Consumer Protection Bureau, the Investor Protection Bureau and the Insurance Consumer Protection Bureau respectively, thereby creating a regulatory organizational structure for protecting the rights and interests of financial consumers. In the meantime, the State Administration for Industry and Commerce, the China Consumers Association and various financial industry associations also undertook their respective functions and duties for protecting the rights and interests of financial consumers.

The PBoC set up the Financial Consumer Protection Bureau, which was comprised of the General Division, the Supervision and Inspection Division, the Financial Consumer Education Division, the Complaints and Investigation Division, and the Systems and Research Division. The Financial Consumer Protection Bureau was tasked to conduct the comprehensive research on major issues of financial consumer protection in China, and work with the relevant competent authorities to draw up a draft for policies and regulations on financial consumer protection as well as standards and norms for overlapping financial operations and services; monitor the risks of overlapping financial instruments, and coordinate and facilitate the consumer protection work; and carry out specific consumer protection work within the remit of the PBoC according to the law.

The former CBRC set up the Consumer Protection Bureau to strengthen the protection of consumer rights and interests. From 2012 onwards, more than 170 institutional and normative documents have been issued to protect consumer rights and interests in the banking sector, including implementing rules, implementing measures, guidelines and circulars. Additionally, a series of departmental rules and regulations have been also promulgated to protect consumer rights and interests in the banking sector, including guidelines, guiding opinions and evaluation measures. In the end, an institutional framework has taken shape, which consists of four major parts, namely statutory documents on consumer rights and interests; specific normative documents on complaint handling, information protection, publicity and education, internal assessment and audit, and code of conduct; institutional framework consisting of legal regimes for protecting consumer rights and interests, and management systems for specific products and services.

Meanwhile, the former CBRC also urged banking financial institutions to assume their respective responsibilities for continuously publicizing and popularizing financial knowledge of the banking sector. For example, the Shanghai Banking Regulatory Bureau explored the establishment of a whole process financial consumer protection system, while the Shenzhen Banking Regulatory Bureau innovated consumer protection training in rotation in an effort to provide reasonable guidance on financial consumer protection.

The Insurance Consumer Rights and Interests Protection Bureau was set up by the former CIRC to undertake the following major tasks: Formulating regulations and policies on the protection of the rights and interests of insurance consumers; studying the working mechanism for protecting the rights and interests of insurance consumers, and working with relevant departments to research and coordinate to grapple with major issues on the protection of the rights and interests of insurance consumers; receiving complaints and enquiries from insurance consumers, and investigating and handling complaints that may jeopardize the rights and interests of insurance consumers; building information systems for insurance consumer education and services, and releasing information on consumer risk alerts; guiding the safeguard of industry integrity; and urging insurance institutions to strengthen information disclosure relating to the rights and interests of insurance consumers.

Since its establishment by Chinese regulators, the Financial Consumer Protection Bureau has proactively promoted institutional building, established a sound complaint handling mechanism and constantly strengthened the oversight and assessment on financial institutions, while attaching great importance to public publicity and education for financial consumers. Despite its tangible results, the Bureau had difficulty in reforming the conventional institutional regulation model in any substantive manner due to its legislative, enforcement, staffing and funding deficiencies arising from its highly dependent and fragmentary institutional structure.

In December 2014, the CSRC approved the establishment of China Securities Investor Services Center under its direct administration as a securities and finance public welfare agency and a non-profit financial consumer protection organization, with the main duty of providing educational, legal, information and technical services for small and medium-sized investors to help them self-defend their rights. This is an important step for the CSRC to overhaul the investor protection system and effectively strengthen the protection of the legitimate rights and interests of small and medium-sized investors. Additionally, it is also a milestone in the move towards the rule of law and maturity of China's capital market.

Nowadays, the legal basis for the protection of financial consumer rights and interests is mainly comprised of two main parts.

Firstly, there are statutory laws such as the Law of the People's Republic of China on the Protection of Consumer Rights and Interests, the Law of the People's Republic of China on Commercial Banks, the Banking Supervision and Administration Law of the People's Republic of China, the Securities Law of the People's Republic of China, and the Insurance Law of the People's Republic of China, as well as administrative regulations such as the Regulations on the Administration of Savings, the Regulations on the Administration of Foreign Exchange, the Regulations on the Administration of the Credit Industry, and the Regulations on the Deposit Insurance System, among others.

Secondly, there are departmental rules and regulations such as the Administrative Measures for the Protection of Financial Consumer Rights and Interests (for Trial Implementation) issued by the PBoC (2013), the Guiding Opinions on Strengthening the Protection of Financial Consumer Rights and Interests (2015) promulgated by the State Council, and the Administrative Measures for Handling Consumer Complaints in the Banking and Insurance Industries (2020) issued by the CBIRC.

Among them, the Guiding Opinions on Strengthening the Protection of Financial Consumer Rights and Interests were issued by the State Council as a deployment for protecting the rights and interests of financial consumers at the central government level. In the Guidance Opinions, the work requirements for financial management authorities, financial institutions and relevant social organizations in the financial sector were set forth respectively, and 20 proposals were put forward in respect of regulating financial institutions, improving the regulatory regime and establishing a sound protection mechanism.

The Central Government has been attaching importance to the protection of the legitimate rights and interests of depositors, which has expedited the process of institutional building and establishing a financial safety network to protect the legitimate rights and interests of depositors, investors and the insured. In addition, this move has played a positive role in optimizing the securities investor protection corporation fund and the insurance security fund system, guarding against moral hazards, regulating and guiding the activities of financial institutions, creating a favorable market environment and social atmosphere, and thus promoting the sustainable and healthy development of the financial sector.

In recent years, the emergence of fintech has spawned novel financial business and lowered the investment threshold for internet finance consumers. However, the legitimate rights and interests of financial consumers have not been effectively protected, and there was a risk of infringement of legitimate rights and interests such as the right to privacy, the right to information and the right to protect the security of personal information. In an era of fintech, it is imperative to effectively protect the legitimate rights and interests of financial consumers.

The relevant legal provisions relating to the protection of consumer rights and interests in fintech and internet finance were set out in the Law of the People's Republic of China on the Protection of Consumer Rights and Interests and the Implementing Measures for Protecting the Rights and Interests of Financial Consumers. Nevertheless, the former only defined the terminology of financial consumers in principle yet rarely covered fintech and Internet finance consumers while the latter aimed to regulate financial institutions from the perspective of general finance consumer protection rather than specifically providing for special provisions on protecting fintech and Internet financial consumers.

In July 2015, ten departments of the State Council jointly issued the Guiding Opinions on Promoting the Healthy Development of Internet Finance, which officially incorporated Internet finance into the regulatory framework. In compliance with the principles of exercising lawful regulation, proper regulation, classified regulation, coordinated regulation and innovative regulation, the concept of protecting the rights and interests of financial consumers was introduced for the first time and unworkable provisions were just roughly set forth. In other words, the provisions were still too general and lacked operability.

Generally speaking, it can be said that currently as it is, a complete legal framework for regulating fintech is still pretty much absent, nor is a set of overarching laws and statutes at a higher level in place yet, a weakness that is to be remedied in a timely manner as this sector grows, so as to ensure a closed loop in terms of legislation for financial regulation, and to expand the coverage of China's finance security network.

Chapter 6
Evolutionary Trajectory of the Opening-Up of China's Financial Sector

From 1949 to 2019, the Chinese government succeeded in opening up its closed financial sector to the outside world through its efforts to reform the foreign exchange control regime, develop a foreign exchange market, and promote the internationalization of the RMB. As such, China's financial sector has progressively integrated into the world economy and it has become a major player in international finance in the process of economic globalization.

6.1 History of the Opening-Up of the Financial Sector

From 1949 to 1978, the Chinese government had limited financial exchanges with the rest of the world due to particular domestic and international environment at the time. From 1978 onwards, when the policy of reform and opening up was implemented throughout China, the Chinese government had the opportunity to start opening up its financial sector to the outside world and has since gone through different stages of opening up and development.

6.1.1 Initial Opening-Up Stage and Attracting Foreign Capital

From 1978 to 1991, China's financial sector entered a period of initiating opening-up and attracting foreign capital by adopting a global strategy of "bringing in" and "going global".

With the opening-up of Shenzhen, Zhuhai, Shantou and Xiamen special economic zones to the outside world, China's financial sector has progressively come out of its long-term isolation. From 1979 onwards, a policy of "bringing in" was adopted

Y. Wu, *A Financial History of China (1949–2019)*, Research Series on the Chinese Dream and China's Development Path,
https://doi.org/10.1007/978-981-99-6571-7_6

to allow foreign financial institutions to set up representative offices and business branches in China. 1979 saw the opening up of China's financial sector to the outside world when Japan's Shinsei Bank Ltd. opened a representative office in Beijing, which set a precedent for foreign banks to establish financial branches since the founding of the People's Republic of China in 1949 and kicked off the opening-up of China's financial sector. In 1982, Nanyang Commercial Bank in Hong Kong established a branch in Shenzhen, becoming the first foreign bank which were allowed to operate in business in China after the founding of the People's Republic of China. Besides, some famous banks from Japan, the United States, Britain, France, Germany, Canada and Sweden all have also successively established representative offices in China.

In the early 1980s, the Chinese government also commenced to open up its insurance industry to the outside world. In 1982, Minan Property and Casualty Insurance Company Limited were approved to set up a branch in Shenzhen. Meanwhile, foreign insurance companies were allowed to set up a representative office in China. By 1988, 10-odd foreign insurance companies such as American International Group Inc. (AIG) had set up 16 liaison offices in Beijing. In September 1992, the AIG set up the Pan-Asian Life Insurance Group (AIA) in Shanghai, becoming the first foreign insurance company which had been approved to operate in the life and non-life insurance business in China. In 1996, Manulife-Sinochem Life Insurance Co., Ltd. was established with approval as the first joint venture life insurance company in China.

In 1985, the State Council promulgated the Regulations of the People's Republic of China on the Administration of Foreign Banks and Sino-Foreign Joint Venture Banks in the Special Economic Zones, bringing in and regulating foreign-funded financial institutions according to the law, and officially allowing foreign banks to set up a business branch in Shenzhen, Zhuhai, Xiamen and Shantou special economic zones. In August 1985, Xiamen International Bank, a Sino-foreign joint venture, was established with a registered capital of RMB1,069 million. Subsequently, the branches of a large number of foreign banks were opened for operation in business in the special economic zones and they were licensed to directly operate in 10-odd business such as foreign currency deposits and loans as well as foreign trade settlements.

Meanwhile, the Chinese government encouraged domestic financial institutions to go global. On January 15, 1980, the ABC joined the International Fund for Agricultural Development (IFAD).

In the initial stages of opening-up, China won the recognition from the world economies and international financial organizations. On April 17, 1980, the Executive Board of the International Monetary Fund (IMF) passed a resolution to restore the seat of the People's Republic of China in the IMF, so did the World Bank on May 15, 1980. As of February 25, 1981, the IMF allocated the quota of SDR 1.8 billion to China.

In April 1988, the Hainan Special Economic Zone was established with approval. In 1990, the CPC Central Committee and the State Council decided to develop the Pudong New Area in Shanghai, allowing wholly foreign-funded financial institutions, Sino-foreign joint venture financial institutions and branches (hereinafter collectively referred to as "foreign commercial financial institutions") to settle in and conduct the licensed business in the Pudong New Area. In the same year, the PBoC promulgated the Measures for the Administration of Foreign-Funded Financial Institutions and Sino-Foreign Joint Venture Financial Institutions in Shanghai City, setting forth the relative procedures for the establishment, registration, business scope and administration of foreign-funded financial institutions. However, foreign-funded banks were only allowed to operate in foreign exchange business at that time.

6.1.2 Progressive Opening-Up and Market Liberalization

The period from 1992 to 2001 was a period of progressive opening-up and exploratory domestic market liberalization for China's financial sector.

The year 1992 was an important year for China's reform and opening-up. In June, 1992, the Chinese government successively designated seven coastal cities such as Guangzhou, Fuzhou, Ningbo, Nanjing, Qingdao, Tianjin and Dalian as pilot cities to bring in foreign-funded banks. Meanwhile, opening-up was also launched in the insurance industry on a pilot basis. On September 25, the AIG set up the AIA with approval in Shanghai, which was the first foreign-funded insurance company established in China.

As of the end of 1992, foreign financial institutions from 29 countries and regions set up 231 representative offices in 14 open coastal Chinese cities, and 68 foreign commercial financial institutions opened for operation in business in 5 special economic zones and the 8 open cities of Shanghai, Tianjin, Dalian, Qingdao, Ningbo, Nanjing, Fuzhou and Guangzhou. In Shanghai, 4 foreign banks and foreign financial companies affiliated to enterprise group were allowed to act as brokers in different foreign exchange adjustment centers.

In 1994, the Chinese government allowed the establishment of foreign commercial financial institutions in 11 inland cities, including Beijing and Shenyang. In 1997, nine foreign banks were allowed to conduct the RMB business in the Pudong New Area on a pilot basis. As of the end of 1997, there were 164 foreign commercial banks in China, an increase of 90 in four years, with a total asset of US$38 billion. From 1997 onwards, the pace of opening up to the outside world slowed down due to the Asian financial crisis and the uncertainty of China's accession to the WTO. Nevertheless, the Chinese government has been pursuing a national policy of opening up to the outside world all the time.

From 1996 to 1998, the Chinese government opened up its RMB business to foreign banks, allowing eligible foreign financial institutions to operate in the RMB business in the Pudong New Area of Shanghai as well as Shenzhen on a pilot basis. Meanwhile, it also further expanded the RMB business scope of foreign banks in Shanghai and Shenzhen.

With a view to steadily promoting the opening-up of the financial sector to the outside world, the PBoC lifted the regional restrictions on the establishment of branches of foreign financial institutions in China to allow more foreign banks to operate in the RMB business in 1999. With the support of this policy, the Shanghai Branch of Bank of New York, the Beijing Branch of Chase Manhattan Bank, the Shenzhen Branch of Citibank and the Shenzhen Branch of the Bank of Tokyo-Mitsubishi UFJ Limited (BTMU) were all allowed to carry out relevant business.

As of the end of September 1999, there were a total of 155 branches of foreign banks, 13 locally registered foreign-funded banks, 7 foreign-funded financial companies affiliated to enterprise group, and 248 representative offices of foreign banks in China.

In 2001, China's securities market made great strides in going global. The CSRC officially allowed some domestic residents to invest in the B-share market with their legally held foreign currencies, so did all of domestic residents on June 1 that year, marking the official opening-up of China's B-share market. As of the end of 2001, it allowed 177 foreign banks to operate in business in China, which held assets totaling US$45 billion. Overall, foreign banks were allowed to conduct the RMB business for a wider range of clients and regions. As such, they have become major players in the Chinese banking system.

On December 11, 2001, China officially joined the World Trade Organization (WTO) and the Chinese government was committed to further opening up China's banking, securities and insurance industries. On December 9, 2001, the PBoC released the Announcement on Issues Regarding Market Access for Foreign-funded Financial Institutions, undertaking to progressively open up the financial sector after China's accession to the WTO. On December 12, 2001, the Regulations on the Administration of Foreign-Funded Finance (the "New Regulations") were revised to stipulate that almost all the business in the financial sector has been or will be opened up to foreign financial institutions, marking that the opening up of the financial sector to the outside world entered a new development stage.

6.1.3 Expanded Opening-Up and Two-Way Interaction

From 2002 to 2017, the opening up of China's financial sector to the outside world entered an expanded openness and synergy period.

In terms of market access for foreign-funded financial institutions, as of the end of 2003, foreign banks set up 191 foreign commercial banks in China, of which 60-odd foreign banks were allowed to conduct the foreign exchange business for all kinds of customers without geographical restrictions, and 53 foreign banks were approved to operate in the RMB business in 9 cities (including Shanghai), and then 13 cities in 2004. Even more, they were allowed to conduct the RMB business for Chinese enterprises. Besides, there were also 2 Sino-foreign joint venture securities companies, 11 joint venture fund management companies, and 67 foreign commercial insurance companies in China. In 2004, three foreign auto finance companies were approved for establishment, while foreign insurance companies were established in 15 cities.

From December 11, 2004 onwards, the Chinese government commenced to comprehensively lift the business scope and geographical restrictions on foreign investments in the insurance industry to fulfill its WTO accession commitments. From 2005 onwards, foreign insurance companies were given national treatment in respect of their business, provided that foreign shareholders were not allowed to hold more than 50% of shareholdings in joint venture life insurance companies, nor were foreign property and casualty insurance companies allowed to operate in compulsory insurance.

As of the end of 2005, there were a total of 254 foreign commercial banks in China, with a total asset of US$87,657 million, accounting for 1.89% of the total assets of the Chin's banking industry. Among them, 154 foreign banking financial institutions were approved to operate in the RMB business in 25 cities in China, and 25 foreign financial institutions had an equity stake in 20 Chinese banking institutions. Additionally, there were 7 foreign securities companies, 20 Chinese holding Sino-foreign joint venture fund management companies, and 40 foreign insurance companies (including 23 Sino-foreign joint venture insurance companies and 17 wholly foreign-funded insurance companies) in China.[1]

On December 11, 2006, a transitional period for China's accession to the WTO ended and China' financial sector commenced to comprehensively open up to the outside world. Specifically, geographical and customer restrictions on foreign banks operating the RMB business in China, as well as restrictions on the establishment of branches and the scope of business of foreign financial institutions were all lifted, Meanwhile, a number of foreign financial institutions were allowed to gain access to China's financial market. As such, China's financial sector has made greater strides in its economic and financial globalization.

On December 1, 2002, the CSRC and the PBoC jointly issued the Interim Measures for the Administration of Domestic Securities Investments by Qualified Foreign Institutional Investors and the qualified foreign institutional investor (QFII) program was officially launched for implementation. On July 9, 2003, QFII program was officially carried out in China's financial market. In 2004, there were 11 foreign financial institutions that had obtained the QFII qualification. In 2005, there were a total of 32 QFIIs in China.

On June 20, 2007, the CSRC issued the Measures for the Administration of Overseas Securities Investment by Qualified Domestic Institutional Investors (For Trial Implementation) to launch the qualified domestic institutional investor (QDII) program, allowing QDIIs to conduct the overseas securities investment business.

Under the foreign exchange control regime, the QFII and QDII programs were launched as important moves for opening up the domestic capital market to the outside world, which has stimulated capital inflows and outflows to and from the capital market.

Following China's accession to the WTO, state-owned financial institutions such as the CCB, BOC, BOCOM, ICBC and ABC all brought in overseas strategic

[1] Financial Stability Analysis Group of the PBoC: China Financial Stability Report 2006, China Finance Publishing House, 2007, p. 6.

investors during their joint-stock regime reforms and successfully went public overseas. This is an important move for China to reform and open up the financial sector.

From 2009 onwards, the PBoC proactively promoted the opening-up of China's inter-bank bond market by encouraging domestic institutions to issue RMB-denominated bonds in Hong Kong and allowing international development financial institutions to issue RMB-denominated bonds in China on a pilot basis. Specifically, derivative products such as commercial paper, credit asset securitization products, medium-term notes, bond forward transactions, and RMB interest rate swaps were successively issued.

In 2014, the Chinese government continued to steadily promote the opening up of its bond market to the outside world by relaxing restrictions on Panda bond issuers and the size of Panda bond issues, and facilitating the successful issuance of SDR-denominated bonds. Meanwhile, efforts were made to promote stock market interconnection between China's mainland and Hong Kong. In November 2014, pilot trading for "Shanghai-Hong Kong Stock Connect" was conducted, so did "Shenzhen-Hong Kong Stock Connect" trading in December 2016. Additionally, the "Shanghai-Hong Kong Stock Connect" trading mechanism has been continuously optimized and the quota regime has been duly scraped. Meanwhile, the Chinese government was also actively promoting the preparatory work for establishing the "Shanghai-London Stock Connect" trading mechanism in the Shanghai and London stock markets.

The Chinese government was committed to opening up China's financial market to Taiwan, Hong Kong and Macao. On August 31, 2012, the cross-strait monetary authorities signed on the Memorandum of Understanding on Cross-Strait Clearing and Settlement Cooperation, in which both sides agreed to establish a cross-strait clearing mechanism in accordance with the principles and cooperation framework set out in the MOU. In August 2015, the CSRC approved the establishment of two joint venture securities companies and one joint venture fund management companies to further opened up China's securities companies and securities investment advisory institutions to Hong Kong and Macao by adhering to the Supplementary Agreement of Closer Economic Partnership Arrangement (CEPA).

As another important move towards the opening up of China's financial market to the outside world, the Shanghai Gold Exchange (SGE), a national financial factor market for gold trading, was established and officially put into operation with approval in October 2002, marking the opening up of China's gold market and the installation of a market-oriented gold production, consumption and distribution regime. From 2007 onwards, the SGE was among the world's top gold spot trading venues in terms of trading volume for ten consecutive years.

On April 19, 2016, the SGE's Gold Benchmark Price Auction was launched, which is the world's first gold benchmark price denominated in RMB. This pricing mechanism was established to promote the innovation, opening-up and going global of China's financial factor market, and accelerate the internationalization of China's gold market.

As of the end of 2018, the SGE had 260 members, including 157 ordinary members (including 28 financial members and 129 general members); and 103 special members (including 7 foreign financial members, 74 international members and 22 special institutional members such as securities companies, trusts, and small and medium-sized banks). It is worth mentioning that all the international members were internationally well-known banks, gold groups and investment institutions.

While promoting the opening up and two-way synergistic development of the financial sector, the Chinese government also encouraged flexible and pragmatic multilateral financial cooperation with foreign countries. From 2008 onwards, the PBoC officially joined the Financial Stability Board, the Basel Committee on Banking Supervision, and the Committee on the Global Financial System, actively engaged in the formulation of international regulatory rules (e.g. Basel Capital Accord III and systemically important financial institutions), and participated in the discussions on major issues such as global economic and financial governance, reform of the international monetary system, and financial regulatory reform.

With a view to promoting the pragmatic cooperation in the bilateral economy, finance and regional finance fields, the Chinese government actively attended major events such as the US-China Strategic and Economic Dialogue, the UK-China Economic and Financial Dialogue, the China-Japan High Level Economic Dialogue, the Working Group between the PBoC and the European Central Bank (ECB), the China-Russia Financial Cooperation Sub-Committee, the China-ASEAN Mechanism, and the ASEAN+3 mechanism.

6.1.4 The New Era of Opening-Up and Globalization

From 2018 onwards, China's financial sector entered a new era of opening to the outside world and continued its integration into the financial globalization process in different manners.

On April 10, 2018, General Secretary Jinping Xi launched a series of new initiatives for further opening up China to the outside world to expedite the opening-up of the China's financial sector. On April 27, 2018, the CBRC issued relevant policies and it also decided to further lower the market access threshold for foreign banks, accelerate the opening-up of the banking and insurance industries, remove the restrictions on the foreign shareholdings in Chinese banks and asset management companies, and enforce the rules and regulations that allowed domestic and foreign companies to have the same equity stake. On April 28, 2018, the CSRC allowed the establishment of joint venture securities companies controlled by foreign investors and progressively liberalized the business scope of joint venture securities companies, ushering in a new era of opening up China's financial sector to the outside world.

In the new era, the financial sector commenced to comprehensively open up to the outside world, with the participation of financial institutions such as banks, insurance companies, securities companies and fund management companies. Specifically speaking, the proportion of foreign investment in insurance companies, securities companies and fund management institutions was liberalized to 51% while investment restrictions were slated for further liberalization and even abolition in the coming years. The level of opening-up was unprecedented. Not only were QFIIs allowed to operate in the insurance agency business and insurance surveyors and loss adjusters business in China, but the business scope of foreign insurance brokers was liberalized to be in line with that of Chinese financial institutions.

On May 2, 2018, the UBS became the first foreign banking institution that applied for controlling a securities company in China. This is a specific case of China's securities industry opening up to the outside world in a new era.

The year 2019 witnessed the comprehensive opening-up of China's financial sector to the outside world. In June, 2019, the Chinese government and the British government officially launched "Shanghai-London Stock Connect" and China's A-shares were included in the FTSE Russell Global Index, accelerating the two-way opening-up of China's capital market. In July, 2019, the Chinese government rolled out 11 measures to promote opening-up by stipulating as follows: Allowing foreign financial institutions to assign ratings to all kinds of bonds in the interbank bond market and the bond exchange market while conducting the credit rating business in China; encouraging overseas financial institutions to establish and invest in the wealth management subsidiaries of Chinese commercial banks; allowing overseas asset management agencies to jointly establish foreign-controlled joint venture wealth management companies together with the subsidiaries of Chinese banks or insurance companies; allowing foreign financial institutions to establish and invest in pension management companies; assisting foreign investors in establishing wholly-owned or having an equity stake of inter-dealer brokers; putting to end the transition period for liberalizing the proportion of foreign equity in life insurance from 51 to 100% from originally scheduled 2021 to 2020 in advance; annulling the provisions that the aggregate shareholding of Chinese insurance companies in insurance asset management companies shall not be less than 75%, and allowing foreign investors to hold more than 25% shares; and liberalizing the access threshold for foreign insurance companies, and waiving the 30-year operating period requirements.

On September 16, 2019, the SAFE announced the abolition of QFII/RQFII quotas. Meanwhile, the restrictions on countries and regions under the RQFII pilot scheme were also lifted. In December, 2019, Amundi Asset Management Co., Ltd. and BOC Wealth Management Co., Ltd. jointly established a joint venture wealth management company with approval in Shanghai, with a contribution ratio of 55% and 45% respectively.

After China's financial sector entered a new era of opening-up, an irreversible trend towards the deeper degree of economic and financial integration between China and other countries has emerged. Specifically, the Chinese financial sector has shifted from "brining in" in the early stages, then to "bringing in" and "going global", and eventually to today's comprehensive opening-up and deeper degree of integration and synergy. In the opening-up process, the Chinese government has expedited the process of going global in China's financial sector, thereby promoting its reform and development, as well as accelerating the pace of its integration into financial globalization.

6.2 Reform and Overhaul of the Foreign Exchange Control Regime

The opening-up of China's financial sector involved institutional reform and restructuring, and the reform of the foreign exchange regulation regime formed the core.

6.2.1 Foreign Exchange Retention and the Exchange Rate Dual-Track Regime

From 1978 to 1993, China's foreign exchange control regime reform got off the ground, aiming to allow enterprises to have greater autonomy in their handling of the foreign exchange and implement an exchange rate dual track regime.

After China's reform and opening-up was launched in 1978, the former regime of unified collection and allocation of foreign currencies was progressively liberalized, and export enterprises gained a certain degree of autonomy in their disposal of their surplus foreign currencies and foreign currency quotas. For the sake of mobilizing the enthusiasm of export enterprises to earn foreign currencies and ensuring the concentrated utilization of limited foreign exchange resources in national economic construction, a foreign exchange retention policy was introduced in 1979. While foreign currencies were centrally regulated in a unified, balanced and prioritized manner, foreign currency-earning export enterprises were duly allocated the quotas for retaining certain foreign currencies earned, and they were allowed to sell or lend their surplus foreign currency quotas to those with insufficient foreign currency quotas. As a result, a foreign exchange adjustment market has taken shape.

As a transitional product of imposing the foreign exchange control regime, foreign exchange certificates were issued for special foreign exchange trading purposes on April 1, 1980. In those days, China imposed a unique dual currency regime, whereby both *renminbi* and equivalent foreign exchange certificates were in circulation in the market. It was not until January 1, 1995 that all of foreign exchange certificates were finally withdrawn from the circulation in the market.

In the absence of reform policies, a "dual track regime" in the foreign exchange market was in place from 1981 to 1984, in which an official exchange rate and an adjustment market exchange rate coexisted. The internal exchange rate for international trading settlement was set at US$1:CNY2.8 and the official exchange rate was applied to non-international-trading foreign exchange settlement. As the first attempt to push through with the reform in China's former rigid fixed exchange rate regime, the "exchange rate dual track regime" was imposed to reward exports and restrict imports by applying dual exchange rates.

On January 1, 1985, the Chinese government decided to abolish the internal exchange rate for international trading settlement and it reverted to the unified exchange rate regime by setting the exchange rate of US$1:CNY2.8. On July 5,

1986, a sudden depreciation in the CNY rate occurred, and the CNY rate was lowered to RMB3.7 for each US dollar. From 1986 onwards, the CNY Exchange Rate was pegged to a basket of currencies under the "pegged exchange rate regime". In practice, however, it eventually transformed into a "pegging-to-the US-dollar exchange rate regime".

The "exchange rate dual track" regime and the "pegging-to-the-US-dollar exchange rate regime" merely functioned as transitional exchange rate regimes, which were not conducive to shifting enterprise business models, leveraging foreign capital, conducting international economic exchanges with the rest of the world, and installing a unified foreign exchange market system. Therefore, it was imperative to put reform into practice.

6.2.2 The Exchange Rate Dual-Track System Reform and the Banking Foreign Exchange Sales and Purchase Regime

The period from 1994 to 2000 witnessed the reform of China's foreign exchange control regime and the imposition of a new regime. On January 1, 1994, the Chinese government decided to launch a unified exchange rate reform and installed a new foreign exchange control regime. The long-term objective was to realize the convertibility of the RMB, while the interim objective was to achieve the convertibility of the RMB under current accounts and launch the inter-bank foreign exchange market. The unified exchange rate reform was primarily carried out in the following aspects:

First, exchange rates were unified and foreign exchange certificates were abolished. The issuance of foreign exchange certificates was ceased, and those issued in circulation were progressively redeemed. On July 1, 1995, foreign exchange certificates were prohibited from redemption. The exchange rate dual track regime was duly abolished when the Chinese government forbade the use of foreign currencies for denomination, settlement and circulation purposes in China. With the establishment of an interbank foreign exchange trading market, the unified CNY Exchange Rate was primarily dictated by the supply and demand in the foreign exchange market. Following the application of a unified exchange rate, China imposed a unified and regulated floating exchange rate regime based on market supply and demand.

Second, a banking foreign exchange settlement regime was imposed. As the foreign exchange retention regime was abolished, all of domestic enterprises, public institutions, government agencies and social organizations must promptly transfer their foreign exchange earnings back to China. According to related provisions, net foreign exchange earnings from foreign exchange business operations which banks were required to turn over, as well as foreign exchange earnings such as foreign exchange profits from overseas labor service contracts and overseas investments that should be transferred to China must be sold to the designated foreign exchange banks at the nominal exchange rate. Meanwhile, the original foreign exchange control regime for retaining, turning over and imposing quotas on foreign currencies was duly abolished accordingly.

Third, a banking foreign exchange sales regime was imposed. Provided that a foreign exchange settlement regime is imposed, approval for normal foreign exchange payment plans under current accounts has been abolished. Instead, domestic enterprises, public institutions, government agencies and social organizations were allowed to purchase foreign currencies at designated foreign exchange banks and make foreign exchange payments under current accounts on the strength of specific valid documents.

Fourth, the inter-bank foreign exchange market was established and the exchange rate formation mechanism was optimized. After maintaining a reasonable and relatively stable CNY Exchange Rate and imposing the banking foreign exchange sales and purchase regime, the Chinese government commenced to establish a unified national interbank foreign exchange market and designated foreign exchange banks were major players in the foreign exchange market. Under the supervision by the PBoC via the SAFE, the interbank foreign exchange market mainly functioned to maintain the net open position of designated foreign exchange banks within prudential limits, and to provide positions closing, filling and clearing services.

After the inter-bank foreign exchange market was established, the PBoC published USD/CNY central parity rate and the exchange rates of CNY against other major currencies by reference to international foreign exchange markets on a daily basis. In view of foreign exchange supply and demand, designated foreign exchange banks handled foreign exchange transactions for their customers at their published exchange rates within a floating range specified by the PBoC.

Following the exchange rate unification reform, the foreign exchange regulatory authority continued to optimize the foreign exchange control and settlement regime. Specifically, it abolished the prudential limit under current accounts, streamlined the audit and approval procedures for selling and purchasing foreign currencies, and increased the annual caps on foreign currencies purchased by individuals, so as to facilitate trade and investment.

Through the unified exchange rate reform, the Chinese government has preliminarily established an institutional framework for foreign exchange control that was compatible with the socialist market economy system, and the foreign exchange supply and demand market was in full swing, reinforcing the fundamental role of the market mechanism for allocating foreign exchange resources.

6.2.3 Two-Way Equilibrium Management of Capital Mobility

From 2001 onwards, a market-oriented foreign exchange management regime was installed to bring in the two-way equilibrium management of capital mobility. As China's foreign exchange reserves spiked after the accession to the WTO, the Chinese government optimized the large-scale foreign exchange reserve management regime by developing a benchmark and investment management model and a risk management framework for operating foreign exchange reserves in a standardized, professional and internationalized manner in 2001. Additionally, the reform of the CNY exchange rate formation mechanism initiated in July 2005 promoted the development of the foreign exchange market. Meanwhile, the Chinese government also shifted the focus of foreign exchange reserve management from managing foreign currency outflows to achieving a balance between foreign currency outflows and inflows, shaping an institutional framework for exercising a balanced management of two-way capital mobility.

As of 2008, according to the newly revised Regulations on the Management of Foreign Exchange, the foreign exchange regulatory authority developed a foreign exchange equilibrium management regime and imposed administrative regulations to explicitly abolish the mandatory foreign exchange sale and purchase regime.

After the financial crisis arose across the world in 2008, the Chinese government promptly launched the emergency handling mechanism, formulated contingency plans for international balance of payments and proactively guarded against financial risks, so as to ensure the overall safety of foreign exchange reserve assets, and withstand the severe impact of the international financial crisis.

From 2009 onwards, with a view to addressing the issues such as the complexity and scale expansion of cross-border capital flows and the growing demand for the convenience of market participants, the foreign exchange regulatory authority has promptly reformed foreign exchange management philosophy and patterns in five areas: shifting from audit and approval to monitoring and analysis, from pre-management to post-management, from behavior management to market participant management, from "guilty until proven innocent" to "innocent until proven guilty", and from "positive list" (whatever is allowed is not forbidden) to "negative list" (whatever is not allowed is forbidden).

The aforesaid reform has achieved the desired effects.[2] Specifically, the number of foreign exchange items subject to administrative approval has been curtailed to 17, down by 80%; the reform of foreign exchange management for trading in goods and services has proceeded smoothly, and the degree of convertibility of the RMB has been further improved; conventional methods and means of foreign exchange management such as foreign exchange item-by-item reconciliation have been phased out; items subject to pre-approval for foreign exchange control have been drastically curtailed and the focus of foreign exchange management has been shifted from pre-management to in-event management and post-management; the cross-border capital flows monitoring and early warning capability has been enhanced, and a system for managing foreign debts and capital mobility under a macro-prudential regulation framework has been progressively established.

[2] State Administration of Foreign Exchange: *Institutional Functions and Historical Evolution*. Please refer to the relevant reports on the official SAFE website for details, http://www.safe.gov.cn/safe/lsyg/index.html. Accessed on August 28, 2018.

By shifting foreign exchange control philosophy and patterns, the Chinese government has further enhanced its capacity to serve the real economy and prevent risk shocks through foreign exchange management.

6.3 Establishing an Open Foreign Exchange Market

From 1949 to 1979, the Chinese government established a unified foreign exchange control system characterized by "unified collection and allocation". In the absence of a free market for foreign exchange, there was only an official market in which foreign currencies were allocated and traded at an official exchange rate. In other words, foreign currencies were collected and allocated in a unified manner without inter-transactions and inter-lending, and the CNY rate was merely used as a bookkeeping and accounting tool instead of having a leverage effect for regulating the economy. Following the reform and opening up, a foreign exchange adjustment market with Chinese characteristics and a regulated inter-bank foreign exchange market progressively took shape, and the RMB exchange rate formation mechanism underwent reform.

6.3.1 National Foreign Exchange Adjustment Market

With a view to encouraging enterprises to increase exports and earn more foreign currencies, the Chinese government installed a foreign exchange retention regime in 1979. By allowing foreign currency-retaining enterprises to sell or lend their surplus foreign currencies or foreign currency quotas to those in need at an official exchange rate, the BoC commenced to conduct the foreign currency adjustment and quota lending and trading business for the sake of adjusting foreign currencies and foreign currency quota surplus and shortage in October 1980, bringing forth a fledgling foreign exchange adjustment market. Additionally, foreign exchange adjustment centers were set up in different regions, and the former "unified mandatory foreign exchange planed control and allocation regime" was duly abolished.

From 1980 to 1987, China's foreign exchange adjustment market was in its infancy, and the Chinese government made explorations in developing a foreign exchange adjustment market. As the adjusted exchange rate was only 10% higher than the official exchange rate, the trading volume was small and more often than not, quotations were offered without transactions in the market. In order to expedite the thriving process of the foreign exchange adjustment market, the Chinese government chose Shanghai as the first pilot city and adjusted the exchange rate to RMB 1 higher than the official CNY/USD exchange rate in the summer of 1985. In other words, the foreign exchange adjustment work was mainly carried out by the SAFE and its regional branches. In addition to enterprises and public institutions engaging in import and export trade, foreign-funded enterprises were also allowed to trade in the foreign exchange market.

In 1986, the State Council reformed foreign exchange retention and adjustment policies, liberalized the floating range of the foreign exchange adjustment rate, and redefined the targets and eligibility for foreign exchange adjustment. Subsequently, foreign exchange adjustment exchanges or foreign exchange adjustment centers were successively set up in different provinces, municipalities, cities specifically designated in the state plan and special economic zones. In November 1986, foreign exchange adjustment centers for foreign-funded enterprises were also set up in Shanghai and other regions respectively.

As the foreign trade system reform proceeded and enterprises generally implemented a foreign trade contracting system, the imbalance between foreign exchange supply and demand was exacerbated. From 1988 to 1993, the foreign exchange adjustment market was booming and reforms were pushed through all along.

In March 1988, the SAFE set forth new provisions on foreign exchange adjustment to allow to set up foreign exchange adjustment centers in different provinces, autonomous regions, municipalities directly under the central government, and cities specifically designated in the state plan, thereby setting off a new round of the development of the foreign exchange adjustment market.

In 1988, the first open market for foreign exchange adjustment was established in Shanghai to adjust the foreign currencies or foreign currency quotas of foreign currency-retaining enterprises, followed by Shenzhen, Nanjing city, Fuzhou city, Xiamen city, Beijing city and so on. In addition to Chinese enterprises and public institutions, wholly foreign-funded enterprises, Sino-foreign joint ventures and overseas Chinese-funded enterprises were all allowed to trade in the foreign exchange adjustment market, so did individuals from December 1, 1991 onwards.

It was not until 1991 that China had a truly national foreign exchange market. Prior to 1991, 90-odd open and non-open foreign exchange adjustment markets of varying size were scattered throughout the country without interconnection.

On August 8, 1992, National Foreign Exchange Adjustment Centre was opened for operation in business in Beijing. In the same year, a joint foreign exchange quotation network consisting of 26 local foreign exchange adjustment centers was put into operation in China as an information network for foreign exchange adjustment quotations and transactions. Through electronics computers networking, more than 100 foreign exchange adjustment markets established across the country were connected for unified foreign exchange transactions. On this basis, 15 regional open foreign exchange adjustment markets were set up in different regions and 1 national open foreign exchange adjustment market were established in Shanghai respectively. As of the end of 1993, a national unified foreign exchange adjustment market progressively took shape, and 80% of foreign exchange resources were allocated via the foreign exchange adjustment market.

On October 25, 1998, the PBoC and the SAFE decided to suspend foreign exchange adjustment business and incorporate all the foreign exchange adjustment business of foreign enterprises into the banking foreign exchange sales and purchase regime, thereby successfully making market-oriented allocation of foreign exchange resources. This marked the phase-out of the foreign exchange adjustment market.

6.3.2 A Unified Interbank Foreign Exchange Market

The monolithic interbank foreign exchange market originated from the exchange rates unification reform initiated on January 1, 1994. On February 15, 1994, the PBoC decided to set up the China Foreign Exchange Trade System (CFETS). On March 1, 1994, the CFETS was put into trial operation. On April 1, 1994, the CFETS was inaugurated in Shanghai to provide a transaction platform for a monolithic interbank foreign exchange market, and local foreign exchange adjustment centers were restructured as China Foreign Exchange Trade Sub-systems which were connected to the CFETS for foreign exchange transactions. On April 4, 1994, the monolithic interbank foreign exchange market was officially put into operation. On April 5, 1994, the National Interbank Funding Center launched the CNY/HKD trading business in the interbank foreign exchange market, eventually forming a national unified, market-oriented and regulated CNY foreign exchange market.

The interbank foreign exchange market served as a modern trading network which was characterized by a membership system, centralized clearing and settlement of domestic and foreign currencies, and an auction trading mechanism of automated quotations and matchmaking trade off. By following the administrative pattern of "separation of three powers", the CFETS was mandated to serve financial institutions and supervise market operations, install the foreign exchange trade system, support and organize foreign exchange transactions, handle the settlement and clearing of foreign exchange transactions, and afford foreign exchange information services; the SAFE was in charge of regulating the foreign exchange market; and the Open Market Operations Office of the PBoC was responsible for tightening up the macro-regulation of the foreign exchange market.

In April 2002, the CFETS launched the EUR/CNY trade in the interbank foreign exchange market subject to the approval from the SAFE. Meanwhile, a market maker regime was imposed for EUR/CNY and HKD/CNY transactions on a trial basis.

As of the end of July 2002, there were a total of 314 members in the interbank foreign exchange market, including 232 proprietary members (60 Chinese members and 172 foreign members) and 82 agency members. In December 31, 2002, the trading volume of the interbank foreign exchange market reached a record high, with a cumulative market turnover of US$97,190 million.

On April 14, 2004, the SAFE approved the CFETS to conduct foreign currency transactions. On May 18, 2005, the CFETS officially launched a foreign currency trading system. On August 15, 2005, it also commenced to handle interbank foreign exchange forward transactions.

On January 3, 2006, the PBoC decided to introduce the market maker and OTC trading mechanism and it empowered the CFETS to publish the central parity rate of CNY against USD, EUR, JPY and HKD each business day. On January 4, 2006, it switched the central parity rate formation model from previously referring to the closing rate of the preceding day to calculating based on a weighted average of rates offered by market makers before the opening of the interbank market each business day. Thereafter, it also officially launched the market maker and OTC mechanism for the quotation-and-order-based interbank foreign exchange market in place of the auction trading mechanism.

On December 7, 2006, the SAFE newly approved 6 new interbank foreign exchange market makers and there were a total of 21 market maker members including 13 Chinese banks and 8 foreign banks in the interbank spot foreign exchange market.

With the improvement of the foreign exchange trading system, transactions in other foreign currencies were successively conducted and new transaction models were rolled out in the interbank foreign exchange market. From 2010 to 2011, the CFETS launched foreign exchange transactions in foreign currencies such as USD/SGD, CNY/Malaysian ringgit, CNY /Russian ruble, Australian dollar/CNY and Canadian dollar/CNY, as well as CNY/Thai Baht regional transactions in the interbank foreign exchange market. From 2012 to 2016, it also operated in direct foreign exchange transactions in CNY against 18 national currencies including the Japanese yen, Australian dollar, New Zealand dollar, British pound, euro, Singapore dollar, Swiss franc, South African rand and South Korean won. Meanwhile, it also debuted various forms of foreign exchange derivatives business.

In terms of institutional reform, the CFETS has optimized the market maker mechanism. On January 3, 2015, the first securities company (Guotai Junnan Securities Co., Ltd.) and fund company (Harvest Fund) entered the interbank foreign exchange market. On November 25, 2015, the first batch of 7 foreign central banking institutions penetrated the interbank foreign exchange market, so did the first batch of 6 foreign participating banks in the RMB purchase and sale business on May 20, 2016. On September 14, 2015, Hawaii Technologies Co., Ltd. entered the interbank foreign exchange market as the second non-financial enterprise spot transaction member. Meanwhile, all the market maker banks netted the OTC transactions in the interbank foreign exchange market. As of June 2020, there were a total of 30 market makers conducting the foreign exchange spot transactions and 27 market makers operating in foreign exchange forward and swap transactions.

China's foreign exchange market has undergone a bottom-up development process from scratch, with trading patterns moving from simple to complex, from decentralised to centralised and from closed to open-up after the reform and opening up. As the mainstay of China's financial market, the national interbank foreign exchange market has eventually taken shape, facilitating the flow of international capital and promoting the development of enterprises going abroad and economic globalisation.

6.3.3 Reform of the CNY Exchange Rate System

From 1949 to 2019, China's exchange rate regime went through reforms for several times. From 1949 to 1952, a flexible CNY Exchange Rate regime was launched, followed by a fixed exchange rate regime from 1953 to 1972, which was superseded by a "pegged exchange rate system" from 1973 to 1980. From 1981 to 1984, a "dual track regime" was installed in the foreign exchange adjustment market where the official exchange rate and the adjustment market exchange rate coexisted. The exchange rates unification reform was instituted in January 1994 to terminate the "exchange rate dual track regime". Thereafter, a unified and regulated floating exchange rate regime based on market supply and demand was put in place.

After several years of operational practice, the floating exchange rate system has undergone transitions. In particular, after the Asian financial crisis in 1997, the RMB exchange rate was in a state of hyper-stability and shifted from a floating exchange rate regime to a unified exchange rate regime pegged to the US dollar. Under such circumstances, the excessive intervention of the PBoC in the operation of the foreign exchange market made it difficult to install a market-oriented RMB exchange rate formation mechanism. In addition, the Chinese government's dominant role in allocating foreign exchange resources exposed it to significant clearing and exchange rate risks.

On July 21, 2005, the Chinese government launched the RMB exchange rate reform for the second time since 1994 to overhaul the RMB exchange rate formation mechanism. The PBoC officially announced the imposition of a regulated floating exchange rate regime and decided to expand the floating range of the RMB against the USD from 0.3 to 0.5% in the interbank spot foreign exchange market. By shifting from a US dollar-pegged exchange rate regime to one pegged to a basket of currencies, the reform was carried out to achieve the conditional convertibility of the *renminbi* under current accounts. This marked the institution and steadily implementation of the reform of the RMB exchange rate formation mechanism.

The RMB exchange rate reform was unleashed comprehensively in July 2005. Subsequently, the PBoC subsequently rolled out a series of supporting measures, including relaxing the eligibility requirements for participants in the interbank spot foreign exchange market, allowing eligible non-banking financial institutions and non-financial enterprises to trade in the interbank foreign exchange market, and installing a market maker regime in the foreign exchange market.

Following the RMB exchange rate reform in 2005, The PBoC steadily and orderly pushed ahead with the market-oriented reform of the RMB exchange rate formation mechanism. The floating range of CNY/US dollar exchange rate in the spot foreign exchange market was adjusted from 0.3% to 0.5%, then to 1% and to 2% respectively for three times on July 21, 2007, April 16, 2012 and March 17, 2014 respectively. As such, the elasticity of the RMB exchange rate has been enhanced and the market-oriented exchange rate formation mechanism has been progressively optimized.

On August 11, 2015, the PBoC launched the third round of RMB exchange rate reform, also known as the "811" exchange rate reform, which mainly reformed the central parity rate quotation mechanism. Thereafter, market makers were allowed to offer a weighted average of rates to the CFETS prior to the opening of the interbank foreign exchange market each business day by referring to the closing rate of the interbank foreign exchange market on the preceding business day, and comprehensively taking account of foreign currency supply and demand as well as the changes in the exchange rates of major foreign currencies.

Following the "811 exchange rate reform", the RMB exchange rate entered a period of appreciation, with the CNY/USD exchange rate once getting close to the level of 6:1. Meanwhile, the central parity rate quotation mechanism was optimized, the market-oriented guidelines were laid down, and therefore a market-oriented RMB exchange rate formation mechanism was installed, making it more possible to impose a regulated floating exchange rate regime, and laying the foundation for achieving the third step objectives in the reform of the RMB exchange rate regime—the free convertibility of currencies under capital accounts.

6.4 Cross-Border Settlement in RMB and Internationalization of the RMB

The internationalization of the RMB was launched in 1996 when the RMB was freely convertible under current accounts. Nevertheless, due to various reasons, the pace of RMB internationalization was slowed down, and the *renminbi* was only in circulation in a few neighboring countries and regions. In particular, it was more often used for cross-border trade payment and settlement.

6.4.1 Cross-Border Payment and Settlement in RMB

As reform and opening up were rolled out nationwide and foreign trade was flourishing, the *renminbi* was initially used as a payment and settlement currency for border and cross-border trade. Subsequently, the *renminbi* was used as a payment and settlement currency for foreign trade in specific countries and regions and then its use was up-scaled in more countries and regions, gaining recognition from a growing number of countries and international businesses.

In the wake of financial crisis in 2008, the Chinese government introduced measures to promote the RMB settlement of cross-border trade and investment, mainly in China's neighbouring countries and regions given the exchange rate risks faced by enterprises. In the end, it has succeeded in settling cross-border transactions in RMB in neighboring countries and regions.

In December 2008, the Chinese government allowed a pilot RMB settlement for trading in commodities with ASEAN in Guangxi province and Yunnan province. From 2008 onwards, it signed bilateral RMB swap agreements of RMB 650 billion with six countries and regions, including South Korea, Hong Kong, Malaysia, Belarus, Indonesia and Argentina. Meanwhile, it also entered into RMB settlement agreements with the central banks of eight neighboring countries and regions such as Russia, Vietnam and Mongolia, allowing commercial banks of the signatories to open agency accounts for RMB settlement.

On April 8, 2009, the Chinese government decided to launch a pilot scheme for cross-border trade RMB settlement in Shanghai, Guangzhou city, Shenzhen, Zhuhai city and Dongguan city. In June 2010 and August 2011, the pilot scheme was further rolled out to 20 provinces and cities including Liaoning province and then across China respectively. Meanwhile, cross-border two-way RMB capital pools and individual cross-border RMB settlement services were put into trial operation in the pilot free trade zones in Shanghai, Fujian province, Tianjin city, Guangdong province and other pilot regions.

On August 22, 2011, cross-border transactions were settled in RMB across China. As of the end of June 2012, Chinese banks handled the RMB settlement business totaling RMB3.2 trillion under current accounts. In September 2013, the BOC officially launched BOC Cross-border RMB Index (CRI) worldwide which served as an authoritative gauge of the usage of the *renminbi* in cross-border and offshore transactions as well as the progress of RMB internationalization.

In Southeast Asia, the *renminbi* was used as a hard currency, second only to U.S. dollar, the British pound, the euro, and the Japanese yen. In China's southwest border areas, the *renminbi* is reputed to be "Mini US Dollar". In other neighboring economies such as Mongolia, Russia, Kazakhstan, Malaysia, Indonesia, the Philippines and South Korea, the *renminbi* was also used as a payment and settlement currency. In Hong Kong and Macao, the *renminbi* was wildly accepted and it was in circulation in a wider range of sectors.

On October 8, 2015, the Cross-border Interbank Payment System (CIPS) Phase I was officially launched and China International Payment Service Corp. was established for CIPS operation in Shanghai. The first batch of direct participants included 19 financial institutions, with 8 participants newly joining in July 2016. In 2015 alone, cross-border RMB receipts and payments totaled RMB12.1 trillion, an increase of 22% year-on-year. Up to date, the RMB Cross-Border Payment System (CIPS) has covered about 90 countries and regions and more than 800 banks.

As of the end of 2015, 170,000 domestic enterprises used the *renminbi* for settlement, and banks from over 124 countries and regions opened RMB interbank accounts in China; 292 overseas financial institutions obtained the quotas of RMB 1.98 trillion in the interbank bond market. As such, cross-border RMB financial transactions were carried out in an orderly manner.

According to the PBoC's statistics, China's cross-border trade RMB settlement business had a turnover of RMB5.11 trillion in 2018, and while direct investment RMB settlement business reached RMB2.66 trillion. The rapid growth of cross-border RMB settlement has laid a solid foundation for expediting the process of RMB internationalization.

As of September 2019, the Macro-prudential Policy Bureau of the PBoC piloted to operate in more convenient cross-border RMB settlement business in 18 free trade zones (FTA) and offer relevant convenient financial services accordingly in the light of the distinct characteristics of the 18 FTAs.

6.4.2 *Offshore Markets and Trans-Regional Financial Cooperation*

The offshore RMB market refers to the RMB financial market outside of China, mainly the offshore bond market and deposit and lending business, etc. From June 2007 onwards, a number of Mainland banks issued RMB-denominated bonds in Hong Kong with a total amount of over RMB20 billion, progressively bringing forth an offshore RMB-denominated bond market. On October 24, 2015, the Mongolian government issued its offshore RMB-denominated bonds of RMB1 billion for the first time, with a coupon rate of 7.5% and a maturity of 3 years.

According to the statistics from the PBoC, RMB-denominated deposits in the Hong Kong market totaled RMB1,003.6 billion in the offshore RMB financial market in 2014, fell to RMB507.3 billion in March 2017 and rose to RMB559.2 billion in November 2017; RMB-denominated deposits in Taiwan reached RMB 338.2 billion in June 2015 and RMB 317.4 billion in November 2017; RMB-denominated deposits in Singapore hit RMB 234 billion in June 2015, and RMB 139 billion in September 2017, suffering a significant decline.

On March 11, 2014, the BOC launched the world's first "BOC Offshore RMB Index", which is another index comprehensively reflecting the internationalization level of the *renminbi* following the launch of the "BOC Cross-border RMB Index" in 2013.

From 2015 onwards, there were a growing number of offshore RMB foreign exchange trading centers around the world. In the second quarter of 2019, the average daily turnover of offshore RMB foreign exchange trading in London exceeded £85 billion (equivalent to RMB 765 billion), a record high of an increase of 22.9% over the same period in 2018, making London the world's No.1 offshore RMB foreign exchange hub, followed by cities such as Hong Kong and Singapore.

Under the current situation, the Chinese government tends to leverage the ASEAN 10+1 economic cooperation framework and "the Belt and the Road" cooperation platform to promote the circulation and use of the *renminbi* in the ASEAN region and in countries and regions along "the Belt and the Road", thereby promoting the regionalization of the RMB and the development of the offshore RMB financial market. Needless to say, this also would help to promote regional economic and financial cooperation as well.

By developing offshore RMB markets, the Chinese government has also promoted regional cooperation in RMB between Guangdong province, the Yangtze River Delta and the Hong Kong and Macao regions.

As the construction of the Guangdong-Hong Kong-Macao Greater Bay Area was in full swing, work was underway to establish an offshore RMB market in a bid to make Macao a RMB clearing centre as well as a RMB-denominated and settled securities market for Portuguese-speaking countries in 2019.

6.4.3 *Measures for Promoting the Internationalization of the Renminbi*

From 2012 onwards, the Chinese government launched various initiatives to promote the internalization of the RMB and it has made significant strides in the following areas:

First, RMB denominated data was incorporated into statistic data by domestic foreign-related economic departments. In February 2013, the GACC tended to release more data on RMB-denominated imports and exports as well as trade balance, and comprehensively published all the statistic data denominated in RMB from 2014 onwards. In January 2014, the SAFE commenced to release RMB-denominated BOP-related statistic data in terms of banking foreign exchange purchase and sales transactions, foreign-related payments and receipts on behalf of customers, BOP statements, as well as direct investments and external debts of financial institutions. In March 2014, the Ministry of Commerce commenced to release more RMB-denominated statistic data on foreign direct investments in China and China's overseas investments.

Second, RMB-denominated international transactions for commodity futures products were promoted. With the approval from the CSRC, the Shanghai International Energy Exchange Co., Ltd. (INE) was officially established in the China (Shanghai) Pilot Free Trade Zone on November 6, 2013. Its scope of business covered organizing and arranging for the business operations in the listing, trading, settlement and delivery of crude oil, natural gas, petrochemical products and other energy derivatives, formulation of business operation management rules and regulations, and provision of related services.

In September 2014, China officially launched international gold trading. In April 2016, the SGE's Gold Benchmark Price auction was conducted, which is the world's first gold benchmark price denominated in RMB. In July 2015, the PBoC set forth specific administrative provisions on the cross-border settlement of domestic crude oil futures transactions, explicitly stipulating that domestic crude oil futures transactions must be denominated and settled in RMB. In March 2018, crude oil futures products denominated in RMB were officially launched.

On October 11, 2019, international iron ore producers Rio Tinto and Vale of Brazil signed trade contracts with two trading and production enterprises in Shandong province to pilot denomination in RMB, demonstrating the inevitable trends of RMB denomination for iron ore trade.

Third, financial products denominated in RMB were continuously developed by launching certificates of deposit, bonds, stocks, foreign exchange futures, funds, trusts, insurance and derivative products, etc. From 2014 onwards, interest rate derivatives and C-Swap were launched in the domestic interbank foreign exchange market. In July and September 2014, foreign central banks (the monetary authorities), international financial organizations and sovereign wealth funds were granted access to China's interbank bond market and interbank foreign exchange market.

The Chinese government allowed overseas institutions to issue RMB-denominated bonds in China, e.g. Panda bonds, which are RMB-denominated bonds issued in China by overseas financial institutions (including those in Hong Kong, Macao and Taiwan).[3] On October 14, 2014, the British government issued RMB-denominated sovereign bonds totaling RMB 3 billion for the first time, with a coupon rate of 2.7% and a maturity period of three years. On October 20, 2015, the PBoC successfully issued central bank bills worth RMB5 billion in London as RMB-denominated ones issued outside of China for the first time, with a maturity of one year and a coupon rate of 3.1%.

From 2019 onwards, major index providers such as Bloomberg, Barclays, JPMorgan, MSCI, FTSE Russell, S&P, Dow Jones all have included China's bonds and A-shares in their index systems or increased the corresponding weights of China's bonds and A-shares.

Fourth, the construction of RMB clearing networks was underway. From 2012 onwards, the Chinese government set up RMB clearing banks in Taiwan, Singapore, the United Kingdom, Germany and South Korea respectively, and countries such as the United States, Russia and the United Arab Emirates followed suit from September to December 2016. Nowadays, there are a total of 23 RMB clearing banks established in Southeast Asia, Western Europe, Central Europe, the Middle East, North America, South America, Oceania, Africa and other regions.

Fifth, the *renminbi* was progressively used as an international payment, settlement and reserve currency. According to the statistics from the Society for Worldwide Interbank Financial Telecommunication (SWIFT), the *renminbi* was ranked third, fifth and fifth in terms of widespread use in global trade and financing, foreign exchange transactions, as well as payment and settlement respectively in December 2015. In addition, balance of payments statistics demonstrated that the *renminbi* was reputed to be the second most widely used and accepted currency in cross-border payments and receipts for five consecutive years.

On November 30, 2015, the Executive Board of the IMF designated the *renminbi* as a freely usable currency. With a corresponding weight of 10.92%, the *renminbi* joined the US dollar, euro, Japanese yen, and British pound sterling in the SDR basket.[4] Along with US dollar, euro, Japanese yen, and British pound sterling, the

[3] RMB-denominated bonds were issued by the International Finance Corporation and the Asian Development Bank as Panda Bonds in the China's interbank bond market for the first time in accordance with international practices in October 2005.

[4] The Special Drawing Right (SDR) is an international reserve asset created by the IMF in 1969 to supplement its member countries' official reserves and SDRs are allocated to member countries in proportion to their quota shares at the IMF. It is worth mentioning that the SDR was initially defined as equivalent to one U.S. dollar. In 1974, the SDR was redefined as a basket of currencies and the value of the SDR was based on a basket of 16 currencies—then 5 currencies in 1981, and

renminbi was included in the SDR basket of currencies as the fifth currency. Additionally, a growing number of foreign central banks (or the monetary authorities) held RMB-denominated foreign currency reserve assets. As of the end of 2015, nearly 50 foreign central banks or monetary authorities held RMB-denominated financial assets in China and incorporated such assets in their foreign exchange reserve holdings.

In January 2016, China officially became the third largest shareholder of the IMF. On October 1, the *renminbi* was officially included in the SDR currency basket, winning the official recognition from the international community. Since then, the Chinese government has embarked on a new journey of RMB internationalization.

In 2014, the *renminbi* was ranked seventh among the world's widely adopted global reserve currencies, and the governments of the United Kingdom, Thailand, South Africa, Russia, Singapore, Tanzania and the Philippines all officially announced that they would hold the *renminbi* in their foreign currency reserve holdings. By the end of June 2016, the PBoC had signed bilateral currency swap agreements with 35 foreign central banks or monetary authorities, with a total amount of over RMB3.3 trillion.

According to incomplete statistics, as of June 2019, China entered into currency swap agreements with nearly 40 countries or regions such as Britain, South Korea, Russia and Japan, with a total amount of over RMB3 trillion.

In accordance with the statistics from the International Monetary Fund (IMF), the amount of the RMB-denominated foreign currency reserves held by the Currency Composition of Official Foreign Exchange Reserves (COFER) reporting countries stood at US$219.62 billion as of the end of the third quarter of 2019, accounting for 2.01% of the total allocated foreign currency reserves and outperforming Australian dollar and Canadian dollar.

From the analysis above, we can learn that, although RMB internationalization has hit new milestones since 2012, there is still a long way to go before the *renminbi* is freely convertible and becomes a sovereign currency for international denomination, payment, settlement and foreign currency reserves. Against the backdrop of the current deteriorating trade environment at home and abroad, the RMB internationalization process may face ups and downs. Meanwhile, choices may need to be made among the three targets of independent monetary policy, fixed exchange rates and free cross-border capital mobility. In the long run, there may arise the "Impossible Trinity" for a sovereign yet international currency. All in a word, RMB internationalization may be a bumpy journey, involving more far-reaching geopolitical issues.

---

4 currencies with the advent of the euro. Nowadays, the value of the SDR is still based on a basket of currencies and the SDR basket is reviewed every five years.

In accordance with the statistics of the International Monetary Fund (IMF), the amount of the RMB-denominated foreign exchange reserves reported by the Currency Composition of Official Foreign Exchange Reserves (COFER) reporting countries stood at US$219.62 billion as of the end of the third quarter of 2019, accounting for 2.01% of the total allocated foreign currency reserves and outperforming Australian dollar and Canadian dollar.

From the analysis above, we can learn that although RMB internationalization has hit new milestones since 2012, there is still a long way to go before the renminbi is freely convertible and becomes a sovereign currency for international denomination, payment, settlement and foreign currency reserves. Against the backdrop of the current deteriorating trade environment at home and abroad, the RMB internationalization process may face ups and downs. Meanwhile, choices may need to be made among the three targets of independent monetary policy, fixed exchange rates and free cross-border capital mobility. In the long run, there may arise the "Impossible Trinity" for a sovereign yet international currency. All in a word, RMB internationalization may be a bumpy journey involving more far-reaching geopolitical issues.

4 currencies with the advent of the euro. Nowadays, the value of the SDR is still based on a basket of currencies and the SDR basket is reviewed every five years.

Miscellany

From 1949 to 2019, China's financial sector went through seventy extraordinary years. In the past seventy years, albeit with twists and turns, China achieved notable accomplishments in the financial sector and its feats bore testimony to the common belief that development is of paramount importance.

First, a stable and credible fiat money and credit money system and a regulated modern central bank system have been established. The *renminbi* was widely accepted and it has established a foothold in the world. Meanwhile, the PBoC was committed to effectively leveraging conventional monetary policy tools, exploring innovative policy tools, and establishing a national financial security network that combined macro and micro-prudential regulation.

Second, a modern financial institution and market system compatible with socialism with Chinese characteristics has been basically established. In thirty years after the founding of the People's Republic of China, there was only one bank and a few credit cooperatives scattered throughout the country's vast urban and rural areas. After more than forty years of reform and opening up, this fragile situation has been fundamentally reversed and the financial sector has entered a period of a rapid development and great prosperity. To date, China has established a system of diversified competitive financial institutions, a multi-tier financial market system, an efficient and viable financial service system combining conventional knowhow and high technologies, and a regulatory regime for effectively safeguarding financial stability.

Third, the financial sector has vigorously supported China's economic development and social progress. Through the direct and indirect financing channels established by the financial sector, funds were regulated between the fund-surplus sectors and the fund-deficit sectors, bringing into play the role of capital funds in facilitating reform and opening up, economic development and social progress, and providing a market mechanism for resource allocation. Meanwhile, financial services have become more accessible, and inclusive finance has made big headways.

Y. Wu, *A Financial History of China (1949–2019)*, Research Series on the Chinese Dream and China's Development Path,
https://doi.org/10.1007/978-981-99-6571-7

Fourth, the financial service industry has grown up and emerged. In the past seven years, China's financial service industry grew from scratch and became the mainstay of the country's economy, basically establishing a financial service system that served the real economy and provided convenient services for the benefit of customers. As such, China was at the forefront of providing basic and convenient financial services in terms of deposit and loan, payment and settlement, wealth management, investment and information enquiry. In the financial market, a holistic system integrating registration, custody, clearing, settlement, credit reference and rating has been established, and the financial infrastructure system has been continuously upgraded.

As of the end of 2016, the value added of China's financial sector accounted for 8.4% of GDP, which was higher than that in countries such as the United States and Japan. From 1979 to 2017, the value added of the financial sector grew by an average of 12.2% per year, 1.7% higher than the average annual growth rate of the service industry.

Fifth, China has integrated into the global financial system and it has taken the initiative to participate in global economic governance. After seventy years of development, China's financial sector has become a major market player in global finance, with a rapidly rising international status and influence, making it possible to make China's voice heard in international financial governance establishment. It is worth mentioning that China's BIG four banks (i.e. the ICBC, ABC, BOC and CCB) were designated as global Systemically Important Banks (G-SIBs) by the Financial Stability Board.

In 2017, Chinese banking institutions had RMB 250 trillion in total assets, ranking No. 1 in asset size in the world. The year 2019 saw China's insurance sector and equity market rank second in the world by market capitalization, and China's bond market rise to the third place globally, second only to the US and Japan. Additionally, China was a leader in mobile payments, digital finance and financial innovations.

In 2019, nearly 40 were Chinese ones among the world's top 1,000 banks in 2019, including six among the top 20, led by the ICBC, CCB, ABC and BOC. This would be unimaginable seventy years ago.

Sixth, China has reformed and improved its financial management and regulatory regimes, taking a crucial step towards building itself into a financial powerhouse. With an attitude of emulating Western countries and being open-minded, Chinese financial practitioners have been seeking to emerge on the world stage by pursuing the "bringing in" and "going global" initiatives to exploit the resources of the international capital markets and make overseas investments. It only took 70 years to create the miracle.

From 1949 to 2019, the Chinese government spared no efforts to make exploration, imposed regulations, pushed ahead with reform, and promoted the development of the financial sector, heralding a new era of displaying independence, upholding reform and opening up, and pursuing the overall strategy of innovation and development. In this regard, we have accumulated the following experience:

First, top-level design at the strategic level was of fundamental importance to the reform and development of China's financial sector. Specifically, top-level design was the prerequisite for nudging in the correct orientation of the financial sector's development and establishing its strategic positioning for improving people's livelihood and serving the real economy.

Second, a viable reform methodology was employed to define the roadmap for the reform in the financial reform in a more rational and effective manner. This methodology allowed the Chinese government to achieve the unity of opposites in the financial system reform process, such as short-term and long-term goals, local and central revenues, innovation and regulation, and equity and efficiency.

Third, progressive reform in the financial sector underwent through a process of "Star Trek" exploration. Like the reform of the economic system, progressive reform of the financial sector was a quest like a Star Trek. As in economic reform, financial reform was also a series of great experiments on a scale from pilot schemes to nationwide roll-out. As Xiaoping Deng once pointed out, "We have to wade through the river by feeling the stones because Marx did not tell us how to carry out reforms, and neither our predecessors nor other socialist countries have done it before. There is no ready-made experience to draw on, and we have to learn by doing and explore in practice[1]".

Fourth, the financial system reform was carried out to effect three "real transformations". This involved building the PBoC into a real regulated central bank, developing state-owned commercial banks into real commercial banks, and reorganizing rural credit cooperatives into real cooperative financial organizations.

Fifth, efforts were made to steadily and prudentially maintain the pace of opening up of the financial market and regulate financial liberalization in an autonomous, progressive and controllable manner. In this regard, we should fully understand the "double-edged sword" of financial globalization, the complexity and danger of systemic financial risks and the long-term tasks of the prevention and control of systematic financial risks, and properly handle the relationship between rigorous regulation and deregulation, as well as financial deepening and globalization, so as to firmly guard the bottom line of non-incurring systemic financial risks.

Sixth, the financial system was a fundamental system crucial for China's socioeconomic development. Finance is at the core of national competitiveness, financial security is central to the country's economic security, and the financial sector is a barometer of the national economy. Therefore, its reform is always on the way.

In the past 70 years, China's financial sector was committed to substantially resolving hurdling difficulties and advancing its reform along the roadmap of market-orientation, integration and financial globalization, targeting at aligning itself with international practice benchmarks. In terms of the opening up of the financial sector, China has evolved from an observer and learner, through a participant, to a promoter and contributor. After seventy years have elapsed, as we get closer to these targets and goals, what will spur on our further reform and development? This triggers such

---

[1] Xiaoping Deng: *Selected Works of Xiaoping Deng*, Vol. 3, People's Publishing House, 1993, pp. 258–259.

major issues as what and how to learn from the Western countries. These are not only historical issues, but also practical ones, requiring our continuous seeking for their solutions in the future.

Postscript

As a book included in the National Belt and Road Book Publishing Program in 2019, its publication in English has been made possible as scheduled, thanks to the generous support and sponsor of Social Sciences Academic Press (China) as well as the collaborative support of Springer Publishing.

In 2018, I published my book entitled "A Financial History of China (1978–2018)". For the present book, I redrew the writing structure, adapted some of the existing contents, and added some new by tracing China's financial history back to 1949. After repeated revisions and refinements, the book has been finally reduced to 150,000 words, as is presented to readers now.

I would like to express my deepest gratitude to Social Sciences Academic Press (China) for including this book into major publication program, and to Ms. Chen Fengling, the editor-in-charge at Social Science Literature Press (China), for her thorough planning, patient and meticulous guidance, as well as tips and encouragement from time to time. Without her generous help and support, I might have ended up halfway. I would like to express my thanks to Ms. Qi Qi from Springer Publishing for all her hard work on the English translation and editing of this book. I am also grateful to the proofreaders, editors and polishers of this book for their conscientious and meticulous work, which has avoided possible errors and omissions. Finally, I would like to pay tribute to all those who have worked so hard for the publication of this book!

The year 2019 marks the 70th anniversary of the founding of the People's Republic of China. Here, I would like to dedicate this book to commemorating this golden era and to develop a readership for the development trajectory of China's financial sector in the past 70 years.

Wu Yunxian
Professor
Business School of
China University of Political Science and Law
In June 2020

Y. Wu, *A Financial History of China (1949–2019)*, Research Series on the Chinese Dream and China's Development Path,
https://doi.org/10.1007/978-981-99-6571-7

References

Chinese Literature

1. Deng X (1993) Selected works of Xiaoping Deng, vol 3. People's Publishing House
2. CCCPC Party Literature Research Office: People's Publishing House (1982) Selected important literature since the third plenary session of the 11th CPC Central Committee. People's Publishing House
3. The People's Bank of China and the CCCPC Party Literature Research Office (eds) (2007) Selected literature on financial work (1978–2005). China Financial Publishing House
4. CCCPC Party Literature Research Office (2018) Selected important literature since the 18th National Congress of the Communist Party of China, vols 1–3. Central Party Literature Press
5. Liu G, Wang L, Mao F, Yang D (2011) Selected data of the People's Republic of China on economy (1958–1965) (volume on finance). China Financial and Economic Publishing House
6. China Legal Publishing House (ed) (2017) Laws and regulations on finance (including relevant policies). China Legal Publishing House
7. National Bureau of Statistics of the People's Republic of China (2018) A new chapter of national rejuvenation after forty eventful years—serial report 1 on the achievements of economic and social development accomplished in the forty years of reform and opening up, August 27
8. Financial Stability Analysis Group of the People's Bank of China (2007–2019) China financial stability reports (2006–2019). China Financial Publishing House
9. China Securities Regulatory Commission and China Futures Association (2017) China futures market yearbook (2016). China Financial and Economic Publishing House
10. The People's Bank of China (2016–2017) Renminbi internationalization reports (2016, 2017). China Financial Publishing House
11. China Securities Regulatory Commission (2016) Annual report of China securities regulatory commission 2016. China Financial and Economic Publishing House
12. The People's Bank of China (2001) Guidelines for financial regulation. China Financial Publishing House
13. Wu X (2008) A chronicle of major events in China's financial reform and opening up. China Financial Publishing House
14. Zhao X (2008) The evolutionary trajectory of China's financial sector (1949–1957). Fujian People's Publishing House
15. Li Y et al (2009) Sixty years of finance in the People's Republic China. China Financial and Economic Publishing House
16. Zhuo X (2013) Market-oriented reform of interest rates. China Development Press
17. Xie P, Xu Z (2013) Rural financial reform in the new century. China Financial Publishing House

Y. Wu, *A Financial History of China (1949–2019)*, Research Series on the Chinese Dream and China's Development Path,
https://doi.org/10.1007/978-981-99-6571-7

18. Chen K (2014) Lost feast: a history of insurance in China 1978–2014. Zhejiang University Press
19. Shen B, Cao Y (2014) China's bond market: thirty years of reform and development, 2nd edn. Peking University Press
20. Zhang J (2015) Institutional logic of China's financial reform. China Renmin University Press
21. Li D (2015) A history of the financial sector in the People's Republic of China, vols 1 and 2. People's Publishing House
22. Lian P, Zhou K (2017) Fintech: a driving force for national innovation. CITIC Press Group
23. Dai X (2018) Recollection of eight years of financial order overhaul. China Finance, Issue 7
24. Yi G (2019) New China's financial sector has accomplished brilliant achievements in the past seventy years. China Finance, Issue 19
25. Liu Z, Liu J (2019) Seventy years of finance in China: historical development trajectory, new contributions and prospects. Contemporary Finance & Economics, Issue 10

Foreign Literature

26. Bowles P, White G (1993) The political economy of Chinas financial reforms: finance in late development. Westview Press, Boulder, Colo.
27. Awrey D (2015) Law and finance in the Chinese shadow banking system. Cornell Int Law J 48(1):1–50. Oxford Legal Studies Research Paper No. 9/2014, Posted: 19 Jan 2014, Last revised: 9 Jan 2017
28. Elliott DJ, Yan K (2013) The Chinese financial system an introduction and overview. The John L. Thornton China Center at Brookings
29. Foreign & Commonwealth Office (2017) Financial services special report: risks in China's financial system
30. Turner G, Tan N, Sadeghian D (2012) The Chinese banking system. Bulletin of Reserve Bank of Australia, September, Quarter 2012, pp 53–64
31. International Finance Corporation (2012) IFC's role in China's financial sector transformation
32. Langlois JD Jr (2001) The WTO and China's financial system. China Q 167:610–629
33. Tam O-K (1987) The development of China's financial system. Aust J Chin Aff 17:95–113
34. Heilmann S (2005) Regulatory innovation by Leninist means: communist party supervision in China's financial sector. China Q 181:1–21
35. Shih V (2011) "Goldilocks" liberalization: the uneven path toward interest rate reform in China. J East Asian Stud 11(3):437–465

MIX
Papier aus verantwortungsvollen Quellen
Paper from responsible sources
FSC® C105338

If you have any concerns about our products,
you can contact us on
ProductSafety@springernature.com

In case Publisher is established outside the EU,
the EU authorized representative is:
Springer Nature Customer Service Center GmbH
Europaplatz 3, 69115 Heidelberg, Germany

Printed by Libri Plureos GmbH
in Hamburg, Germany